# Lin May Saeed
## *Arrival of the Animals*

# Lin May Saeed

# *Arrival of the Animals*

Clark Art Institute
Williamstown, Massachusetts

DISTRIBUTED BY
Yale University Press
New Haven and London

# FOREWORD and ACKNOWLEDGMENTS

The Clark Art Institute is honored to present the first museum exhibition dedicated to the work of Lin May Saeed. Saeed believes deeply in and has dedicated her artistic practice to advocating for nonhuman animals and is one of the foremost artists of her generation commenting on the status of the animal throughout history. Not only is Saeed's work conceptually rich, based in the literature of animal liberation, zoology, and theology, it is also accomplished across a wide range of media and formats, moving fluidly from drawings to sculptural reliefs in a range of nontraditional materials.

Saeed's ideals are rooted in research and theory, but one of her great strengths is her ability to use artistic media to convey, compassionately and legibly, her respect for the animal kingdom. One need not be familiar with Saeed's full range of sources to be moved by her *Calf*, liberated from the wooden crate upon which it stands, or to observe the cunning glint in the swimming feline's eyes in *Panther Relief*. In *Lin May Saeed: Arrival of the Animals*, there are points of connection to be found for everyone.

Sterling and Francine Clark held the natural environment in high regard, a respect that motivated the museum's placement in the Berkshires. As such, it is only fitting that this exhibition should honor the natural world and the fauna that live among us. During an era in which climate change has endangered many of the earth's species, including those that live on and near the Clark's campus, Saeed's work could not be more timely. It is our hope that this exhibition remains with our visitors after they leave the galleries, and that it prompts them to see other animals in a new light.

Credit for bringing Saeed's work to the Clark and to a wider public can be extended to Robert Wiesenberger, associate curator of contemporary projects, who has selected Saeed for his first large-scale contemporary exhibition since joining the institute. Our deep gratitude is also due to Mel Y. Chen, former Robert Sterling Clark Visiting Professor at Williams College and associate professor of gender and women's studies at the University of California, Berkeley, who penned an insightful essay on Saeed's practice for this monograph. We would also like to thank Saeed's galleries, Jacky Strenz, Frankfurt, and Nicolas Krupp, Basel, for their support of the exhibition.

The Clark is, finally, deeply grateful to the unyielding commitment of our members and sponsors. We wish in particular to acknowledge the generous support of Denise Littlefield Sobel and Katherine and Frank Martucci, as steadfast friends of the Clark.

Olivier Meslay
Hardymon Director

This exhibition and publication would not have been possible without the hard work and support of many people. I'd first like to thank Denise Littlefield Sobel and Katherine and Frank Martucci for their generous support of this project.

At the Clark, the Exhibitions team led by Kathy Morris moved mountains to see this project through. Angela Liporace, with Mattie Kelley, secured passage for Lin May Saeed's work from Berlin to Williamstown just under the wire: though humans were no longer allowed to travel, at the onset of a global pandemic the animals still arrived. For their resourcefulness and good humor, I want to thank our preparators Paul Dion, Tom Merrill, and Nathan Ahern, along with Tim Johnson, John Peitso, and Michael Rousseau, who installed this show under adverse conditions. For keeping the wheels on as the project rolled forward, I'm grateful for the project management of Teresa O'Toole and Julie Blake. Anne Leonard and Kristie Couser generously lent their time and knowledge of works on paper in the Clark's collection. For his documentation of the exhibition, in short order, thanks go to photographer Thomas Clark. I am deeply appreciative of deputy director Larry Smallwood; head of public programs Teal Baskerville; Robin Sher in Finance; Ronna Tulgan Ostheimer, Amanda Bell Goldmakher, Keely Kempster Sarr, and Chelsea Neveu in Education; Vicki Saltzman, Sally Morse Majewski, Rebecca Cross, Nora Considine, Min Li, Amy Coon, and David Edge in Communications; Thomas Woodward, Maureen Hart Hennessy, Emily Daunis, Tucker Bair, Catherine Whitney, and Caedy Schultz-Loomis in Advancement; and Bill Powers, Dante Morgano, Mike Pereira and Matt Noyes in Buildings, Facilities, and Grounds. In the library, Susan Roeper, Karen Bucky, Terri Boccia, Michele Slowey, and the entire team make doing research at the Clark a pleasure. Caroline Fowler and Samantha Page, of the Research and Academic Program, created a generous and rigorous environment in which to workshop this material. From the Williamstown Art Conservation Center, I want to thank Helene Gilette-Woodard, Rebecca Johnston, and Montserrat Le Mense. In particular, I am grateful to Kevin Bicknell, who, with Anne Roecklein, brought care, patience, and sound judgement to every editorial aspect of this exhibition and publication. I would also like to thank Olivier Meslay and Esther Bell for their consistent support and sage counsel.

For the form and content of the exhibition, I want to thank several people outside the Clark. I am grateful to Mel Y. Chen for their insightful essay in this catalogue. Thank you to Frank Gregor for his kind permission to publish Birgit Mütherich's writing and Nathaniel McBride for his translation of the text. Mark Owens brought his expert eye to the publication and exhibition graphics, and James Jarzyniecki and Mandy Johnson created an elegant exhibition design that reconciles the visual languages of Saeed's work and Tadao Ando's galleries. For her research and insights over the life of this project, I want to thank curatorial intern Mallory Cohen, of the Williams College Graduate Program in the History of Art, and also Kimberlean Donis of Williams College. Several trusted interlocutors also deserve thanks here, as partners in thinking through this project. They include Catherine Damman, Joanna Fiduccia, Linda Johnson, Sophie Nichols, Kirsten Scheid, Gregor Quack, and Leah Whitman-Salkin.

I'd finally like to thank the artist, Lin May Saeed, for her quiet and committed practice, which has changed my own relationship to other animals, and for her kind collaboration throughout the project. I am grateful to her gallerist since 2006, Jacky Strenz, of Frankfurt, as well as to Nicolas Krupp, Basel, and Daniel Sperry and Alivia Zivich of What Pipeline, Detroit. The world looks very different than it did at the start of this project. It is a testament to Saeed's work that its meanings have only deepened since then.

Robert Wiesenberger
Associate curator of contemporary projects

# SPECIESISM

## *On the Work of Lin May Saeed*

Robert Wiesenberger

For the past seventeen years, Lin May Saeed has worked on the third floor of a Weimar-era printing plant in an unscenic but recently hip part of Berlin. I first meet her there in July 2017. She sets out small plates of seed-studded bread and dates, coffee and nut milk. We graze and chat. An even, kickdrum thump from below distracts me. The studio sits above a small office-supply manufacturer that specializes in plastics, and I assume it's a press or mold of some kind setting the beat. Below the table, however, are two enormous rabbits, and one seems to be rhythmically stretching its legs. Saeed doesn't *own* these adopted bunnies, she would say, distancing herself from the question of captivity. Rather, they live with her.

My mistake was Cartesian, taking a nonhuman animal for a convincing automaton.[1] It's what led the Enlightenment philosopher to endorse live dissections of "unfeeling brutes," their cries notwithstanding, while reserving sentience for humans alone.[2] That view would qualify as psychopathic, today, if directed at a house pet, but it remains a basic if unspoken premise of industrial agriculture, which churns through more than seventy billion animals each year, or nearly two hundred million per day.[3]

Rabbits rarely appear in Saeed's work, but they often appear on it. While her practice is dedicated to animals, she finds these creatures too cute for her purposes. Still, if she doesn't tidy up the reams of paper on her desk—philosophies of animal ethics, histories of the animal liberation movement, anthropologies of Fertile Crescent culture, and her own preparatory drawings—the bunnies will move it one step closer to bedding. And if she leaves out the blocks of Styrofoam that are her material of choice, the animals have been known to burrow. This resulted in Saeed's first collaboration with and for nonhuman animals, and her first abstract sculpture: a slab of foam, whose concavity, once cast in bronze, formed a birdbath (fig. 1).

In all of her work, Lin May Saeed focuses on the lives of animals and human-animal relations. In sculptures and reliefs, drawings and paintings, she tells stories of animal subjugation, liberation, and cohabitation with humans, working toward a new iconography of interspecies solidarity. Using nontraditional or "poor" materials[4] such as Styrofoam—easy for her to acquire and work, and in desparate need of transformation—Saeed creates worlds past and future that are, in their urgent mix of empathy and humor, starkly contemporary.

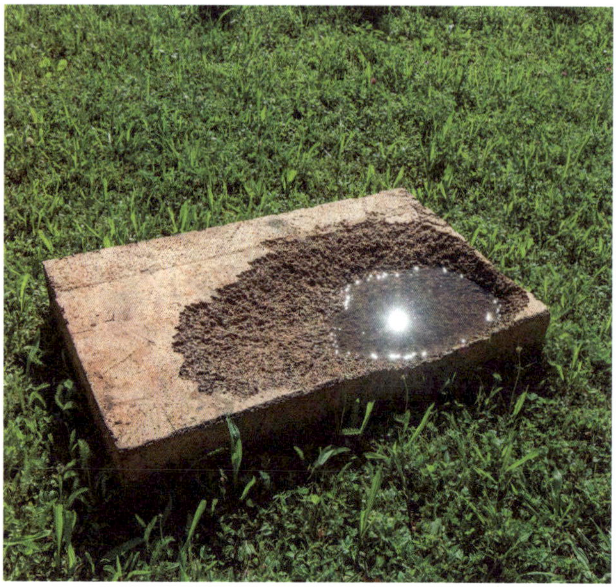

Fig. 1. Lin May Saeed, *Die Mulde/The Hollow*, 2019. Bronze, 5 ⅞ × 38 ⅝ × 24 ¾ in. (15 × 98 × 63 cm)

1
The phrase "nonhuman animal," which is common in animal studies, is used here interchangeably with the more concise "animal." The former is cumbersome, and defined in negative, anthropocentric terms, but is a useful reminder of biological kinship. For a piercing analysis of the concept of the animal, see Birgit Mütherich's *The Social Construction of the Other: On the Sociological Question of the Animal*, excerpted and published here in English translation for the first time (p. 87). Saeed, who finds this text useful, commissioned its translation and has made it available as a handout in her gallery exhibitions.

2
For a recent discussion of René Descartes's position on animals, see Peter Sahlins, *1668: The Year of the Animal in France* (New York: Zone Books, 2017).

3
For an ethnography of the abattoir, see Timothy Pachirat, *Every Twelve Seconds: Industrialized Slaughter and the Politics of Sight* (New Haven: Yale University Press, 2013). For data on global livestock production, see "FAOSTAT," Food and Agriculture Organization of the United Nations, www.fao.org/faostat/en/#home.

4
These nontraditional, low-grade materials recall the late curator Germano Celant's coinage "arte povera" (poor art) to describe an artistic tendency of the 1960s. See Germano Celant, *Art Povera* (New York: Praeger Publishers, 1969).

"Arrival of the Animals," the subtitle of the Clark Art Institute's exhibition, is borrowed from a short story of the same name by the multihyphenate, Nobel Prize–winning author Elias Canetti. Saeed admires Canetti's writing for exposing might-makes-right power structures in general, and anthropocentrism in particular.[5] The titular story chronicles an elementary school field trip to a slaughterhouse and a young boy's dawning awareness of the cruelty in his midst.[6] Animals have indeed arrived, in recent years, and in the sense of Canetti's title, in the moral consciousness of many.[7]

Animals have also arrived in the academy, as scholars reconsider the central term in the humanities.[8] The once crisp category of the human, eroded on the one side by our technological prostheses, gives way on the other to regular reminders that capacities thought to distinguish us—whether language, tool use, or complex emotion—are shared by others, from whom we differ mainly by degree. Animals have also arrived in the visual arts: the so-called "animal turn" of the past two decades has seen artists considering animality in new ways.[9] As Filipa Ramos succinctly puts it, "Art thinks, and invites us to think, the other, and does this in ways that are other. In doing so, it contributes to expanding the humanities beyond the human."[10]

At the same time, metaphorical arrivals notwithstanding, animals have disappeared. Our time qualifies as a mass extinction, fueled by habitat destruction and climate collapse. Some predict that by the end of the century, between one-fifth and one-half of all living species of flora and fauna will be no more.[11] Against this backdrop, animals arrive in Saeed's work to live with humans, to rebel against them, or to reoccupy the spaces that were once theirs; in other words, they return.

The exhibition at the Clark starts and ends in caves—one of the past, the other of the future—both with a cage-like aspect. The first, a "graphic cave," contains drawings and prints from the Clark's collections, spanning four centuries of European art history. Sterling Clark, the institute's co-founder, was an avid equestrian who owned prize-winning race horses, and the institution's first seal reflects this (fig. 2). So do the collections. By far the best represented animals in it are horses, prized by Sterling for their beauty and breeding, power and prestige, and submission to human will. These are not Saeed's concerns.

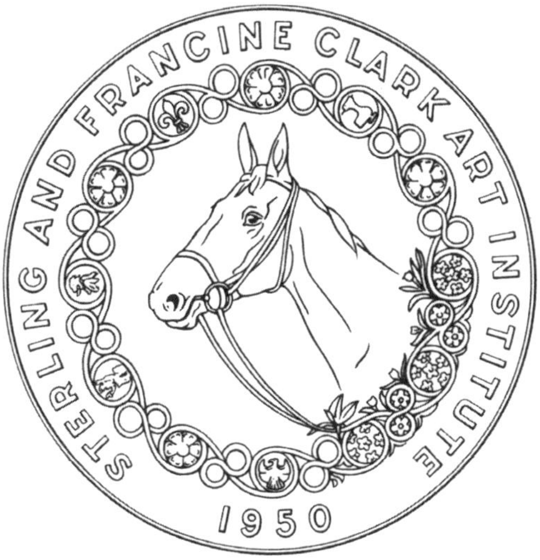


Fig. 2. Original seal of the Sterling and Francine Clark Art Institute, c. 1950

5
Born to Sephardic Jewish parents in Bulgaria, Canetti studied in Austria and Germany, escaped Nazi persecution in England, and lived out his last years in Switzerland. Throughout his career he wrote in German. See Dagmar C. G. Lorenz, ed., *A Companion to the Works of Elias Canetti* (Rochester, NY: Camden House, 2004).

6
Elias Canetti, "Ankunft der Tiere," in *Über Tiere* (Munich: C. Hanser, 2002), 70–97.

7
The year 2019, for example, was to be "The Year of the Vegan," according to *The Economist*, https://worldin2019.economist.com/theyearofthevegan.

8
See, for example, Mel Y. Chen, *Animacies: Biopolitics, Racial Mattering, and Queer Affect* (Durham, NC: Duke University Press, 2012), and works by Cary Wolfe, such as *What Is Posthumanism?* (Minneapolis: University of Minnesota Press, 2010).

9
See Filipa Ramos, ed., *Animals: Documents of Contemporary Art* (Cambridge, MA: MIT Press, 2016); and Ana Teixeira Pinto, "The Post-Human Animal," *Frieze*, April 21, 2015, https://frieze.com/article/post-human-animal (reprinted in Ramos, *Animals*).

10
Ramos, *Animals*, 14.

11
See Elizabeth Kolbert, *The Sixth Extinction: An Unnatural History* (New York: Henry Holt, 2014).

Rather, a selection of objects was made with the artist that surface stranger moments in the human-animal relationship. One of the prints also gestures toward the Orientalism that runs deep in the collection, and its tendency to animalize the non-Western Other. These works show animals as curiosities and nemeses, metaphors and muses, objects and subjects. Together, they form a bridge from the Clark's historical galleries, through the woods to the site of the exhibition on Stone Hill, and into the worlds Saeed creates.

The cave of the future, the exhibition's final space, belongs to *Seven Sleepers*, Saeed's largest sculpture group to date (pl. 21). This new, site-specific installation returns to a legend the artist has explored at several points in her career: the Seven Sleepers of Ephesus exists both in the medieval Christian tradition and in the Islamic Qur'an. The tellings vary, but in both, a group of young Christians in the third century CE, persecuted by the Roman emperor, retreats to a cave for protection. They pray and pray before falling asleep, for what becomes three hundred years. Upon waking, they emerge from the cave to find that their faith has become the state religion. Depending on who tells it, the men are either guarded by a dog at the cave's mouth or joined by one in its interior. Saeed is struck by the story as both trans-religious and interspecies. *Seven Sleepers* might seem to venture a quietist counterpoint to the activism of Saeed's other works, suggesting, in effect, that we sleep—or pray—on our present plight. And yet sleep also implies refusal, opens onto the strangeness of dreams, and, eventually, yields to reawakening.[12]

## PLASTICITY

Lin May Saeed was born in 1973 in Würzburg, a city roughly equidistant between Frankfurt and Nuremberg. She is reticent to share personal biography, but this much can be said: Saeed's German-Jewish great-grandmother was shielded from Nazi persecution through her marriage to the non-Jewish owner of a business deemed essential to the war effort (*kriegswichtiger Betrieb*). Saeed's father immigrated to Germany from Iraq in the 1960s to work as an electrical engineer. She lost him at a young age. Saeed remembers him as being intent on assimilating into German society fully, and not speaking or reading Arabic in the house. Saeed never learned the language growing up, but it later appeared in her work, perhaps, she suggests, reflecting a sense of loss. In early drawings and reliefs, Arabic registered as purely formal marks, some of them invented. Saeed is now teaching herself the language, and it sometimes appears in roughly Germanized transliteration. *Mureen/Lion School* (pl. 17), for example, includes a speech bubble meant to read "In paradise, the snow falls slowly." Saeed considers herself German-Iraqi. She visited Iraq once when she was young, but has not returned since out of safety concerns. Most of her family left the country shortly after the 2003 U.S.-led invasion.

Language, it was long thought, is one of the capacities that differentiates humans from other animals. Yet nonhumans have it, whether or not we can understand it.[13] Saeed's titles are often based on the Arabic name of the animal depicted, such as *Thaealab* (fox, pl. 18) or *Djamil* (camel, pl. 15), or she treats her animals as individuals, with Arabic first names such as *Bilal* or *Khulood*. "Names are often like short poems," she says. "They seem to tell a story about something that is far away and give an idea of the sound and characteristics of a language."[14] For her part, Saeed does not speak publicly and rarely writes about her work; with the exception of some diagrammatic compositions, replete with legends, her practice remains mostly wordless—affective, instinctive, and in large part open-ended, as far as what is happening in a given scene. She

12
On the radical dimensions of sleep, see Jonathan Crary, *24/7: Late Capitalism and the Ends of Sleep* (London: Verso, 2014). On the Seven Sleepers legend and political reawakenings, see Anna Della Subin, *Not Dead But Sleeping* (New York: Triple Canopy, 2016).

13
See Frans de Waal, *Are We Smart Enough to Know How Smart Animals Are?* (New York: W. W. Norton & Company, 2017).

14
Email exchange with the author, December 1, 2019.

has, however, written short, parable-like texts, some of which are included in this volume, and commented on by Mel Y. Chen. "For lack of a better term," Saeed explains, "I have always called the texts fables. The logic of fables is usually that they deal with human themes that are negotiated through animal figures. My fables are about animals."[15] Nevertheless, it is Saeed's human voice that narrates these spare and often darkly funny stories.

Before coming to studio art, Saeed worked in theater, assisting with stage and costume design. Building sets—as an economical, improvisational, and multimedia exercise in (mostly frontal) worldmaking—shaped her artistic approach, and she found more freedom there than in the art world. Saeed brought that freedom to the Kunstakademie Düsseldorf, where she was a student of British sculptor Tony Cragg. The immaculate, quasi-digital quality of Cragg's work looks nothing like Saeed's, but when she started making emphatically rough sculptures from plaster, he was encouraging. In elementary school, Saeed had studied Latin, English, and ancient Greek, in that order, and a class trip to Athens, where she saw the Parthenon friezes, was especially formative. These, in addition to the low-relief sculptures of Ancient Egypt and Mesopotamia, a region that included much of present-day Iraq, helped shape Saeed's style, which borrows also from the naïve forms of neolithic art, in which more attention was often paid to the rendering of animals than humans.

To imagine her ancient, natural scenes, Saeed uses the modern, synthetic material of expanded polystyrene foam—better known by Dow Chemical's trade name of Styrofoam. Discovered by an apothecary in nineteenth-century Berlin, the material was first commercialized in the mid-twentieth century by the German chemical company BASF. Styrofoam is quintessentially futuristic, not just because it emerged from mid-century promises of "Better living through chemistry,"[16] or because it looks the molded, white Space Age part, but because it will remain after us, indefinitely. Saeed concedes that this nonbiodegradable, petroleum-based product containing toxins like styrene and benzene probably shouldn't exist. She generally finds hers, or is given it from construction sites—a byproduct of Berlin's building boom. Designed to take up space and cradle consumer goods orbiting Earth, Styrofoam might be the signature material of the Anthropocene, our current geological epoch—which has been indelibly marked by humans' petrocapitalist adventures. (The term "plasticene," while not causally oriented like "capitalocene," does acknowledge the stratigraphic signature our era will leave.[17])

As Heather Davis observes: "The use of the term 'plastic arts' was first recorded in 1624. Until the invention of the synthetic polymer that we have come to know as plastic, the arts held a virtual monopoly on artifice; now it is chemical engineers who remake and refashion the earth."[18] Yet the association with malleability is unfortunate: "Plastic, once it has been formed through the miracles of the chemical industry, remains recalcitrant both to biological processes [and] to human creativity. It is the materialization of the horror of identity, of the stability of form, of a futurity without change."[19]

Nevertheless, Saeed forms the material to her will. She is not alone among contemporary artists using Styrofoam, either directly or for casting, but her practice with the

15
Email exchange with the author, December 26, 2019.

16
This slogan is associated with the DuPont chemical company, before its merger with Dow.

17
On the plasticene, see Christina Reed, "Dawn of the Plasticene Age," *New Scientist* 225, no. 3006 (January 31, 2015): 28–32. See also T. J. Demos, *Against the Anthropocene: Visual Culture and Environment Today* (Berlin: Sternberg Press, 2017), 95. On the capitalocene, see Jason W. Moore, ed., *Anthropocene or Capitalocene? Nature, History, and the Crisis of Capitalism* (Oakland, CA: PM Press, 2016). On other terms, see Donna J. Haraway, *Staying with the Trouble: Making Kin in the Chthulucene* (Durham, NC: Duke University Press, 2016), 30–57.

18
Heather Davis, "Life & Death in the Anthropocene: A Short History of Plastic," in *Art in the Anthropocene: Encounters Among Aesthetics, Politics, Environments and Epistemologies*, ed. Heather Davis and Etienne Turpin (London: Open Humanities Press, 2015), 348.

19
Davis, "Life & Death," 351–52. See also Amanda Boetzkes, *Plastic Capitalism: Contemporary Art and the Drive to Waste* (Cambridge, MA: MIT Press, 2019).

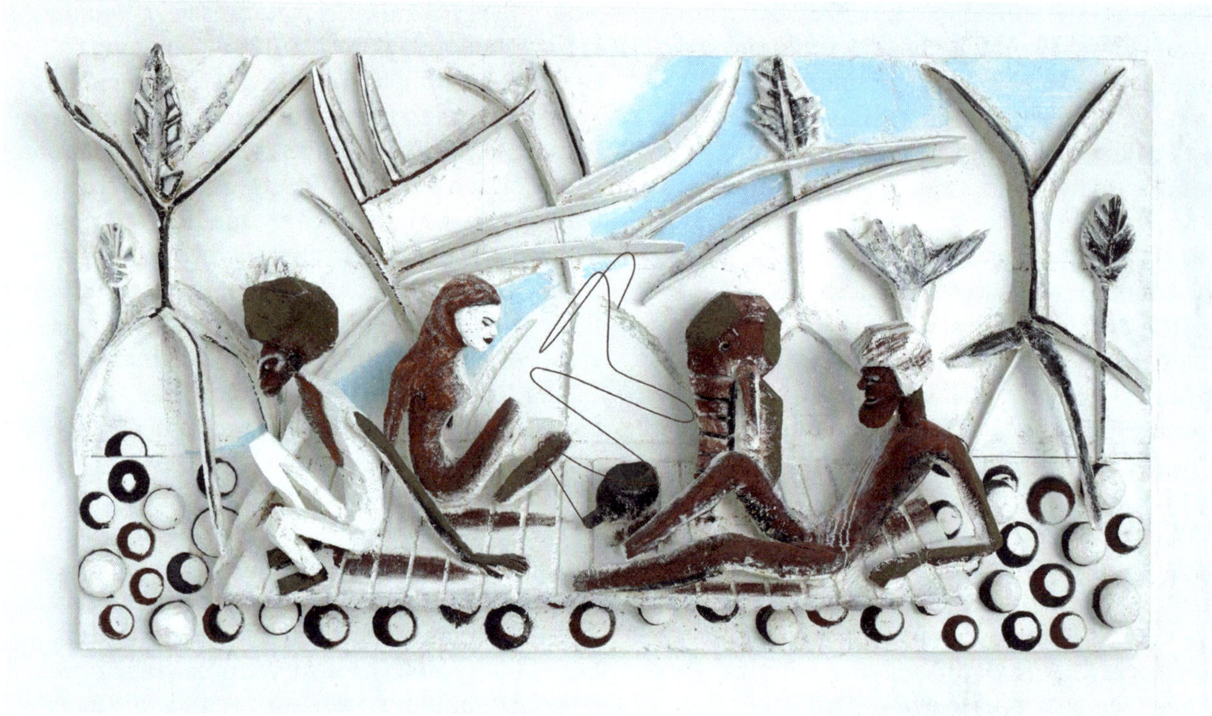

Fig. 3. *Auf dem Floß/On the Raft*, 2006. Polystyrene foam, acrylic paint, steel, 55 ⅛ × 103 ⅞ × 22 ⅞ in. (140 × 264 × 58 cm)

material has been one of the most sustained.[20] Styrofoam lets her work cheaply and at large scale by herself, without the need for studio assistants or fabricators. She carves it with knives and rasps, adheres it with glue, structures it with welded steel armatures, and finishes it with acrylic paint. The material crunches, squeaks, and breaks easily; it is remarkably delicate, given its lifespan. Styrofoam is not, Saeed admits, terribly pleasant to touch, work, or, in its raw state, behold. Its formal limit is the irreducible spheres that comprise it—polystyrene beads that have been placed in molds and puffed up with steam. Figurative details, for example, the fur of an animal, stop at that low resolution.

Yet for her, the ugliness is also the point. As Saeed explained to her friend, the photographer and biologist Jochen Lempert: "It bothers me sometimes, especially as I was brought up in the theater, that in the visual arts everything has to be made so genteel. Or to put it another way: art tends to ennoble everything, to valorize it." That process has occurred for most materials: "Plaster, cardboard, and paper have already long been ennobled. Even Rodin declared plaster a valid artistic material. That never seemed possible for polystyrene or Styrofoam; they're just too trashy. It isn't easy to like this material." Revaluing the material is Saeed's interest: "I think it's a good thing when you can make something different out of something that is complete and utter trash. That's a genuine transformation. Carving a relief out of a beautiful piece of fruitwood makes no sense. Having ugliness as your starting point is far more interesting."[21]

Using Styrofoam, Saeed has long favored the relief format, in which forms emerge from, while remaining attached to, their support. Perhaps its most committed champion, the sculptor Adolf von Hildebrand espoused the merits of "plastic relief," with reference to its Classical history, as "a mold in which the artist casts the form of nature." Proposing it as a

20
Contemporary sculptors using Styrofoam prominently include Huma Bhabha, Nicole Eisenman, Iza Genzken, Katherina Grosse, Rachel Harrison, Eva Rothschild, and Kara Walker.

21
Lin May Saeed and Jochen Lempert, unpublished conversation, Berlin, June 17, 2017.

kind of improved painting, Hildebrand saw the relief as the best solution to "the problem of form," namely, how to achieve compositional unity in an artwork.[22]

In some cases Saeed incises her foam slightly to make low reliefs, often as simple as a drawing; in others, she carves it deeply, undercutting it to create shadows; and in still others, she attaches new elements to the surface that project out into the viewer's space. In general, she paints the surfaces, usually in soft colors, nodding to the polychrome sculpture of antiquity, and especially Greek and Roman marble statuary, so long assumed to idealize whiteness.[23] By contrast, Saeed's human figures are generally of color, and represent the diverse skin tones of the Fertile Crescent. *Auf dem Floß/On the Raft* (fig. 3), for example, depicts three nonwhite humans, one nonhuman animal, and one nonhuman spirit, or genie, wafting as a wire from a bottle. They might be refugees, Saeed allows, but the context is unclear.

The nonhuman, for Saeed, are not just animals. In *Ghost Ship Relief*, a mostly monochrome piece with blushes of washy color (pl. 3), a skeletal, phantom clipper, delineated in steel, sails the seas perpetually without crew (one might think of Wagner's *Flying Dutchman*). Below water are two quiet witnesses to the scene above, whose forms rhyme with one another. One is the rarely seen oarfish—a creature of the deep, and a present-day reminder of deep, or geological, time. Beside it is the billowing, iron-sulfide-rich cloud of a "black smoker," a deep-sea hydrothermal vent thought by some to be the origin of life on Earth.[24] The smoker is an example of what Jane Bennett calls "vibrant matter," a term that evokes "the capacity of things—edibles, commodities, storms, metals—not only to impede or block the will and designs of humans but also to act as quasi agents or forces with trajectories, propensities, or tendencies of their own."[25] Saeed's nonhuman bodies—ship, fish, and cloud—collapse time; they are at once ancient and perpetual.

Another aqueous world, more clearly set in the future, is *Weather Relief*, of 2017, which contends directly with climate crisis (fig. 4). A storm pierces the sickly colored sky, and prehistoric palms thrash in the wind. Evoking the tactile grit of a sooty cave wall, Saeed has picked out the details of a "world without us."[26] In the lower left, an ovine animal looks out from the grotto in which it has taken cover. The graduated lines of a thermometer, or other meteorological index, mark the lower right corner. In the foreground is a beach strewn with relics of human civilization, such as an overturned truck. Here a jackal—Saeed has in mind Anubis, Egyptian god of the underworld—occupies a beach chair, in lieu of the customary sarcophagus that serves

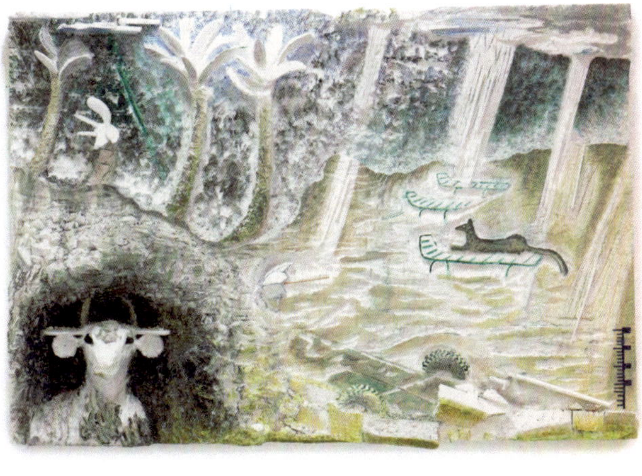

Fig. 4. *Weather Relief*, 2017. Polystyrene foam, acrylic paint, gypsum, wood, paper, 53 ½ × 79 ⅛ × 9 in. (136 × 201 × 23 cm). Private collection, Palm Beach, United States

22
Adolf von Hildebrand, *The Problem of Form in Painting and Sculpture*, trans. Max Meyer and Robert Morris Ogden (New York: G. E. Stechert & Company, 1907), 83.

23
See Vinzenz Brinkmann, Renée Dreyfus, and Ulrike Koch-Brinkmann, *Gods in Color: Polychromy in the Ancient World* (Munich: Prestel, 2017); and Sarah E. Bond, "Why We Need to Start Seeing the Classical World in Color," *Hyperallergic*, June 7, 2017, https://hyperallergic.com/383776/why-we-need-to-start-seeing-the-classical-world-in-color/.

24
Günter Wächtershäuser, "Life as We Don't Know It," *Science* 289, no. 5483 (August 25, 2000): 1307–8.

25
Jane Bennett, *Vibrant Matter: A Political Ecology of Things* (Durham: Duke University Press, 2010), viii.

26
Alan Weisman entertains the thought experiment of how earth might look were humans suddenly to disappear from it, in *The World Without Us* (New York: Picador, 2007).

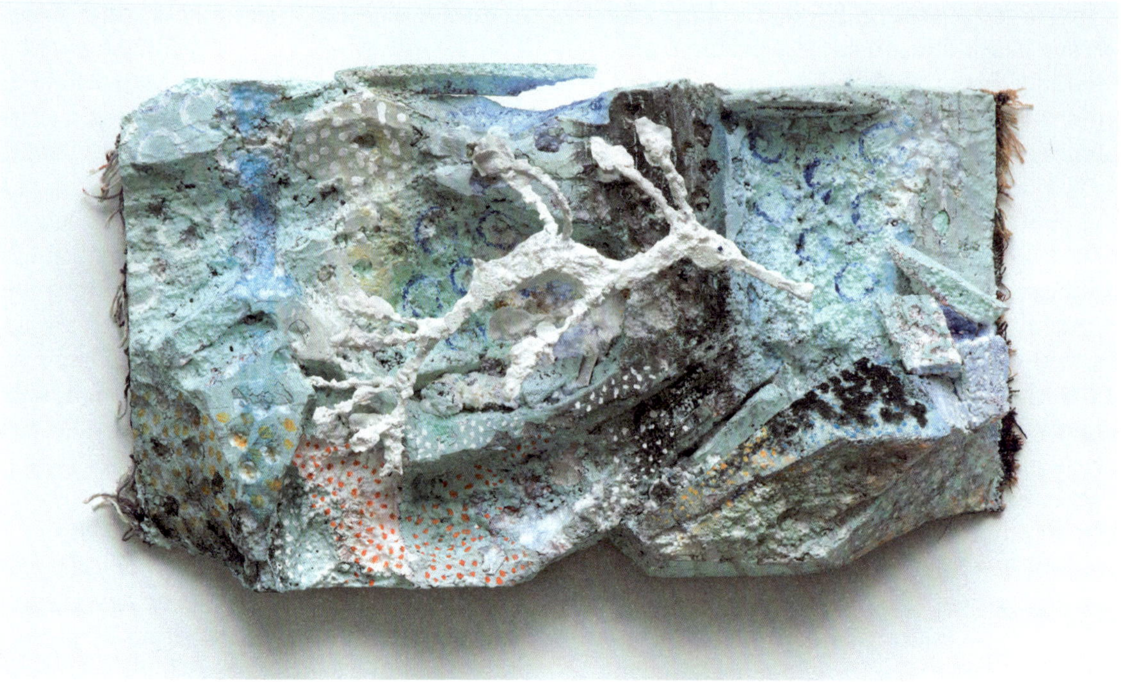

Fig. 5. *Teneen Albaher/Sea Dragon Relief II*, 2016. Polystyrene foam acrylic paint, steel, jute, 19⅝ × 32 × 6¾ in. (50 × 80 × 17 cm). Private collection, Darmstadt, Germany

as a plinth. The fact of climate change striking the most vulnerable—and least responsible for it—first and hardest applies both to human and nonhuman animals.[27] Likewise, Saeed's half-round *Panther Relief* frames a postdiluvian world (pl. 4). A big cat wades through a polluted stream in the foreground—blues and greens tinted by Saeed's muddy brush water. This may be the remains of a Persian Gulf megacity, with ruined glass skyscrapers, barbed wire, and minarets. Fan-shaped foliage in the foreground, meanwhile, evokes the lotus forms of ancient Egyptian ornament.

Saeed records a small gesture of compensation for human violence in *Cleaner* (pl. 16): the rescue of an oil-slicked animal by a hazmat suit–clad human. The first, its body limp, is injured or expired; the second, huddled on the floor, back to the wall, appears exhausted and in mourning. It is, as one colleague put it, a kind of Pietà for the Anthropocene—or plasticene, as it were. Here a peculiar Swiss watering can forms the mask of a creature rendered alien in the environment of its own making, its Tyvek plastic suit protecting it from another petroleum product. *Cleaner* updates the "St.Jerome and the Lion" motif that appears in a Dürer print (pl. 25), and in one of Saeed's steel "gates" (pl. 1), at the exhibition's start, in which the saint is said to have charitably removed a thorn from a lion's paw, and thus gained the animal as a lifelong companion. In *Cleaner*, the thorn is human-made and structural. The work of the cleaner here—whether court ordered or voluntary—marks a small act of aid, of the kind Saeed sees as urgent, if not redeeming.

## FRIENDSHIP

The leafy sea dragon is a marine fish related to the seahorse, but in a genus of its own; it is found only in the waters off southern Australia. Saeed has created a series of sea dragon reliefs

27
It is a cruel irony that global livestock production is one of the largest drivers of climate change. See Damian Carrington, "Huge Reduction in Meat-Eating 'Essential' to Avoid Climate Breakdown," *The Guardian*, October 10, 2018, https://www.theguardian.com/environment/2018/oct/10/huge-reduction-in-meat-eating-essential-to-avoid-climate-breakdown.

(fig. 5), titled with the animal's Arabic name, *Teneen Albaher*. The fish's frilly appendages help to camouflage it as a piece of seaweed or coral. In German, the sea dragon is known as a *Fetzenfisch*, literally "rag fish" or "shredded fish." For Saeed, this is both a one-word joke and a profoundly beautiful, if improbable, creature. Humans respond to symmetry, in faces and in bodies, and the rag fish undermines this. "It's good when something doesn't look like an animal," Saeed says; there's less of a sentimentalized "aww" factor.[28]

Taking pleasure in representing animals is the subject of Saeed's *Freundschaft/Friendship* (fig. 6). It shows two humanoid figures making art socially, rendering nonhuman animals—the subject matter of choice in prehistoric art—on cave walls. There is much to learn from this art, as Barbara Ehrenreich observed recently when quoting archaeologist Jean Clottes: "In the Paleolithic world, humans were not at the center of the stage."[29] Ehrenreich sees the Lascaux paintings, discovered accidentally by children in Nazi-occupied France, as a redemptive lesson amid our latter-day democratic and environmental crises: to reject both ego and anthropocentrism, and to maintain a healthy dose of gallows humor about the human project. "Our Paleolithic ancestors," she writes, "with their faceless humanoids and capacity for silliness seem to have known something we strain to imagine. They knew where they stood in the scheme of things, which was not very high, and this seems to have made them laugh. I strongly suspect that we will not survive the mass extinction we have prepared for ourselves unless we too finally get the joke."[30]

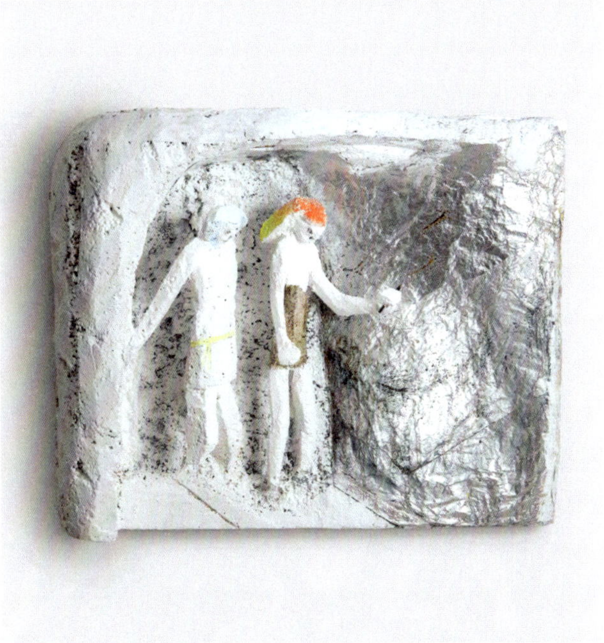

Fig. 6. *Freundschaft/Friendship*, 2010. Polystyrene foam, wood, aluminum foil, acrylic paint, 17 ¾ × 22 ⅜ × 6 ⅛ in. (44 × 57 × 15.5 cm). Private collection, Paris, France

Saeed gets the joke. And her drawings, in particular, make this clear. These are quick sketches, in graphite or charcoal, with a cartoonish quality. In the Clark exhibition is a set of six on brown paper (pl. 7–12). *Noel* (pl. 7), for example, retells a familiar tale, traditionally set in a manger, but with a different focus. The donkey in the foreground munches away on hay at a world-historic moment—not necessarily oblivious, but certainly not captivated, either. In *Davos* (pl. 8), a pair of mountain goats surveys the wreckage of a chair lift and a tangle of skis in the Swiss resort town and site of the World Economic Forum. Other drawings come from Saeed's dreams, with little explanation. *Anmar* (pl. 10) shows a locust in a chariot pulled by an ox, speeding full tilt through a rocky landscape. As Saeed notes, the locust, or *Heuschrecke*, has come to refer in popular German discourse to

28
Conversation with the artist, September 30, 2019.

29
Barbara Ehrenreich, "The Humanoid Stain," *The Baffler*, November 2019, https://thebaffler.com/salvos/the-humanoid-stain-ehrenreich.

30
Ehrenreich, "The Humanoid Stain." Days after the publication of Ehrenreich's essay, cave art discovered in Indonesia appeared to be more than twice as old as the Lascaux paintings, at about 44,000 years. (Figurative art had been thought to have originated in modern Europe, grounding claims of Western cultural superiority, when in fact this was simply where most researchers were looking.) The works have been greeted as depictions of hunting and yet, as one researcher not involved in the study observed: "This scene may not be a depiction of an actual hunting scene but could be about animistic beliefs and the relationship between people and animals, or even a shamanic ritual"; see Becky Ferreira, "Mythical Beings May Be Earliest Imaginative Cave Art by Humans," *The New York Times*, December 11, 2019, https://www.nytimes.com/2019/12/11/science/cave-art-indonesia.html.

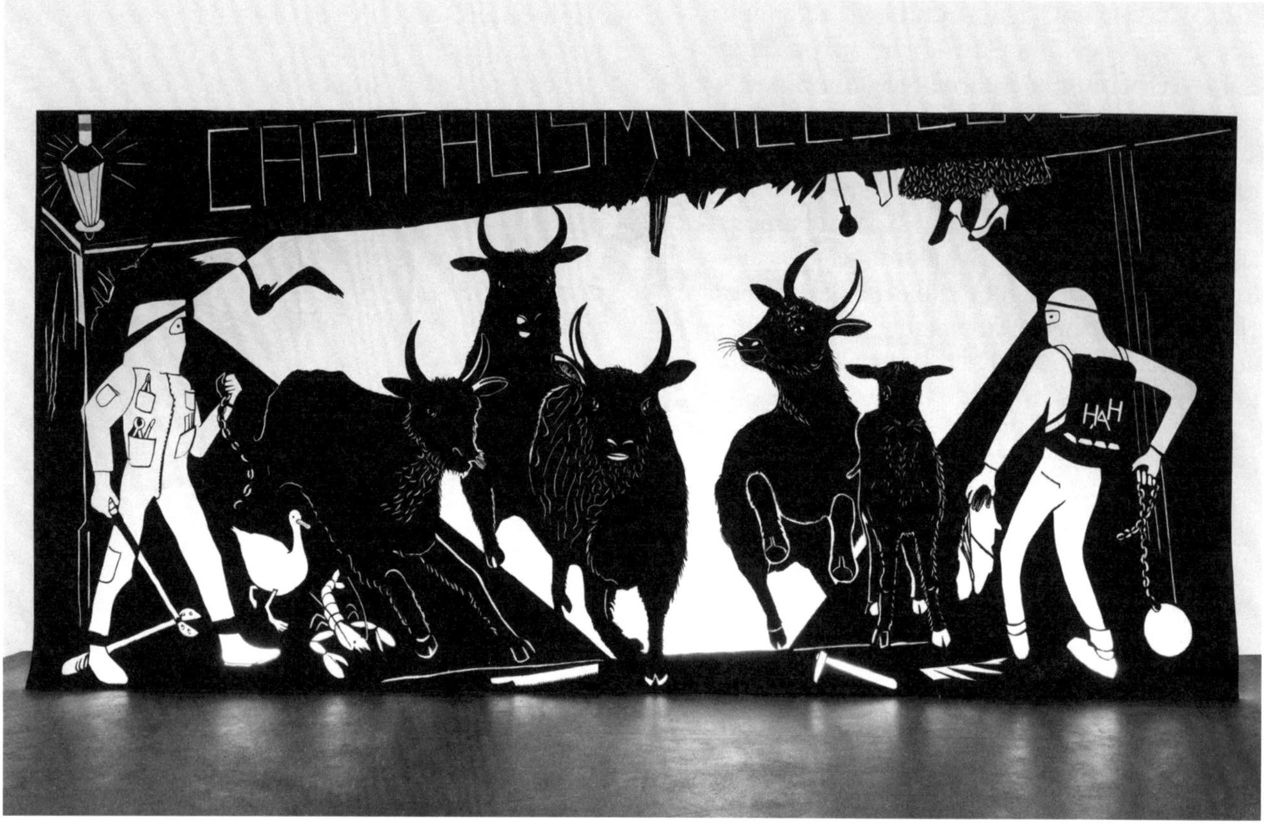


Fig. 7. *The Liberation of Animals from Their Cages XVI*, 2014. Cardboard, paper, wood, fluorescent lights, 110 ¼ × 246 ½ × 19 ⅝ in. (280 × 626 × 50 cm)

a "plague" of private equity firms buying up and gutting German companies, but the exact meaning of the drawing is obscure.[31]

Saeed also draws with paper, and not just on it. Since 2007, she has created what she refers to as "silhouettes," large-format, mural-like works made of transparent paper glued together and suspended, backlit, on the wall (fig. 7). These have the graphic quality and scale of agitprop, and their crispness recalls Expressionist woodcuts, a frequent reference for Saeed. She also sees an affinity here with the German director Lotte Reiniger (1899–1981), whose cut-paper silhouettes represent some of the first animated films. For *Arrival of the Animals*, Saeed has created a new, site-specific silhouette. *Hammar Marshes* (pl. 6) is named for an ancient marshland in Iraq, fed by the Tigris and Euphrates Rivers, and thought by many to be the model for the Garden of Eden, in part for its spectacular biodiversity.[32] Over centuries, the area's human inhabitants have built distinctive floating reed structures they inhabit alongside domesticated water buffalo. In the 1990s, the marshes were dammed and drained by Saddam Hussein, allegedly to root out Shiite rebels, and a major civil engineering project later helped restore them. Now they have started to dry up again, this time from growing cities bordering Iraq and drought brought by a warming planet. Still, for Saeed, the idea of a modern-day Eden in a war-torn country stands as a small pocket of utopia in the present.

31
"The Locusts: Private Equity Firms Strip Mine German Firms," *Spiegel Online*, December 22, 2006, https://www.spiegel.de/international/the-locusts-privaty-equity-firms-strip-mine-german-firms-a-456272.html.

32
Peter Schwartzstein, "Iraq's Famed Marshes Are Disappearing—Again," *National Geographic*, July 9, 2015, https://www.nationalgeographic.com/news/2015/07/150709-iraq-marsh-arabs-middle-east-water-environment-world/.

## LIBERATION

Saeed first became aware of the animal rights cause as a child in the 1980s, when she saw activists wielding graphic images of animal experimentation. In the 1990s, she joined the protests, this time against fur. As a response, Saeed featured animals in her earliest artwork. Yet she was troubled by the problem of how to represent not just animals, but also the abstract construct of animal *rights*. Her solution came around the time the animal rights movement in Germany recast itself in terms of "animal liberation," a cause with a built-in narrative. The term comes from Peter Singer's 1975 classic *Animal Liberation*. "A liberation movement," he explained, "is a demand for an end to prejudice and discrimination based on an arbitrary characteristic like race or sex."[33] Animal liberation took its cues from the liberation movements of the 1960s—which followed in the footsteps of Black Liberation—and set its sights on the arbitrary discrimination it termed speciesism. Singer didn't invent the term, but his writing popularized it, through an unemotional, reason-based case against the exploitation and suffering of nonhuman animals.[34] In the book, Singer recalls describing his and his wife's ethical position to a self-avowed animal lover and, in the moment, ham-sandwich eater: "Neither of us had ever been inordinately fond of dogs, cats, or horses in the way that many people are. We didn't 'love' animals. We simply wanted them treated as the independent sentient beings that they are, and not as a means to human ends."[35]

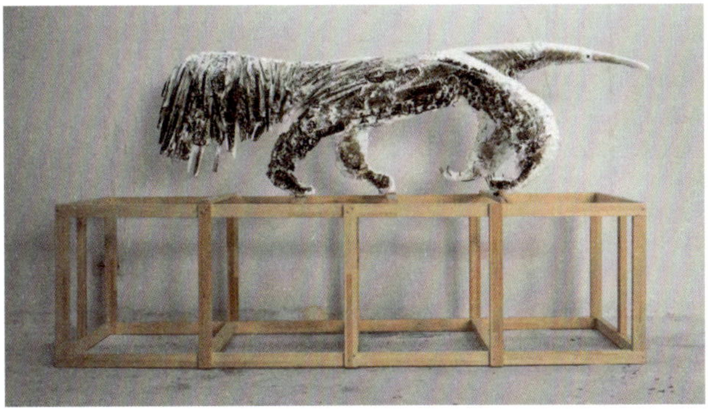

Fig. 8. *Ameisenbär/Anteater*, 2018. Polystyrene foam, steel, acrylic paint, charcoal, 51 ⅛ × 88 ¼ × 19 ¼ in. (130 × 224 × 49 cm)

"Liberation" here was in the sense of movement politics, and not literal emancipation or rescue by activists, about which Singer is ambivalent.[36] For Saeed, however, the term resonates both figuratively and literally. She is in regular dialogue with scholars and activists, and has made posters whose sale supports animal studies conferences, as well signs and objects used in protests. "My work," she explains, "is formed by conversations with activists, and dedicated to activists."[37]

Beginning around 2006, Saeed began to create life-size Styrofoam sculptures of animals standing triumphant atop their wood shipping crates, the cages having become plinths. *The Liberation of the Animals from Their Cages* series continues, with common, charismatic megafauna—such as *Calf* (pl. 13)—as well as peculiar, even comical-looking ones, such as the needle-nosed, bushy-tailed *Anteater* (fig. 8). Late in 2019, Saeed began *Pangolin* (pl. 14) for the Clark's exhibition. Since then, pangolins have made headlines as potential hosts of the virus causing COVID-19, a zoonotic disease that—like Ebola, MERS, or SARS—is transmitted via nonhuman animals, often in the process of their slaughter, sale, or consumption. This might be the pangolin's revenge, it has been suggested, for being the most trafficked mammal in the world.[38]

33
Peter Singer, *Animal Liberation* (New York: Ecco, 2002), xxii.

34
After coining the term in a campus flier in 1970, Oxford scientist Richard Ryder first published it in his essay "Experiments on Animals," in *Animals, Men and Morals: An Enquiry into the Maltreatment of Non-Humans*, ed. Stanley and Roslind Godlovitch and John Harris (London: Gollancz, 1971). Many animal rights advocates today have distanced themselves from Singer, for his subsequent ethical positions.

35
Singer, *Animal Liberation*, xxi.

36
Direct Action Everywhere (DxE) is an example of a nonviolent activist organization that conducts open rescue operations on behalf of ailing animals. Saeed does not align with activist organizations, and instead only individuals.

37
Email exchange with the artist, December 1, 2019.

38
Wufei Yu, "Coronavirus: Revenge of the Pangolins?," *The New York Times*, March 5, 2020, sec. Opinion, https://www.nytimes.com/2020/03/05/opinion/coronavirus-china-pangolins.html.

As elsewhere in her practice, Saeed here questions the traditional role of the plinth, base, or pedestal in sculpture, namely to elevate objects off the ground, above the realm of the ordinary, and to the status of art. In some cases, she places her figures directly on the floor, or spanning floor and wall, and in others she explores alternatives to the pedestal. In *Freie Liebe/Free Love* (fig. 9) apparent friends occupy the common level of a park bench. "I was interested in seeing the park bench as a democratic form of a pedestal. Usually a pedestal makes a sculpture higher, this one makes it lower. It also defines the space around the sculpture as an outside and public space, like a park. Less elite, more egalitarian than an art space."[39]

Raising and lowering and de- and refamiliarizing the nonhuman animal reflects an unresolved tension in Saeed's approach: "*Das Tier ist das Unerreichbare*" (the animal is the unreachable), she writes, concluding a short text decrying Carsten Höller's use of live animals in his 2010 exhibition *Soma*.[40] By "unreachable," Saeed seems to mean both unavailable to full comprehension and sacrosanct, or inviolable. John Berger's landmark essay "Why Look at Animals?" took up the question of the animal's increasing marginality in advanced capitalist society, but also began with the observation that its "lack of common language [with humans], its silence, guarantees its distance, its distinctness, its exclusion, from and of man."[41] In other words, human and animal must return to a proximity long since lost, but also not attempt to fully bridge it, as much out of mystification as respect—or survival. As the indigenous Alaskan man interviewed in Werner Herzog's 2005 film *Grizzly Man* knows, commenting on the title character's fatal mauling by the animals he so loved, there are certain lines one must not cross.

Saeed is a student of the history of the animal rights movement. She is particularly struck by the consistent leadership of women in it. This is one reason, she thinks, why the male-dominated history of art has so rarely taken up subject matter sensitive to animals, and instead represented them as the prey in hunting scenes, the main course in *vanitas* paintings, or, generally, as the allegorical foil to man's biblically warranted dominion. Saeed is also alive to the long history of common cause among abolitionists, suffragettes, labor activists, and animal welfare reformers, aligned against exploitation of different kinds, often perpetrated by the same interests.[42] A recent interest of hers has been the Brown Dog Riots, a violent chapter in English history touched off by an experimental surgery performed on an allegedly conscious brown terrier at the University College London in 1903.[43] The event pitted medical students against anti-vivisection activists, most of whom were also suffragettes and trade unionists, all galvanized by the plight of the least powerful. A bronze memorial to the dog built by activists in Battersea Park (fig. 10) further exacerbated the conflict, and defenders of animal testing destroyed it a few years later. Saeed is fascinated by the story but doesn't expect to make art about it. For her, the original monument, though long since gone, suffices.

If some of Saeed's narratives have humans fighting on animals' behalf, others show animals defending themselves. *War*, of 2006 (pl. 20), literalizes the human assault on the natural world, with one species against all others. Arrayed opposite soldiers with helmets and rifles is a multispecies phalanx, from birds and butterflies in the air to a turtle, spider, and crayfish on the ground. This dream is joined by other drawings in which animals revolt. In *Arrival of the Animals I*, 2009, various creatures

39
Email exchange with the artist, December 9, 2019.

40
Lin May Saeed, "Anlässlich der Ausstellung *Soma* von Carsten Höller im Hamburger Bahnhof, Berlin (November 5, 2010–February 6, 2011)," 2011, www.linmay.de/index_e.html.

41
John Berger, "Why Look at Animals?," in *About Looking* (New York: Pantheon Books, 1980), 4.

42
See Carol J. Adams, *The Sexual Politics of Meat: A Feminist-Vegetarian Critical Theory* (New York: Continuum, 2010); and Bénédicte Boisseron, *Afro-Dog: Blackness and the Animal Question* (New York: Columbia University Press, 2018).

43
See Coral Lansbury, *The Old Brown Dog: Women, Workers, and Vivisection in Edwardian England* (Madison: University of Wisconsin Press, 1985); and Susan Hamilton, ed., *Animal Welfare and Anti-Vivisection, 1870–1910: Nineteenth-century Woman's Mission* (London: Routledge, 2004).

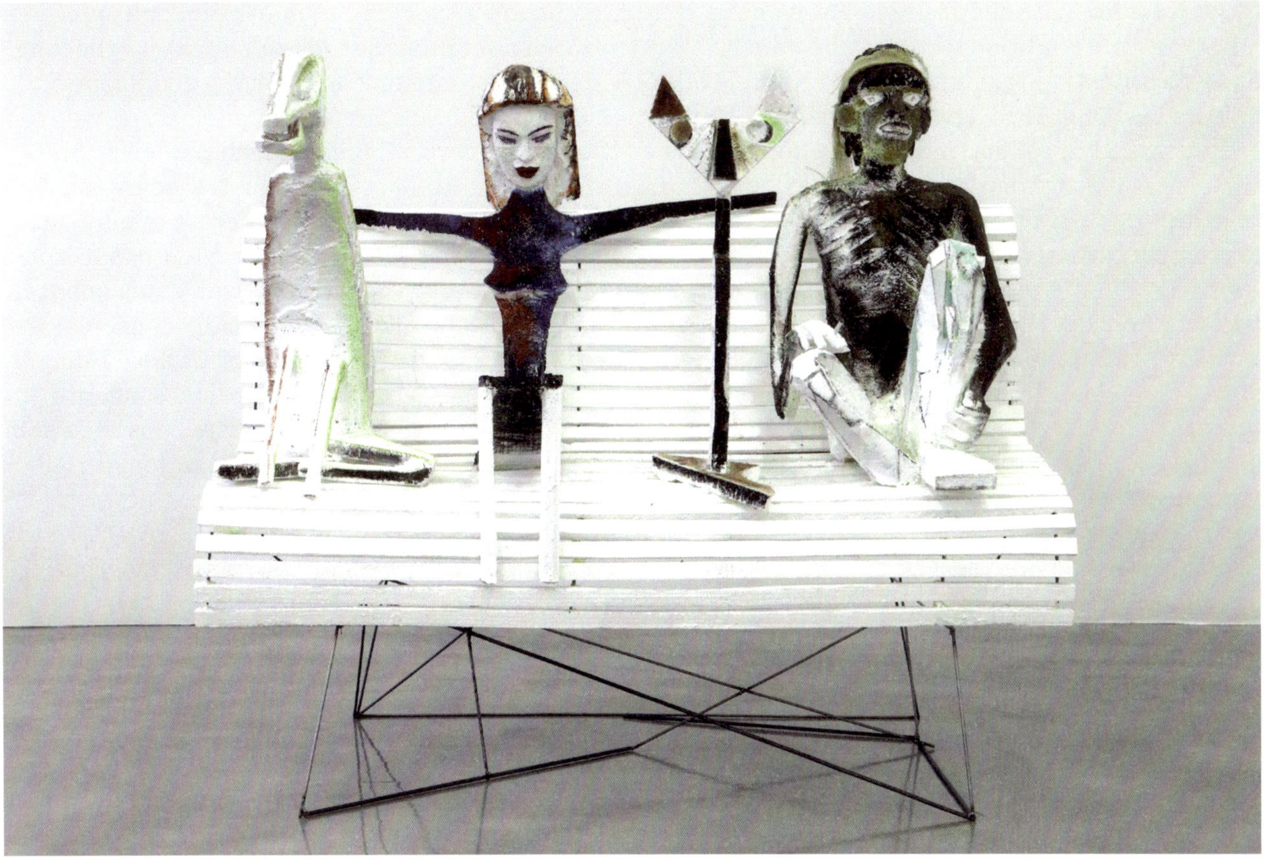

Fig. 9. *Freie Liebe/Free Love*, 2006. Polystyrene foam, acrylic paint, steel, cigarette, jute, 55 7/8 × 64 7/8 × 34 5/8 in. (142 × 165 × 88 cm). Collection Gaby and Wilhelm Schürmann, Herzogenrath, Germany

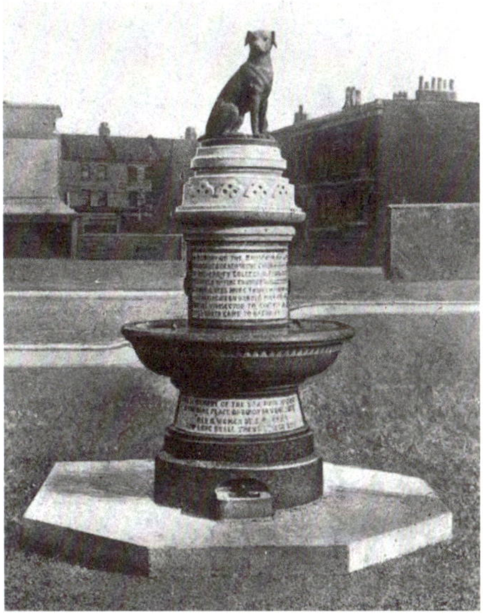

Fig. 10. Joseph Whitehead (English, 1868–1951), *The Brown Dog*, 1906. Bronze

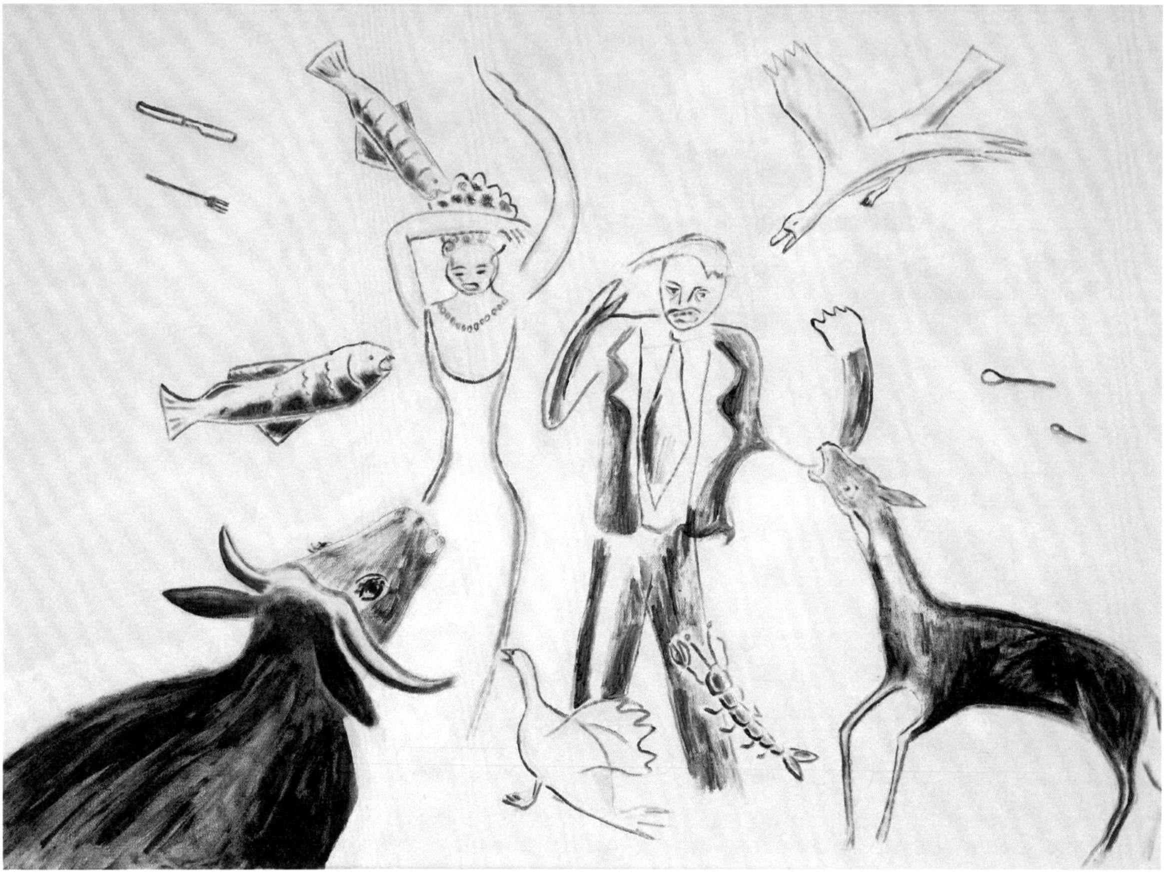

Fig. 11. *Ankunft der Tiere/Arrival of the Animals I*, 2009. Acrylic paint on canvas, 27 ½ × 39 ⅜ in (70 × 100 cm)

fly in the face of a bourgeois human pair (fig. 11). Saeed plays here on the title of one Canetti story and links it to the action of another. Such resistance and revolt are a more common phenomenon in everyday life today, as animals increasingly "arrive" in new environments, homeless and hungry, following the destruction of their own habitats.[44]

Saeed's closest precursor is probably Sue Coe, the British-born artist and illustrator. Since the late 1970s, Coe has made explicitly anti-racist, anti-capitalist, and anti-war drawings and paintings with a special focus on nonhuman animals. "I make art for people on the front lines. That's my family: a community of activists who are not artists but who want to use art as a weapon."[45] Coe grew up in bombed-out, post–World War II Britian, and directly behind a slaughterhouse, whose stench and animal screams she recalls vividly. "As a child, I was forced to see the correlation between war, violence, and fascism, and animal cruelty and abuse. Once I figured that connection out, so early on, I realized that the Other is always at risk." Coe's blunt, lurid works—generally in black and white, with blood-red details—recall both the earnest anguish of Käthe Kollwitz's graphic works and the biting satire of John Heartfield's photomontages. Coe is known for drawings like *Modern Man Followed by the Ghosts of His Meat* (fig. 12), and regularly depicts both the grisly, dehumanizing condition of usually nonwhite, and often non-citizen, slaughterhouse workers as well as the megafarm owners enriched by their labor.[46] Saeed, whose approach is less explicit, does not want her art to feel aggressive. "Many people feel guilty about animals anyway, and [these feelings] make them angry."[47] Instead, her power lies in a different kind of communication.

As a corrective to the history of art, and the limits of our own imaginations, Saeed creates a new mythology and a new iconography, retelling old stories and introducing new ones. Lest our relationship to other animals or the earth ever seem settled, or naturalized, by "since the beginning of time" narratives, Saeed unearths artifacts of an alternative past and a possible future. Here, sentient earthlings stand shoulder to shoulder, sometimes literally,

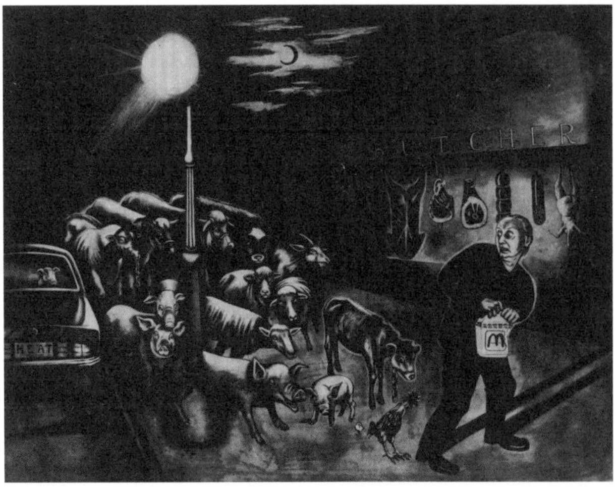

Fig. 12. Sue Coe (British, b. 1951), *Modern Man Followed by the Ghosts of His Meat*, 1990. Photoetching on paper, 13 × 18 ¾ in. (33 × 47.6 cm). Walker Art Center, Minneapolis, MN, Gift of the Walker Art Center Teen Arts Council, 1998. Copyright © 1991 Sue Coe. Courtesy Galerie St. Etienne, New York

united by a common destiny. As Saeed understands, imagining another world will require new—and often old—habits, traditions, and culture. Indeed, this rewriting and re-forming is the plasticity on which all life depends.

44
See Jason Hribal, *Fear of the Animal Planet: The Hidden History of Animal Resistance* (Oakland, CA: CounterPunch, 2010); and Fahim Amir, *Schwein und Zeit: Tiere, Politik, Revolte* (Hamburg: Edition Nautilus, 2018).

45
Lauren O'Neill-Butler, interview with Sue Coe, *Artforum*, August 21, 2018, https://www.artforum.com/interviews/sue-coe-talks-about-her-ongoing-animal-rights-activism-and-political-art-76307.

46
See Stephen F. Eisenman, *The Ghosts of Our Meat: Sue Coe* (New York, NY/Carlisle, PA: DAP/The Trout Gallery, Dickinson College, 2013).

47
Una Meistere, "Why Haven't Animals Revolted against Humans Yet? A Conversation with German-Iraqi Artist and Animal Activist Lin May Saeed," Arterritory.com, January 8, 2020, http://www.arterritory.com/en/texts/interviews/8612-why_havent_animals_revolted_against_humans_yet/.

# PLATES

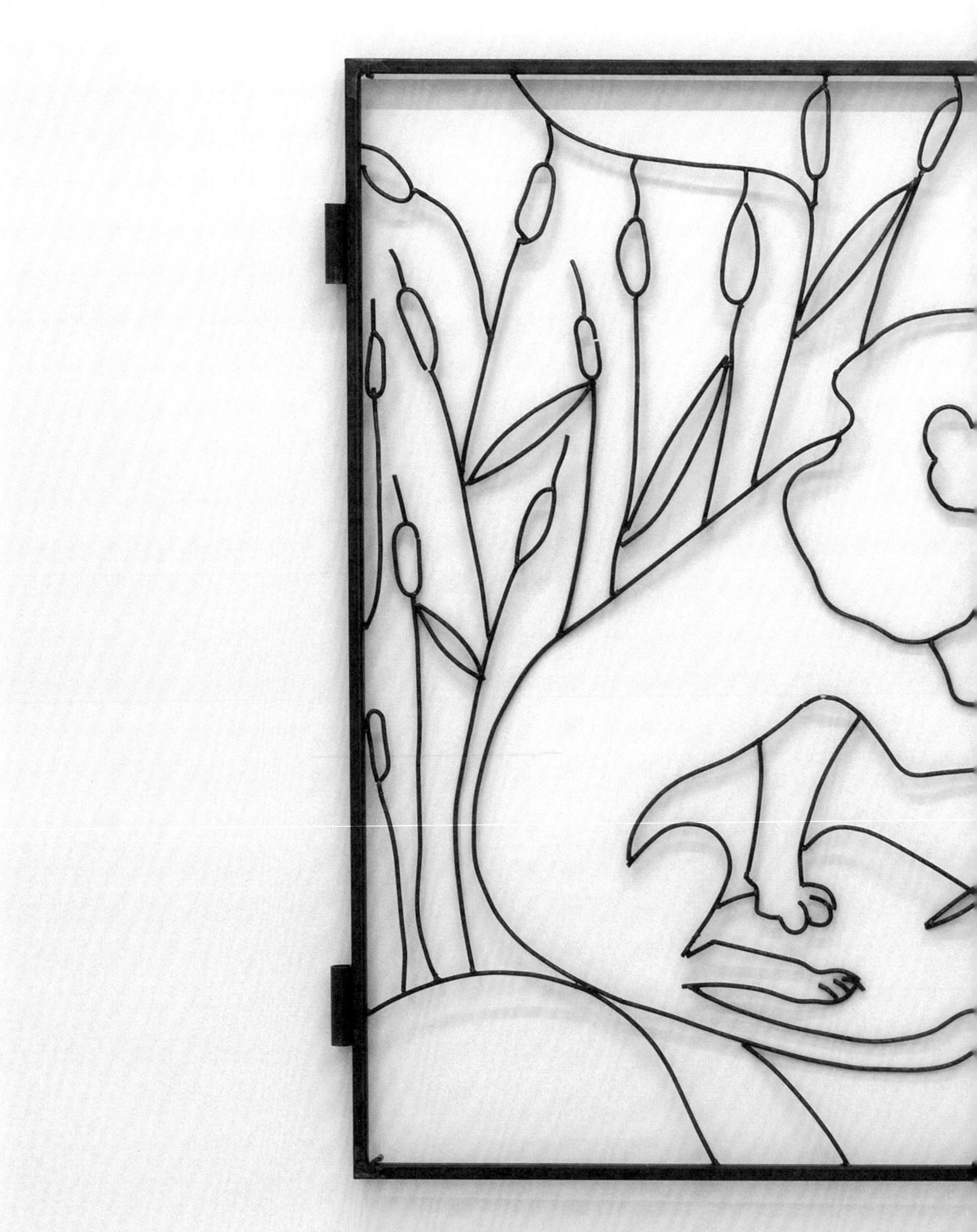

Plate 1. *St. Jerome and the Lion*, 2016
Steel, lacquer, 59 × 73 ¼ × 3 ⅞ in. (150 × 186 × 10 cm)

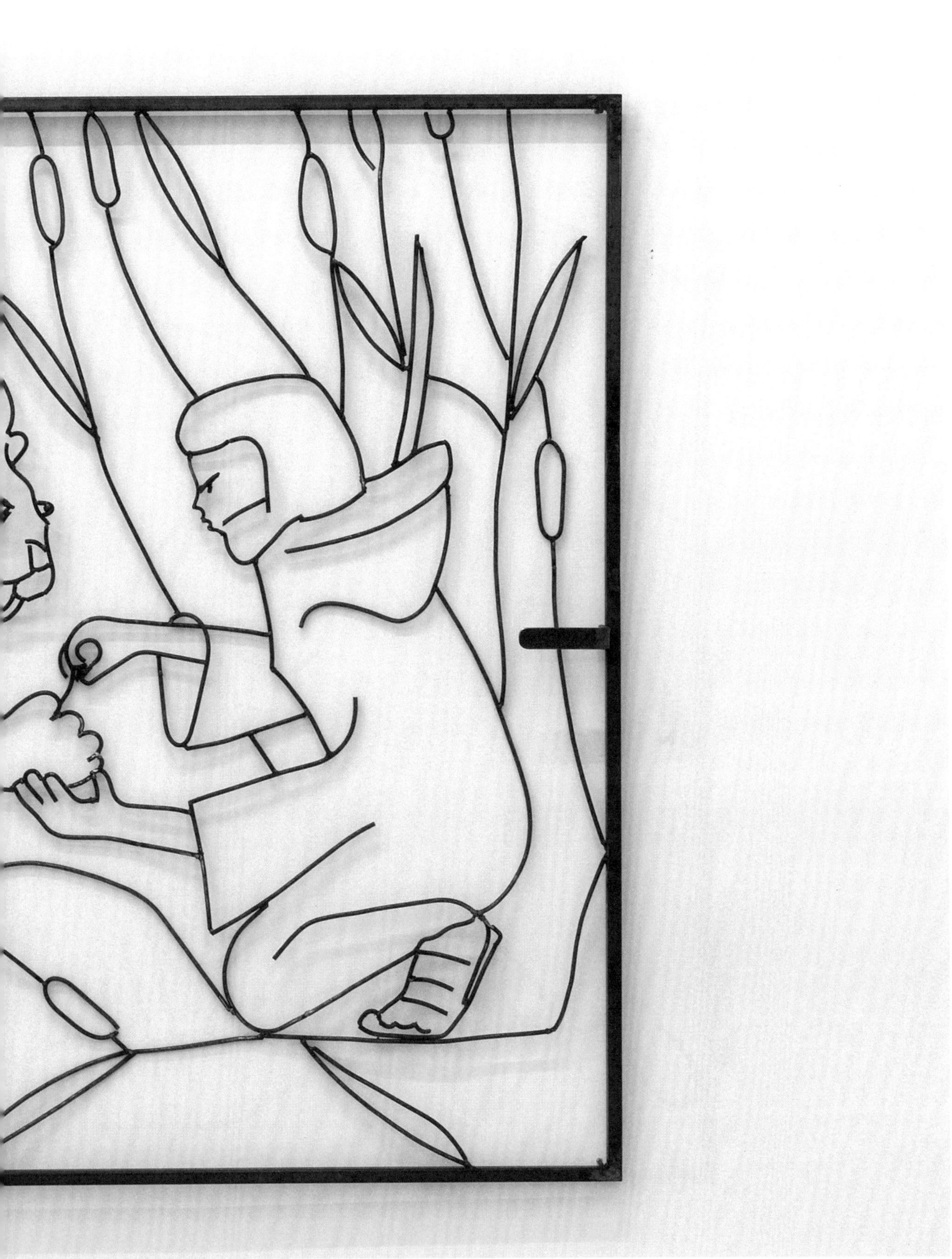

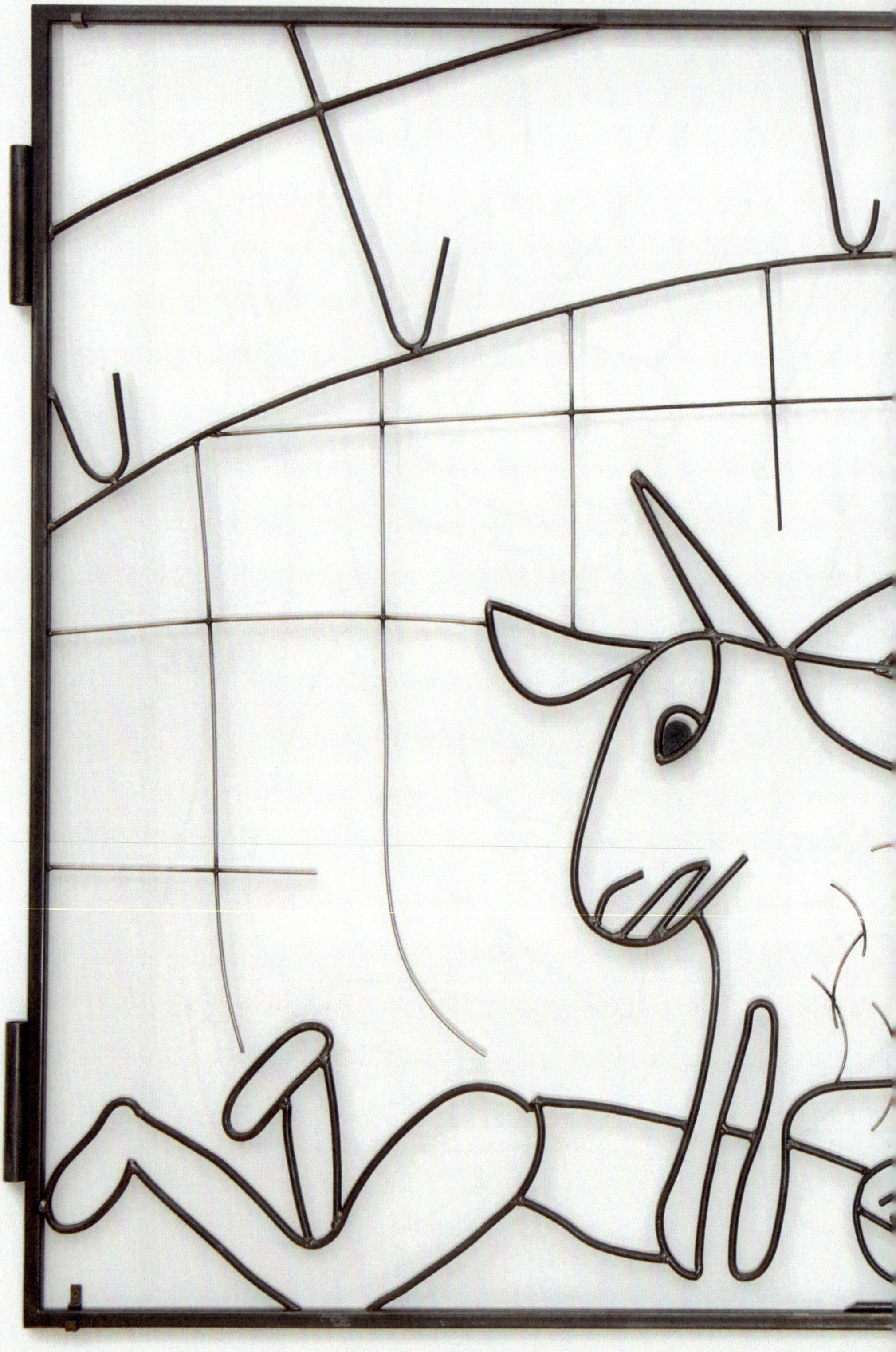

Plate 2. *Toreador Gate*, 2019
Steel, lacquer, 59 × 83 ⅞ × 3 ½ in. (150 × 213 × 9 cm)

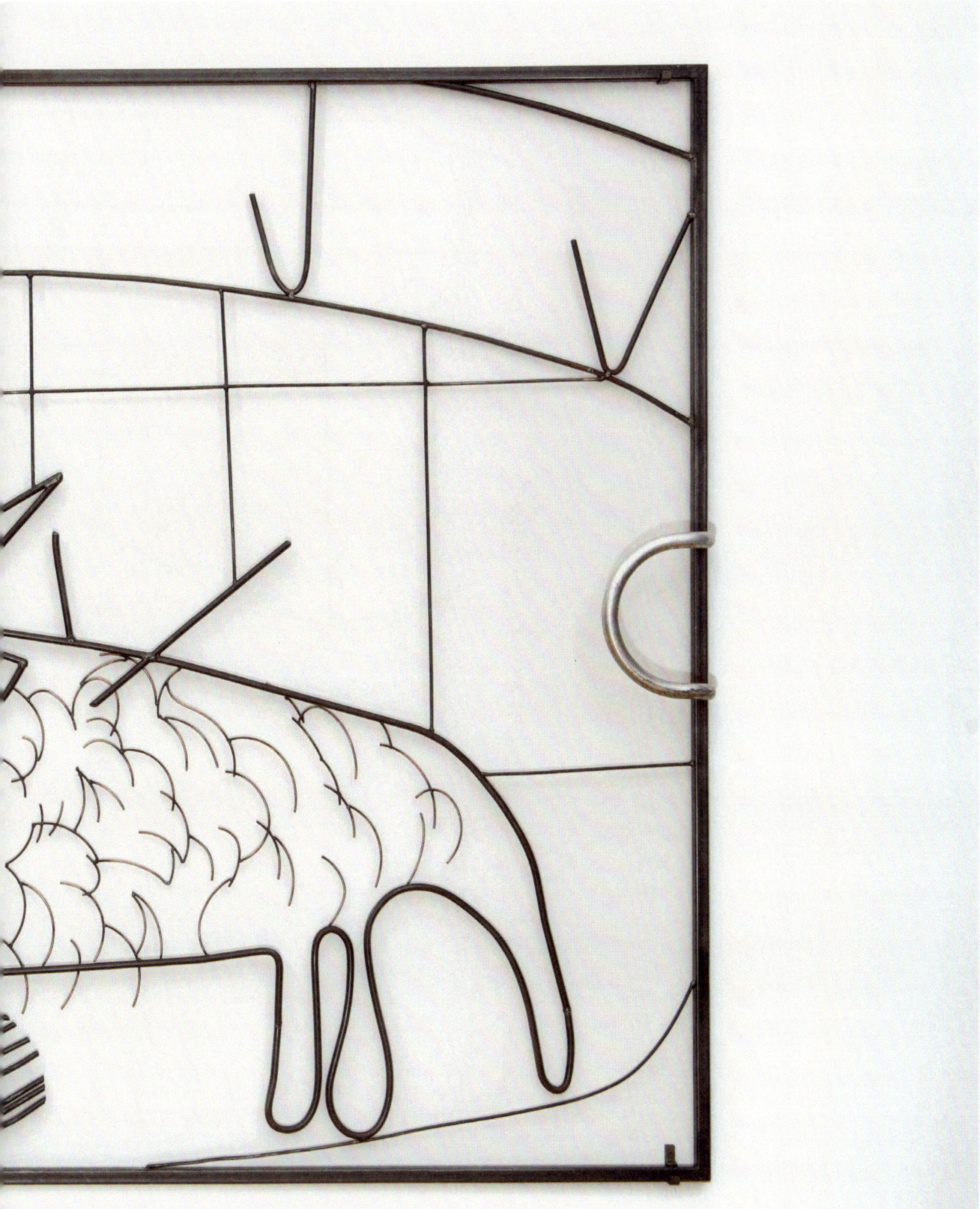

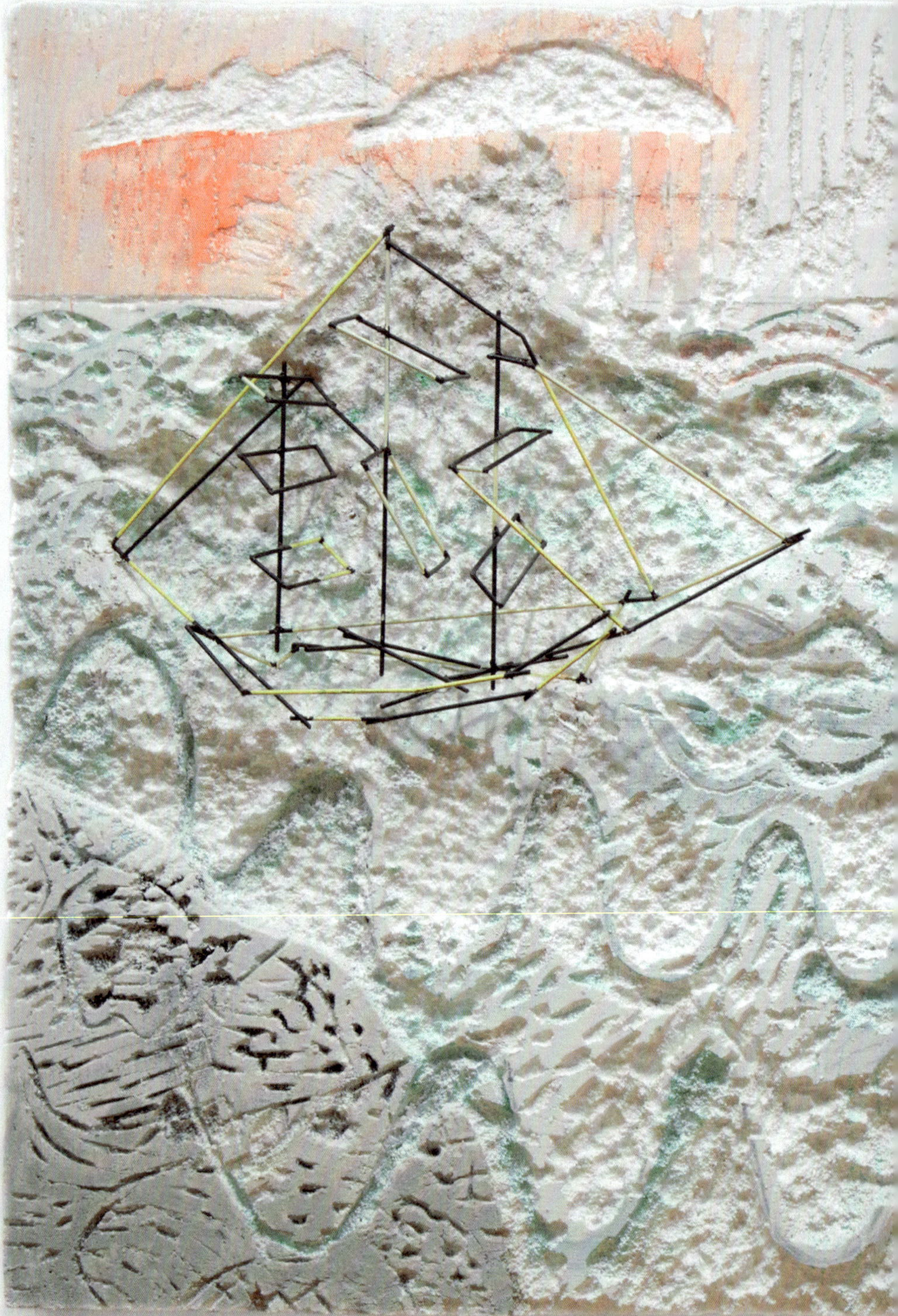

Plate 3. *Ghost Ship Relief*, 2013
Polystyrene foam, acrylic paint, steel, plaster, paper, 69 ¼ × 98 ⅞ × 13 ½ in. (176 × 251 × 34 cm)

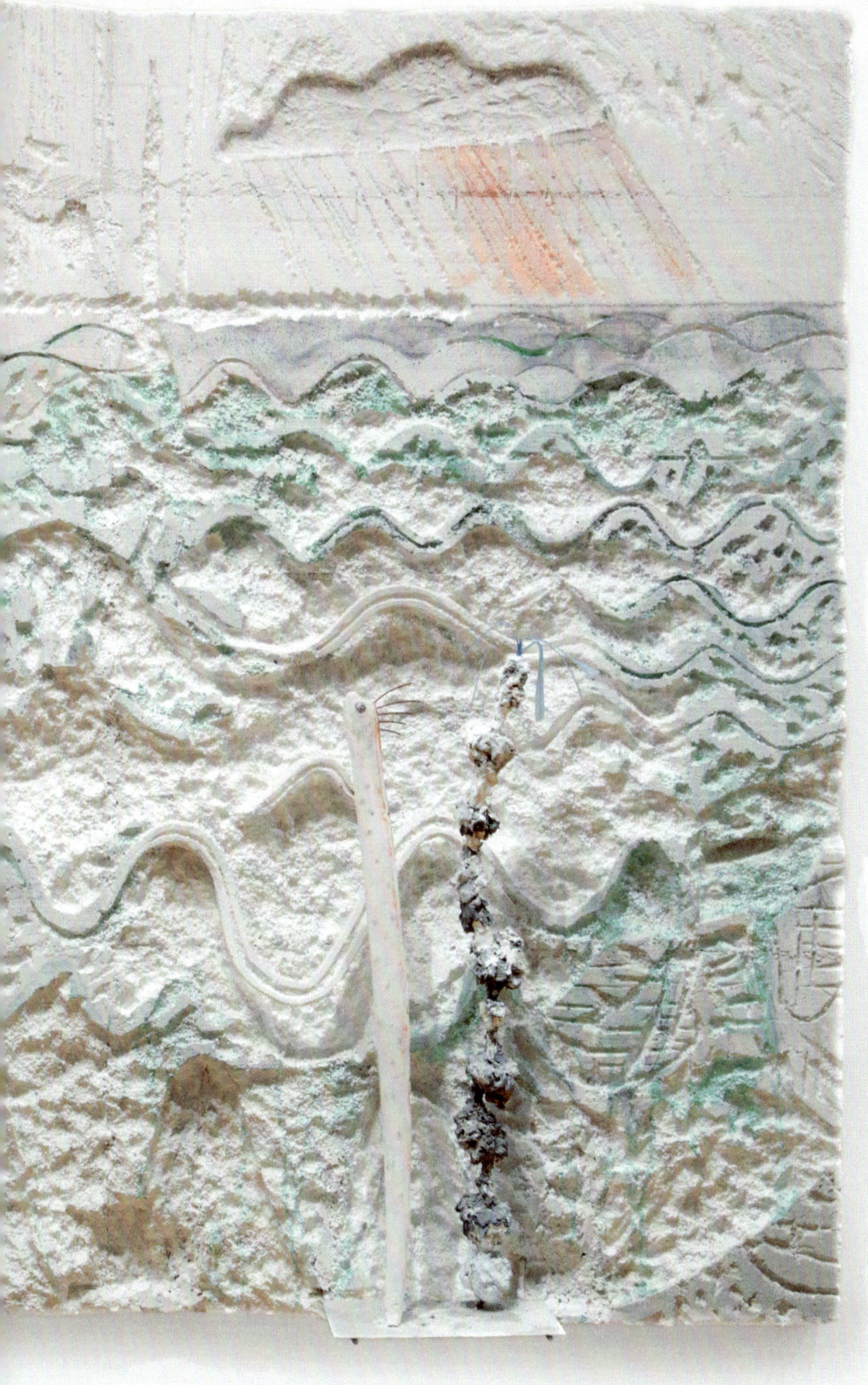

 *Ghost Ship Relief* (detail), 2013

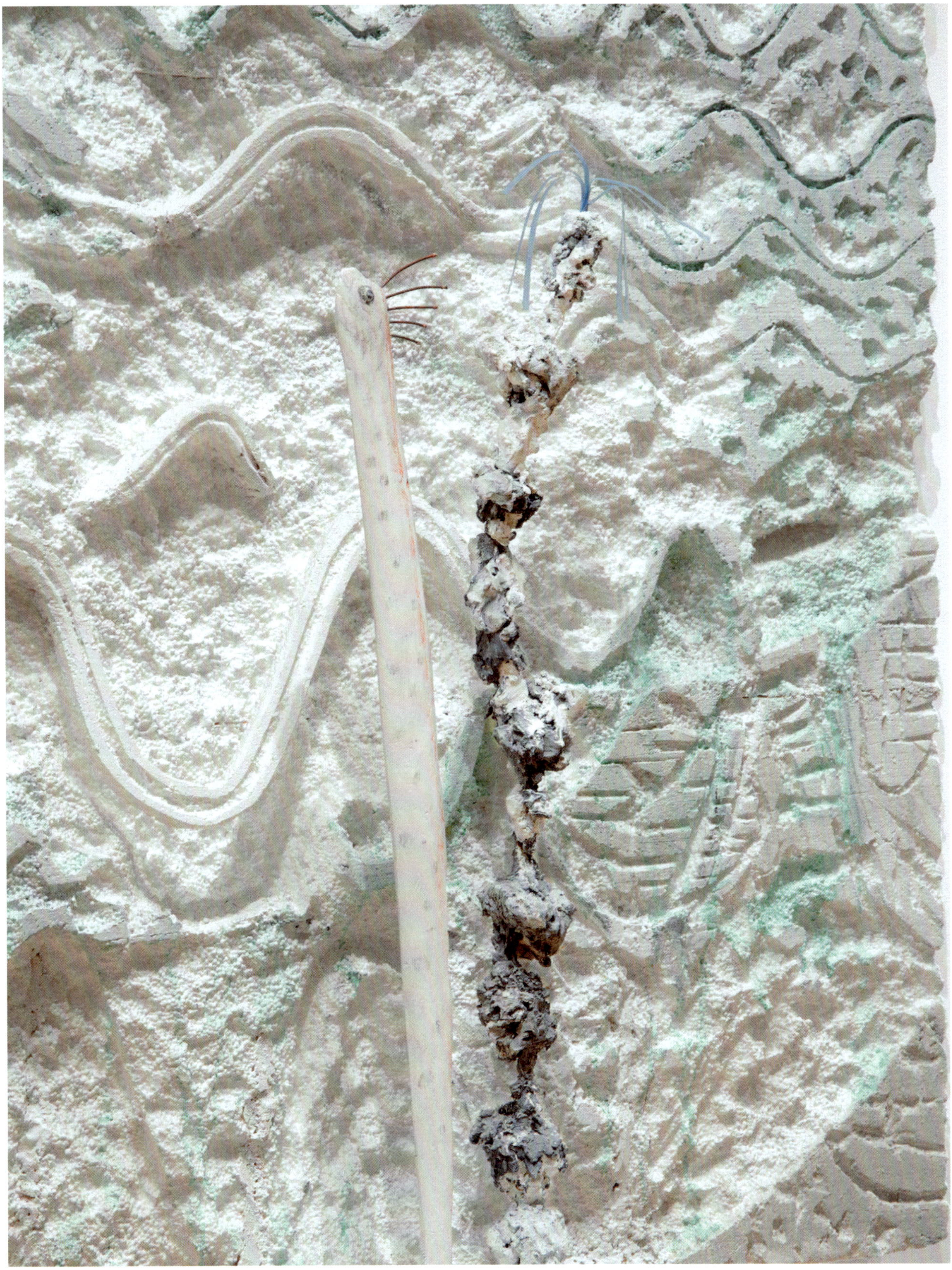

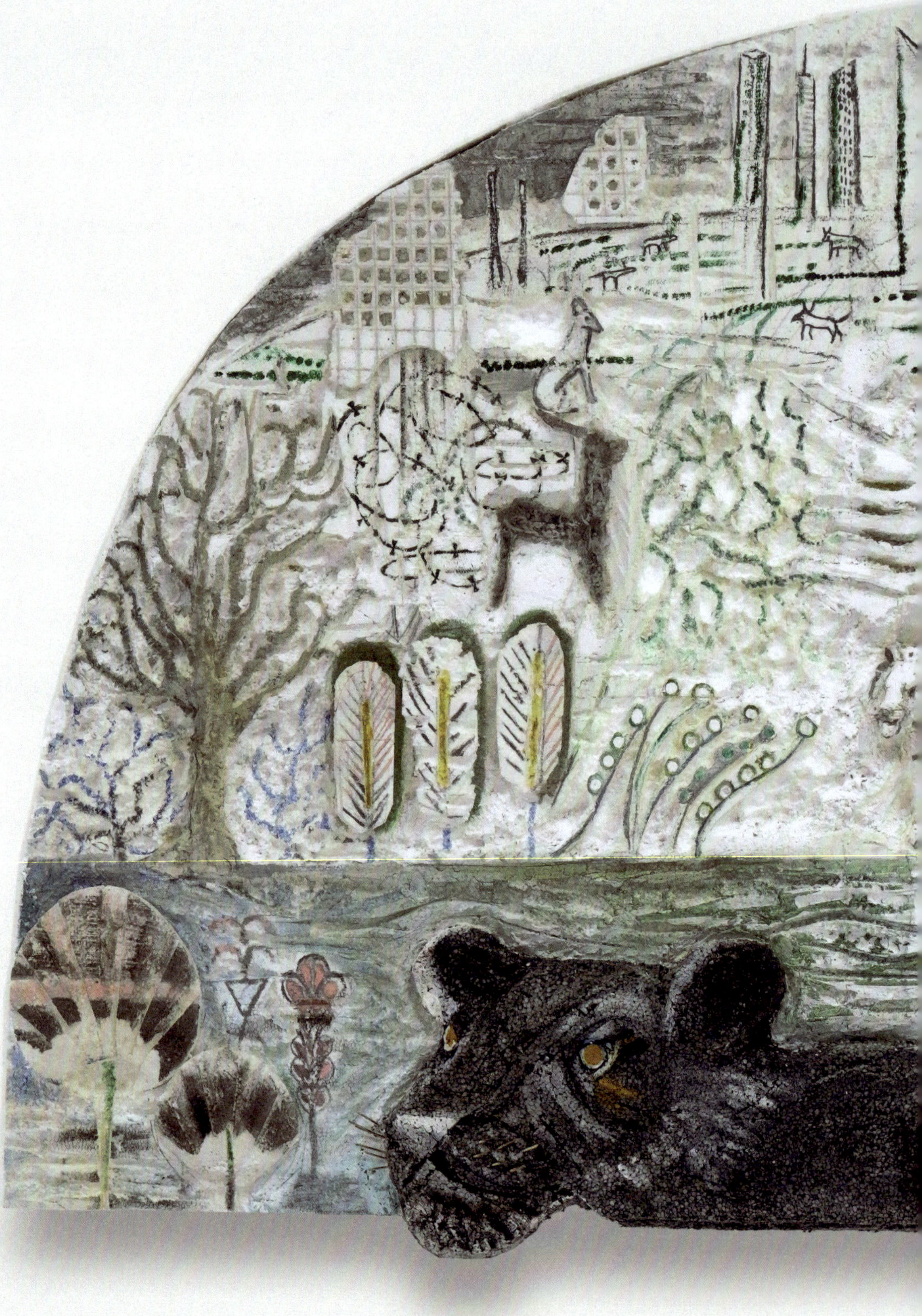

Plate 4. *Panther Relief*, 2017
Polystyrene foam, acrylic paint, wood, 44 ⅛ × 72 ½ × 4 ⅛ in. (112 × 184 × 10.5 cm)

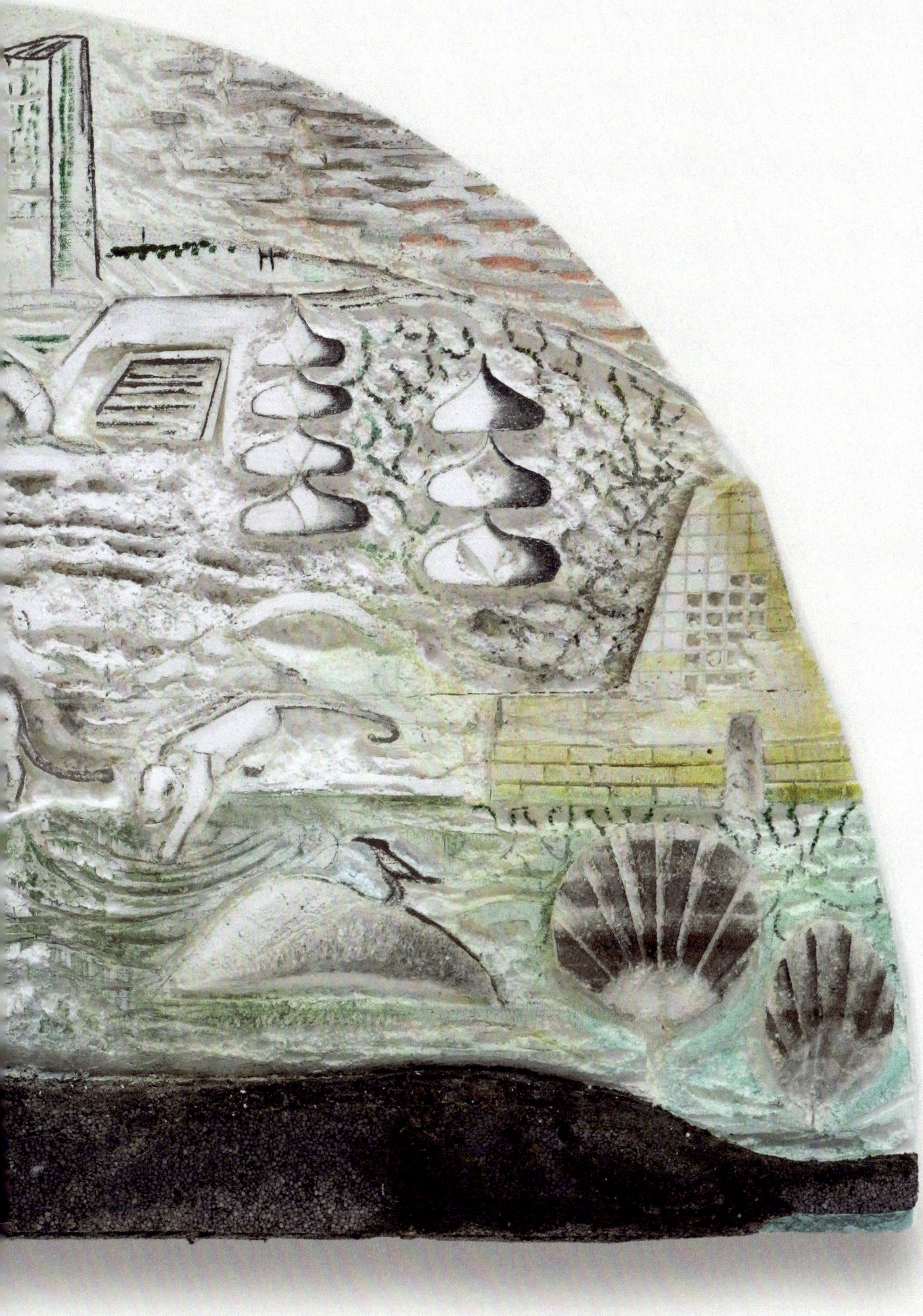

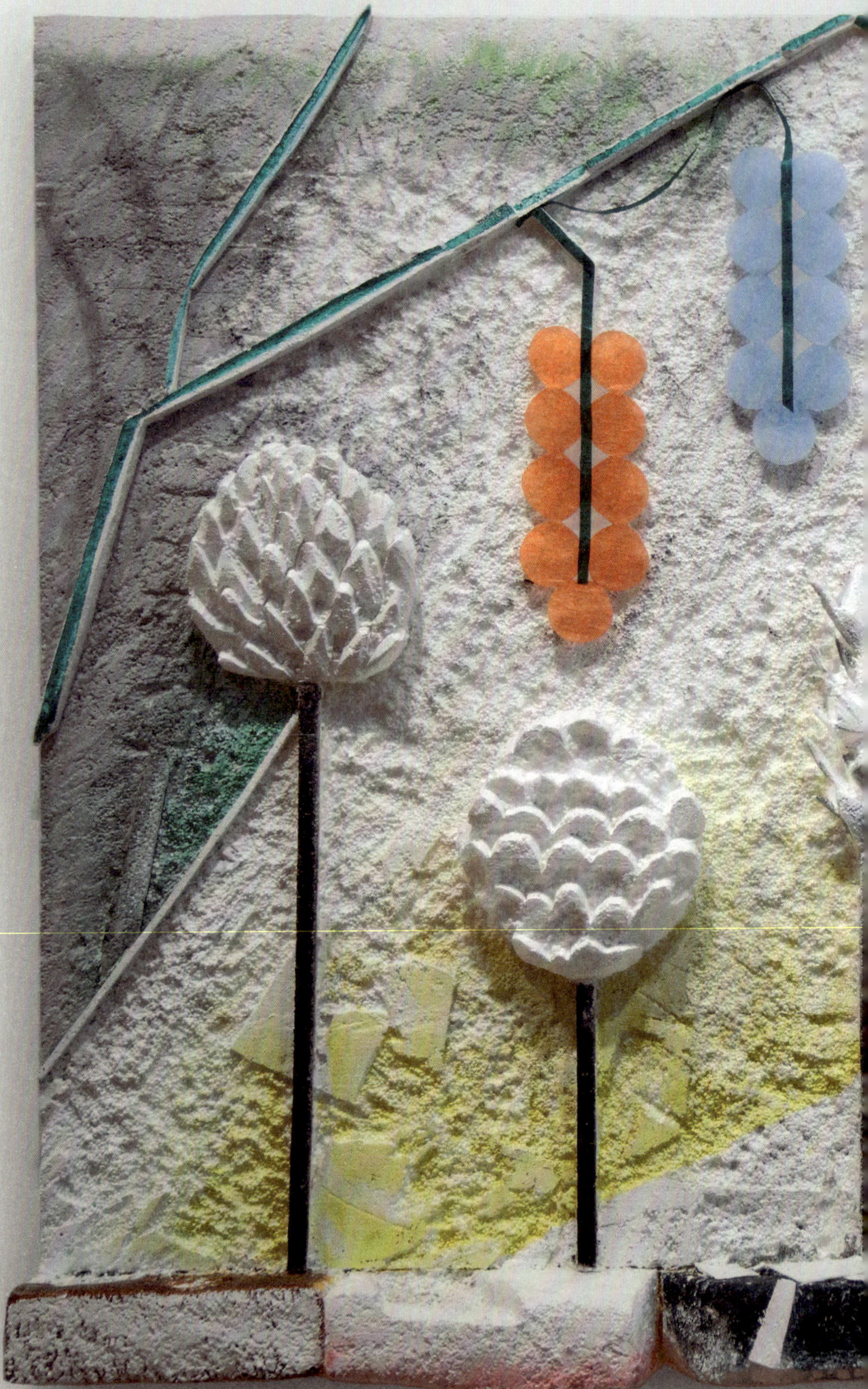

Plate 5. *Bee Relief*, 2018
Polystyrene foam, acrylic paint, steel, wood, paper, 53 ⅛ × 70 ⅞ × 8 ⅝ in. (135 × 180 × 22 cm)

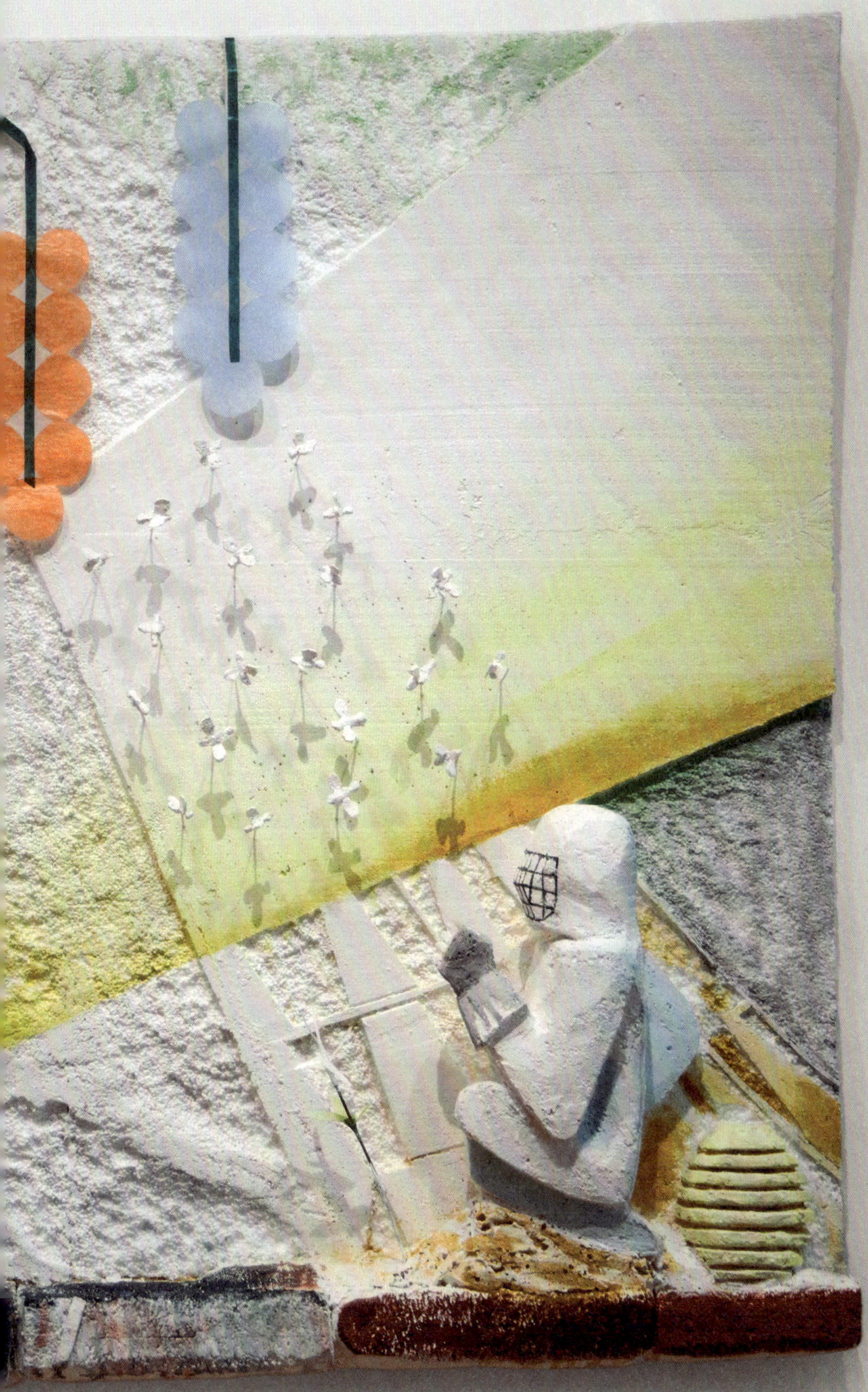

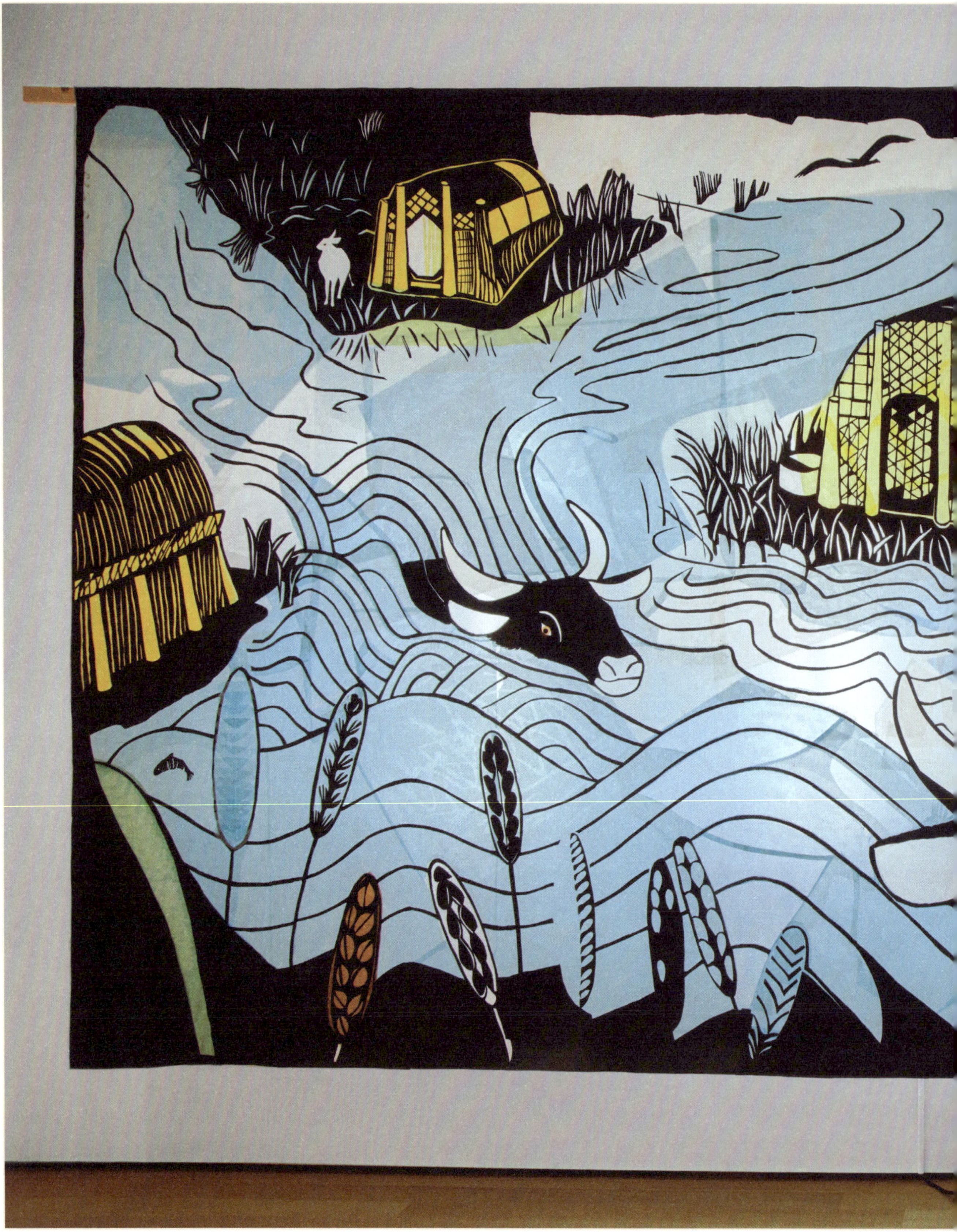

Plate 6. *Hawr al-Hammar/Hammar Marshes*, 2020
Cardboard, paper, wood, fluorescent lights, 102 ⅜ × 200 ¾ × 25 ⅝ in. (260 × 510 × 65 cm)

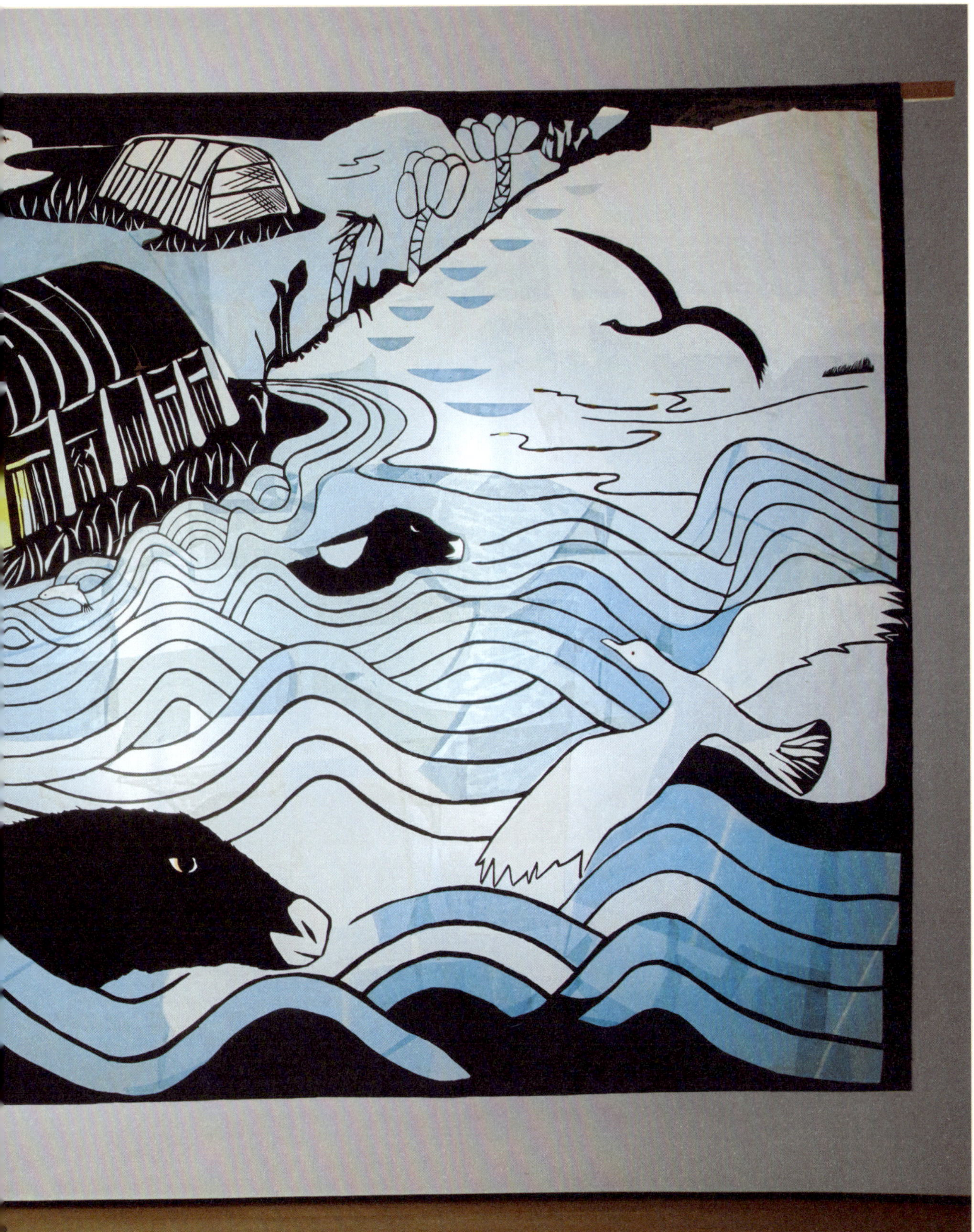

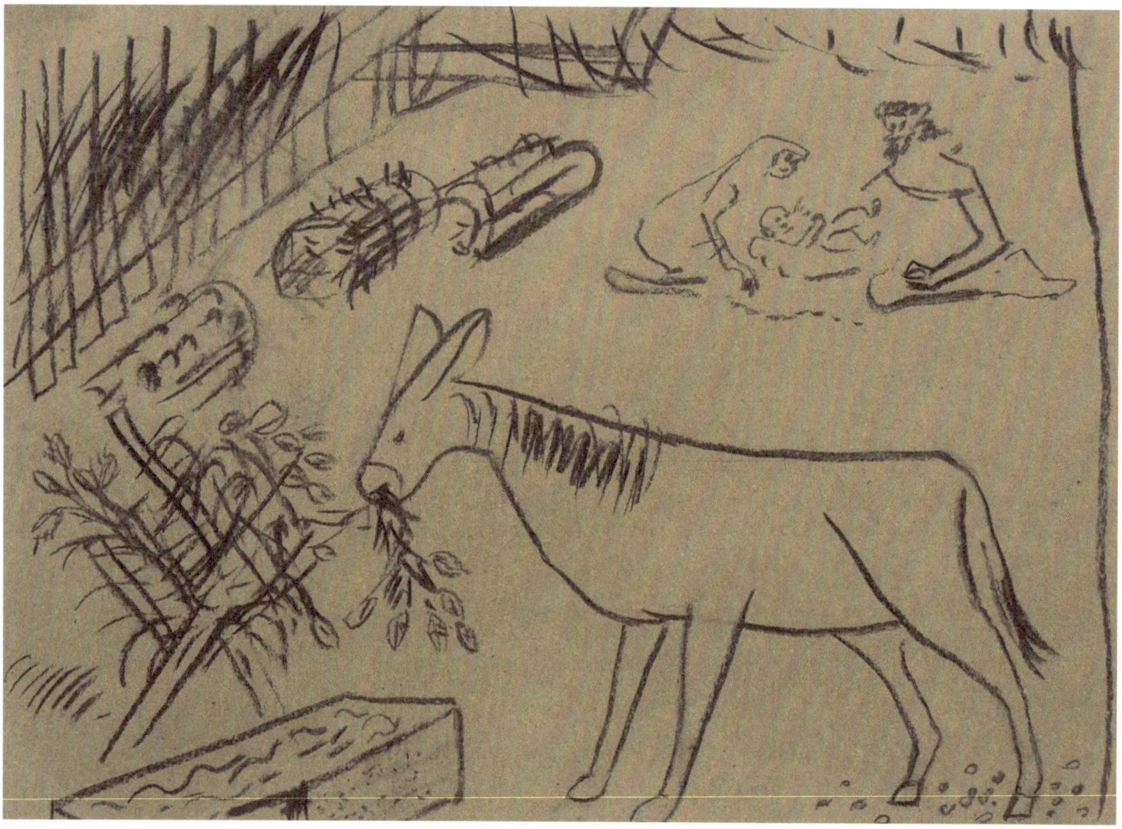

Plate 7. *Noel*, 2019
Charcoal on brown paper, 9 ½ × 13 ⅜ in. (24 × 34 cm)

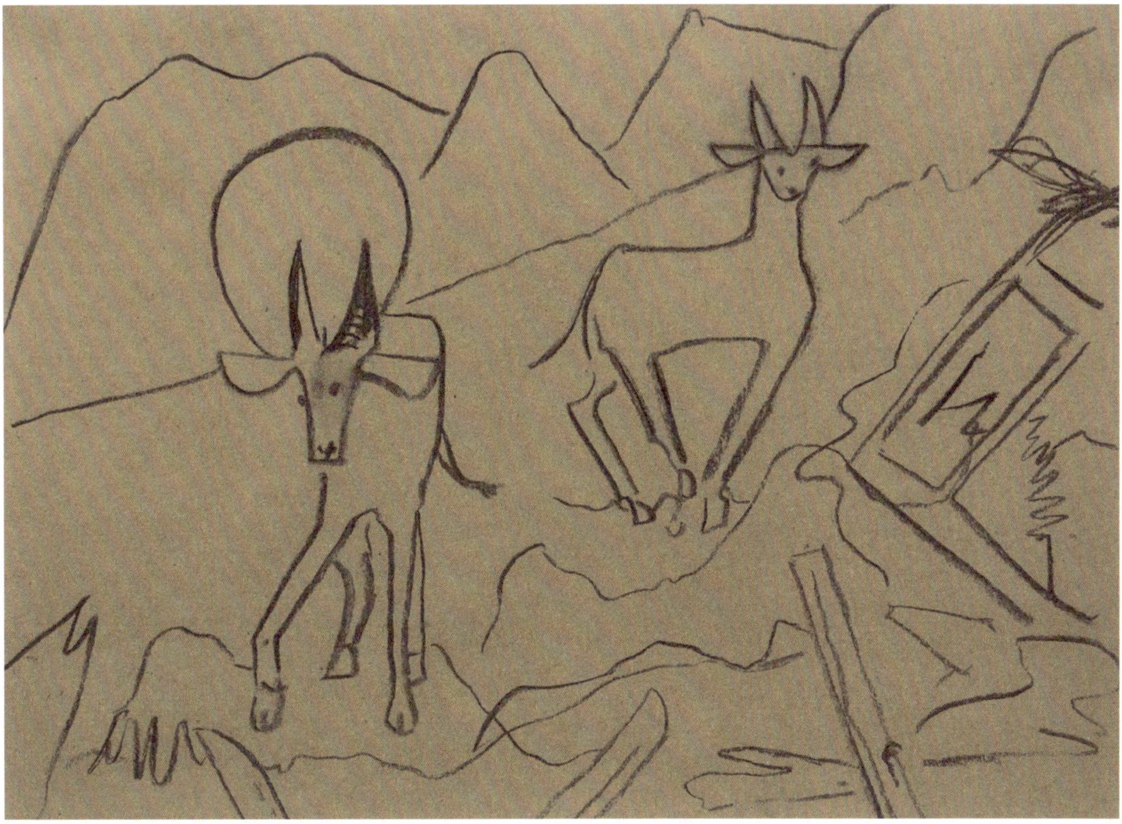

Plate 8. *Davos*, 2019
Charcoal on brown paper, 9 ½ × 13 ⅜ in. (24 × 34 cm)

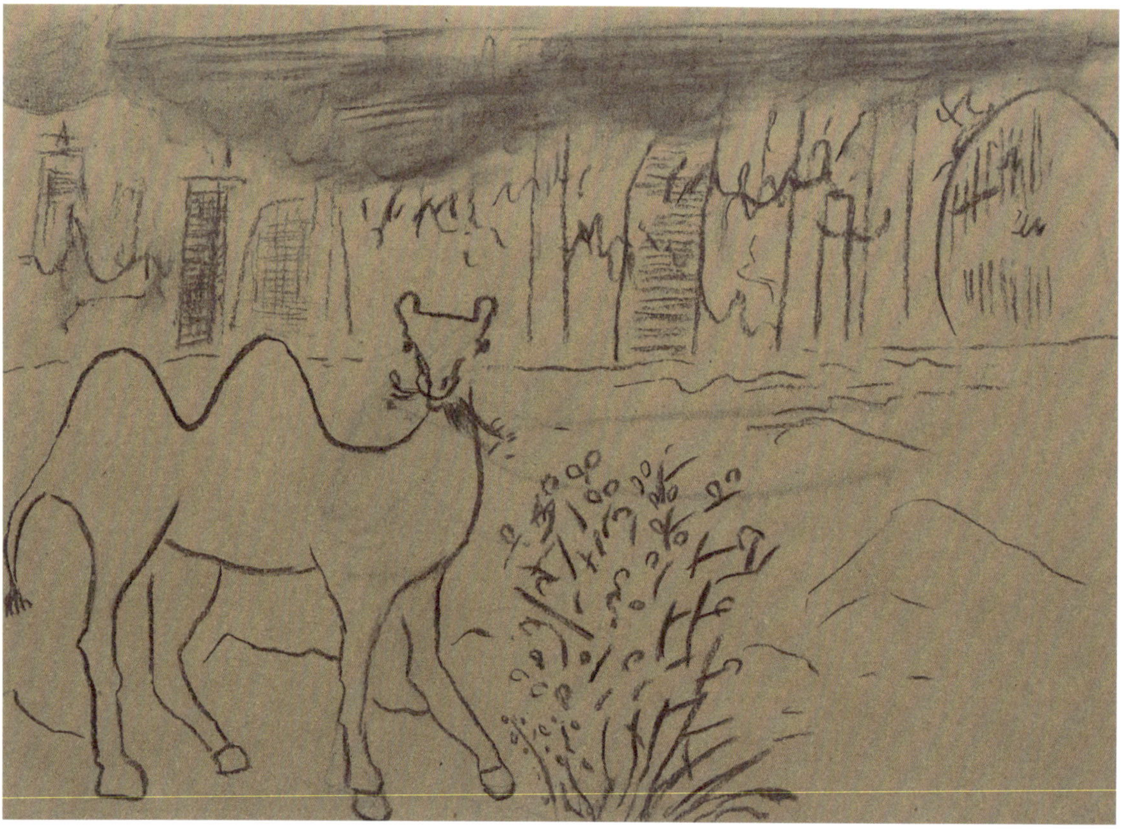

Plate 9. *Doha*, 2019
Charcoal on brown paper, 9 ½ × 13 ⅜ in. (24 × 34 cm)

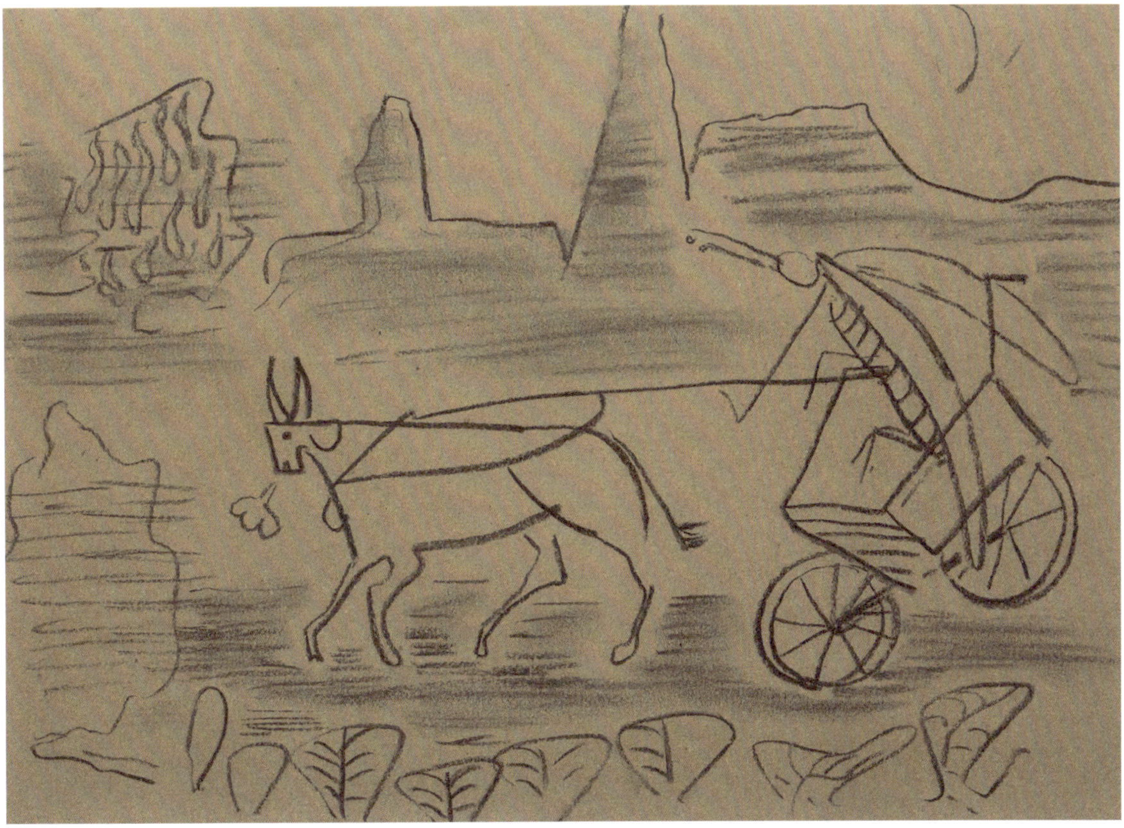

Plate 10. *Anmar*, 2019
Charcoal on brown paper, 9 ½ × 13 ⅜ in. (24 × 34 cm)

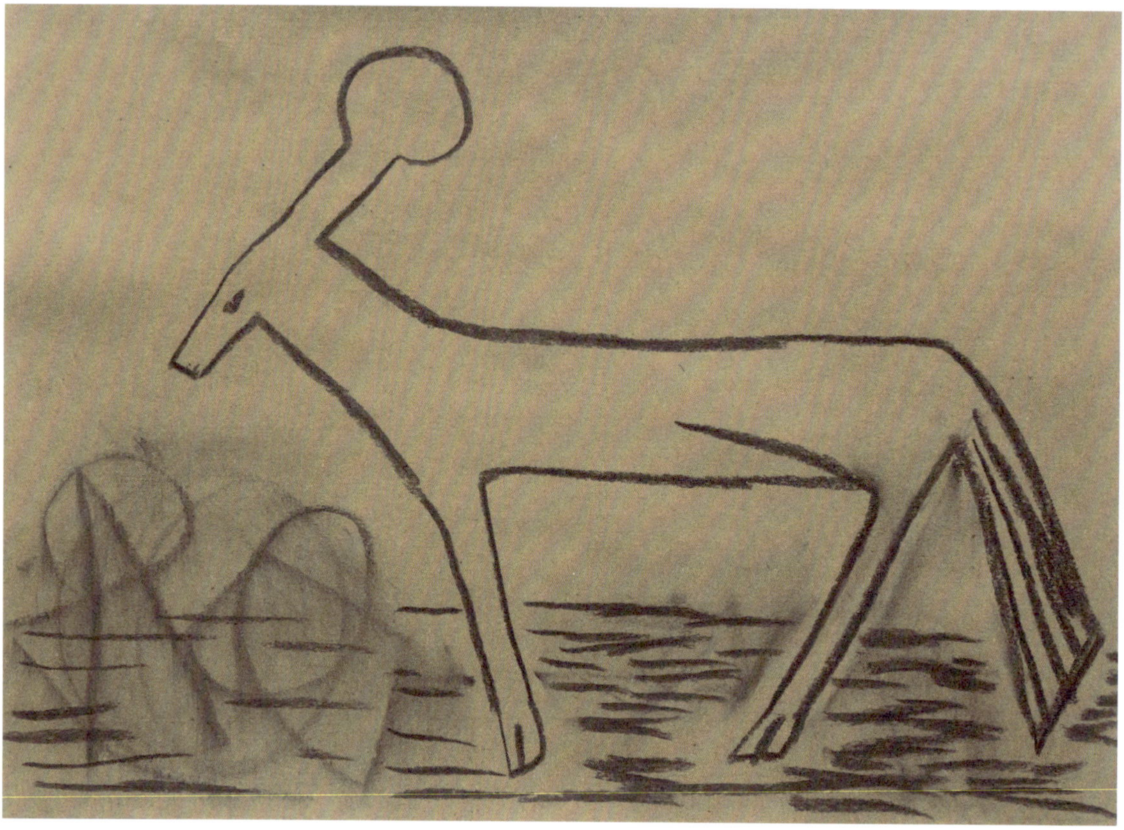

Plate 11. *Hathor*, 2019
Charcoal on brown paper, 9 ½ × 13 ⅜ in. (24 × 34 cm)

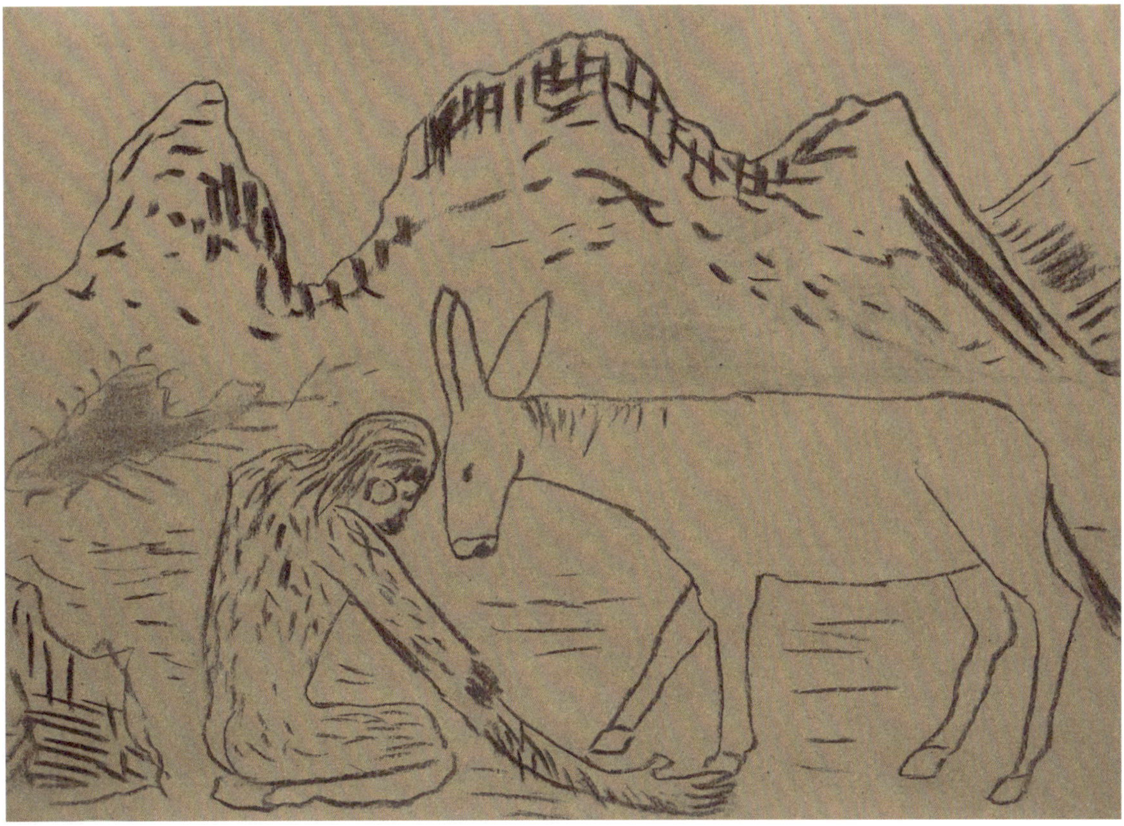

Plate 12. *Cro-Magnon*, 2019
Charcoal on brown paper, 9 ½ × 13 ⅜ in. (24 × 34 cm)

Plate 13. *Calf*, 2018
Polystyrene foam, steel, acrylic paint, charcoal, clay, wood
Overall: 72 ⅞ × 70 ⅞ × 27 ½ in. (185 × 180 × 70 cm); calf: 50 ¾ × 66 ⅞ × 26 in. (129 × 170 × 66 cm)

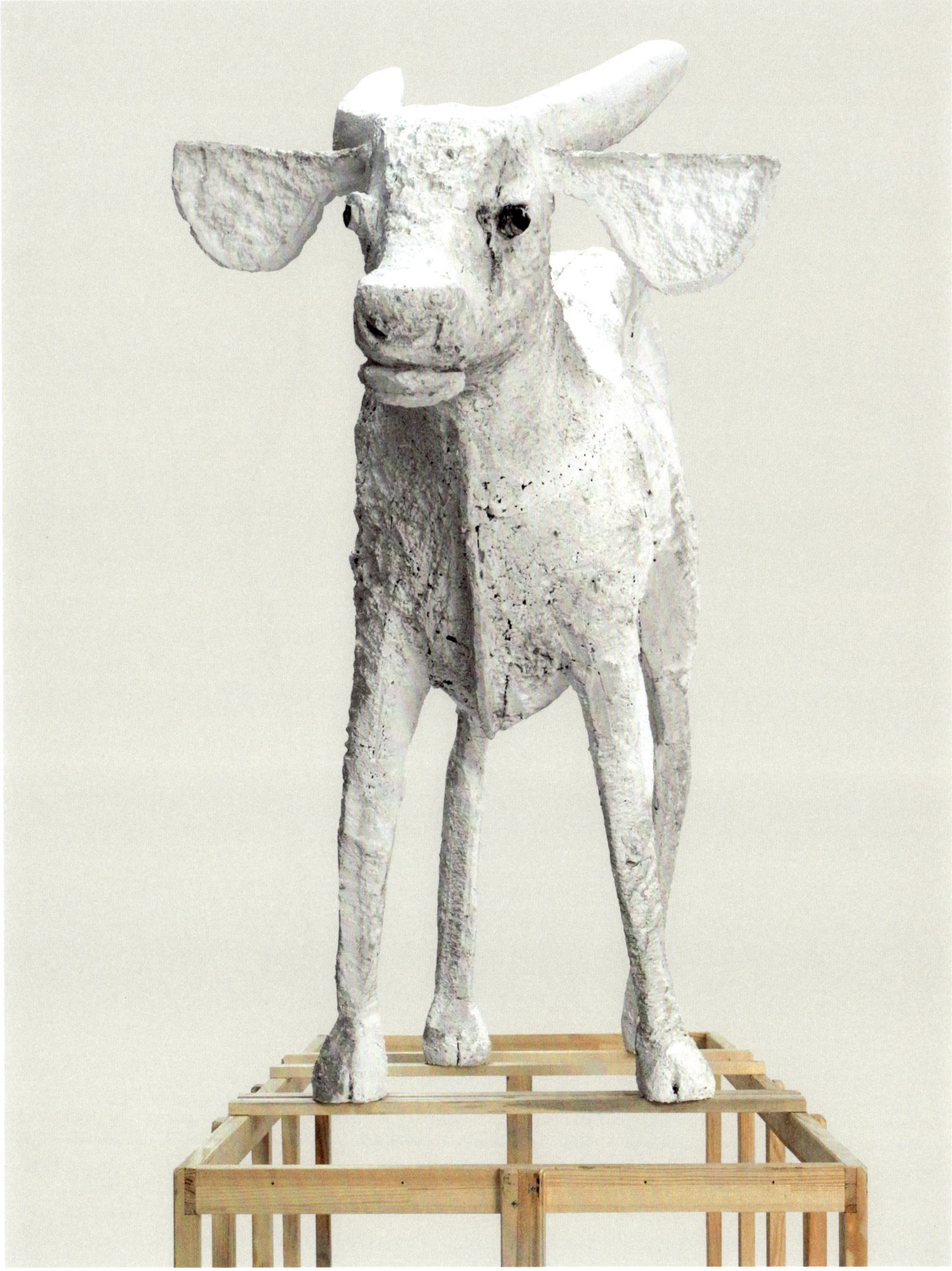

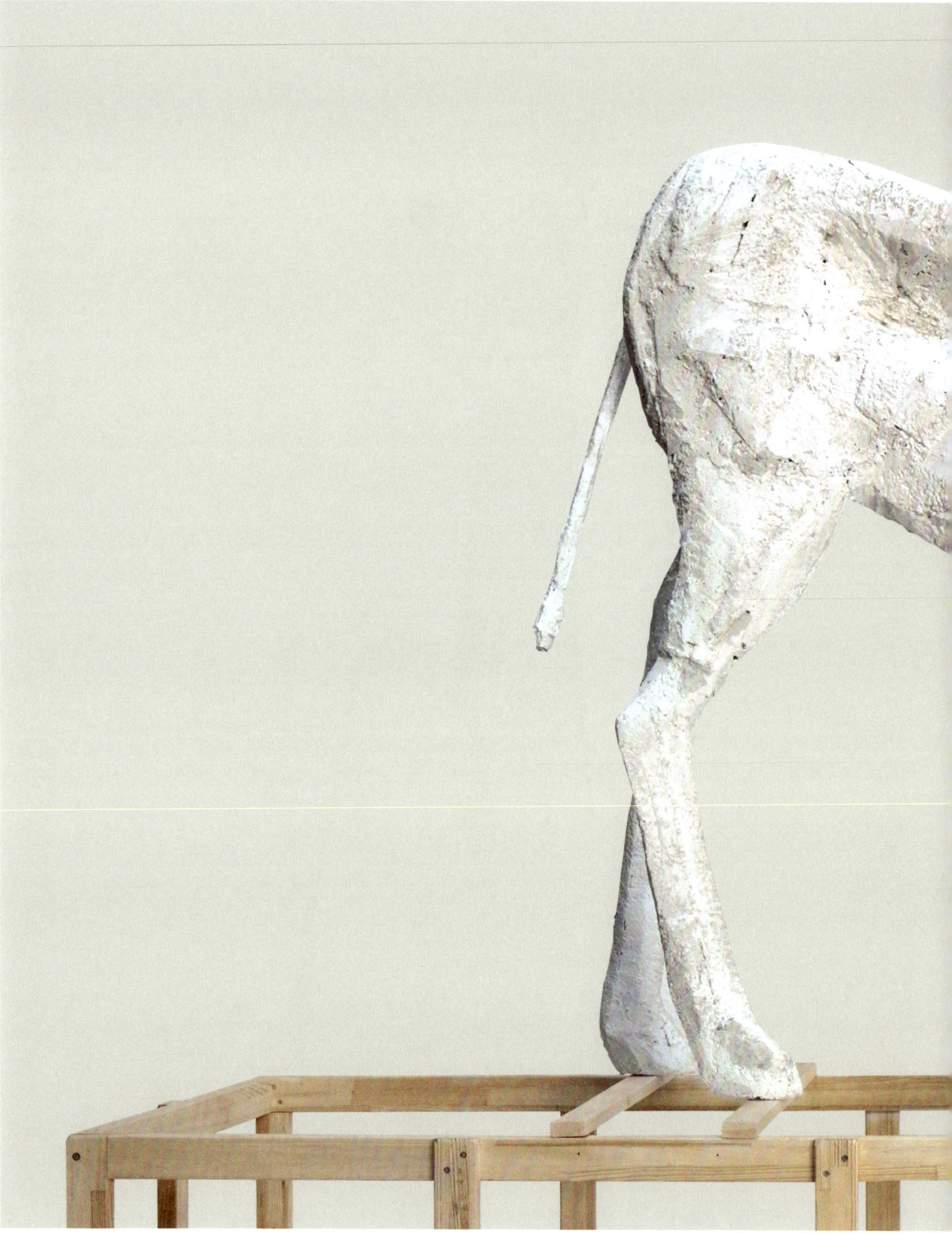

 *Calf*, 2018

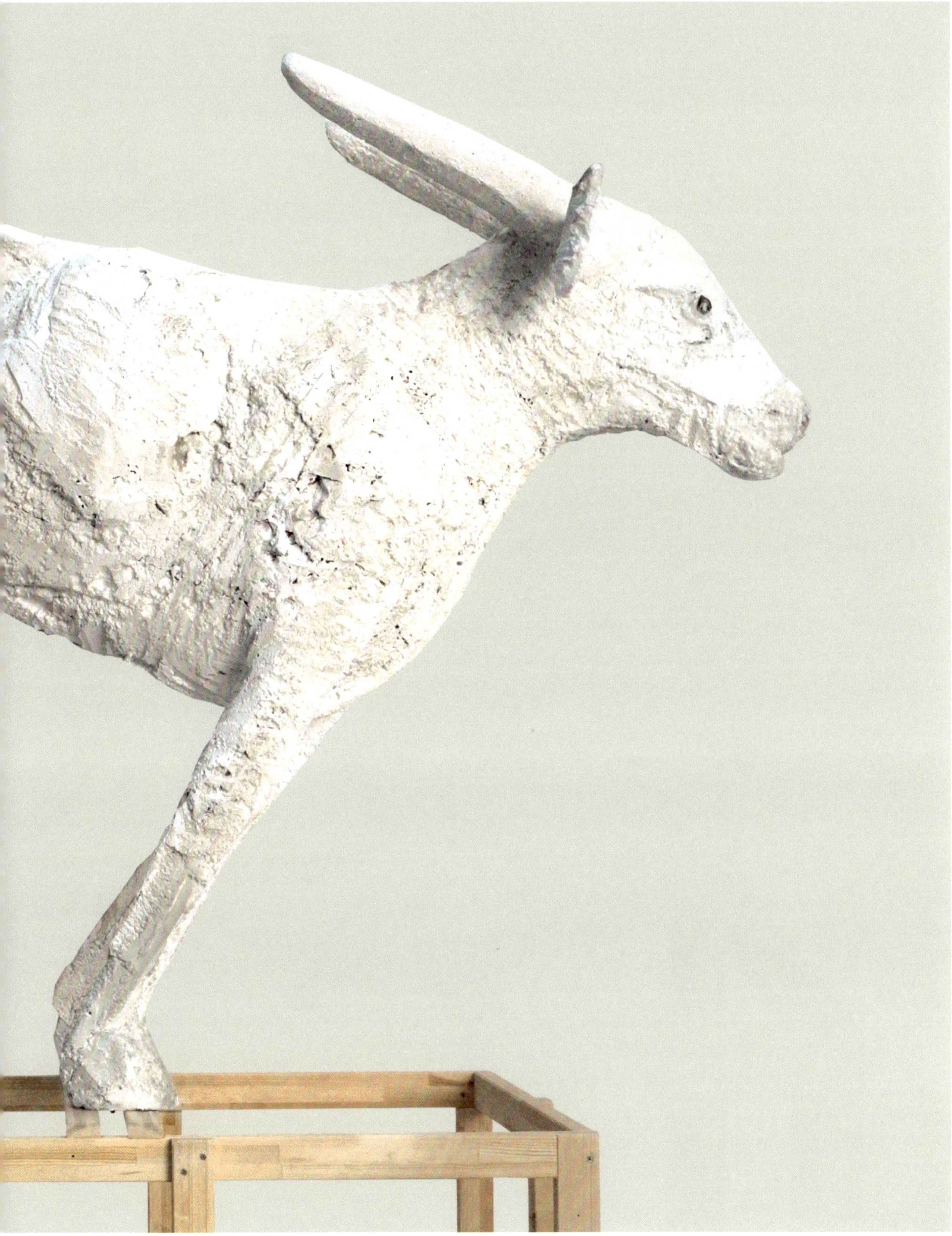

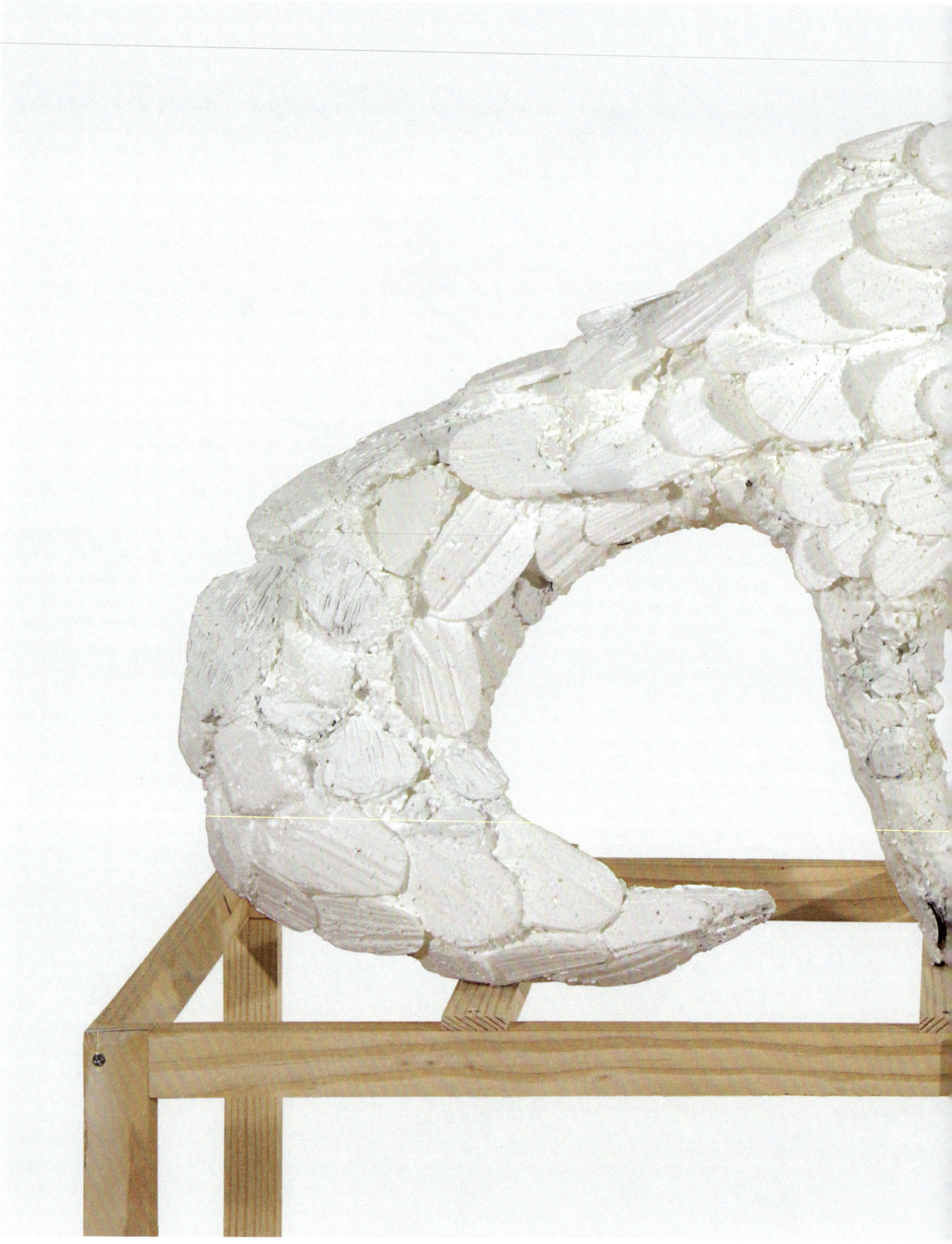

Plate 14. *Pangolin*, 2020
Polystyrene foam, steel, plaster, acrylic paint, wood
Overall: 53 ⅞ × 42 ½ × 14 in. (137 × 108 × 36 cm); pangolin: 20 ½ × 41 × 11 ⅜ in. (52 × 104 × 29 cm)

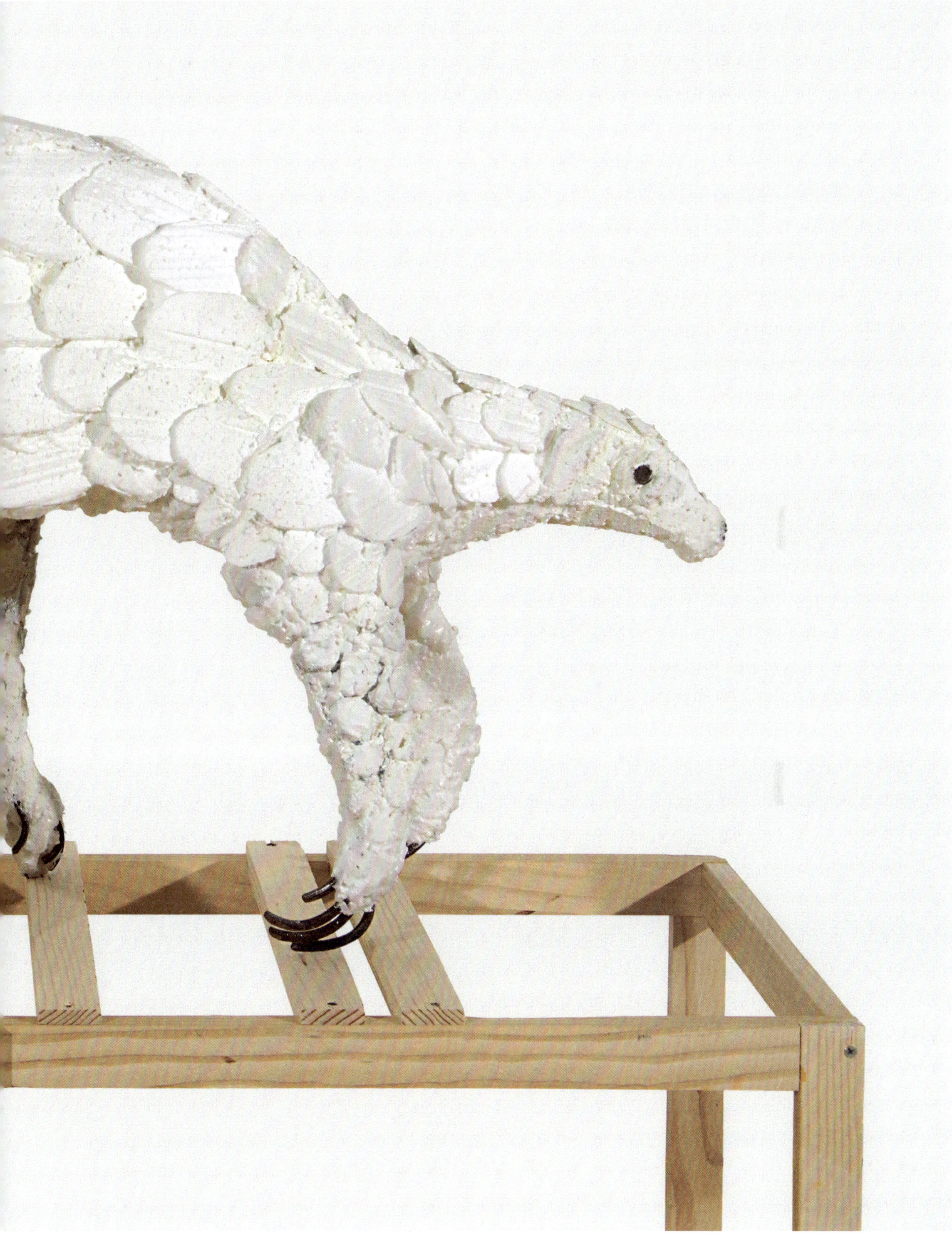

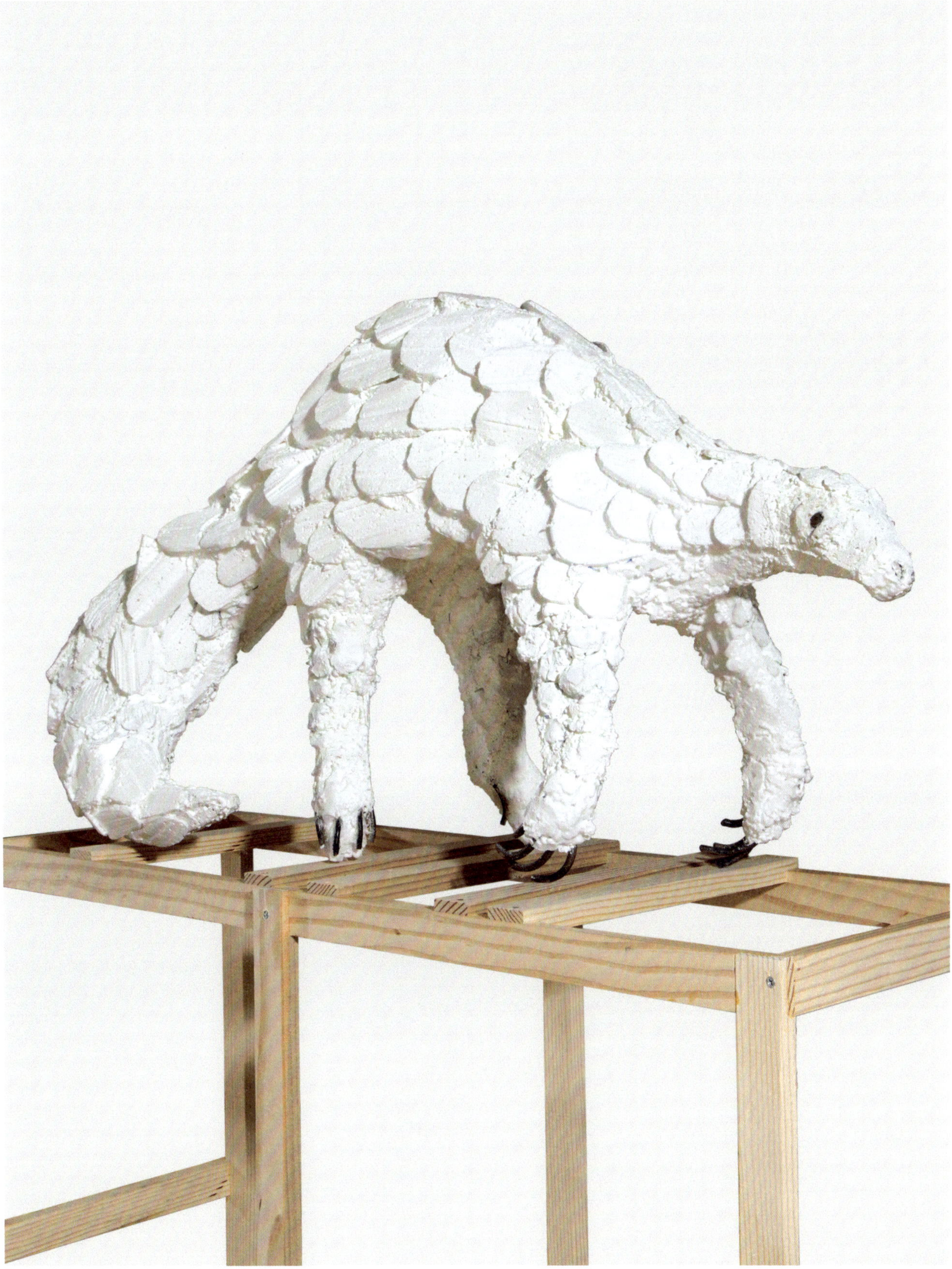

Plate 15. *The Liberation of Animals from Their Cages XXIII / Djamil Gate*, 2020
Steel, lacquer, 82 ⅝ × 61 ¾ × 3 ⅞ in. (210 × 157 × 10 cm)

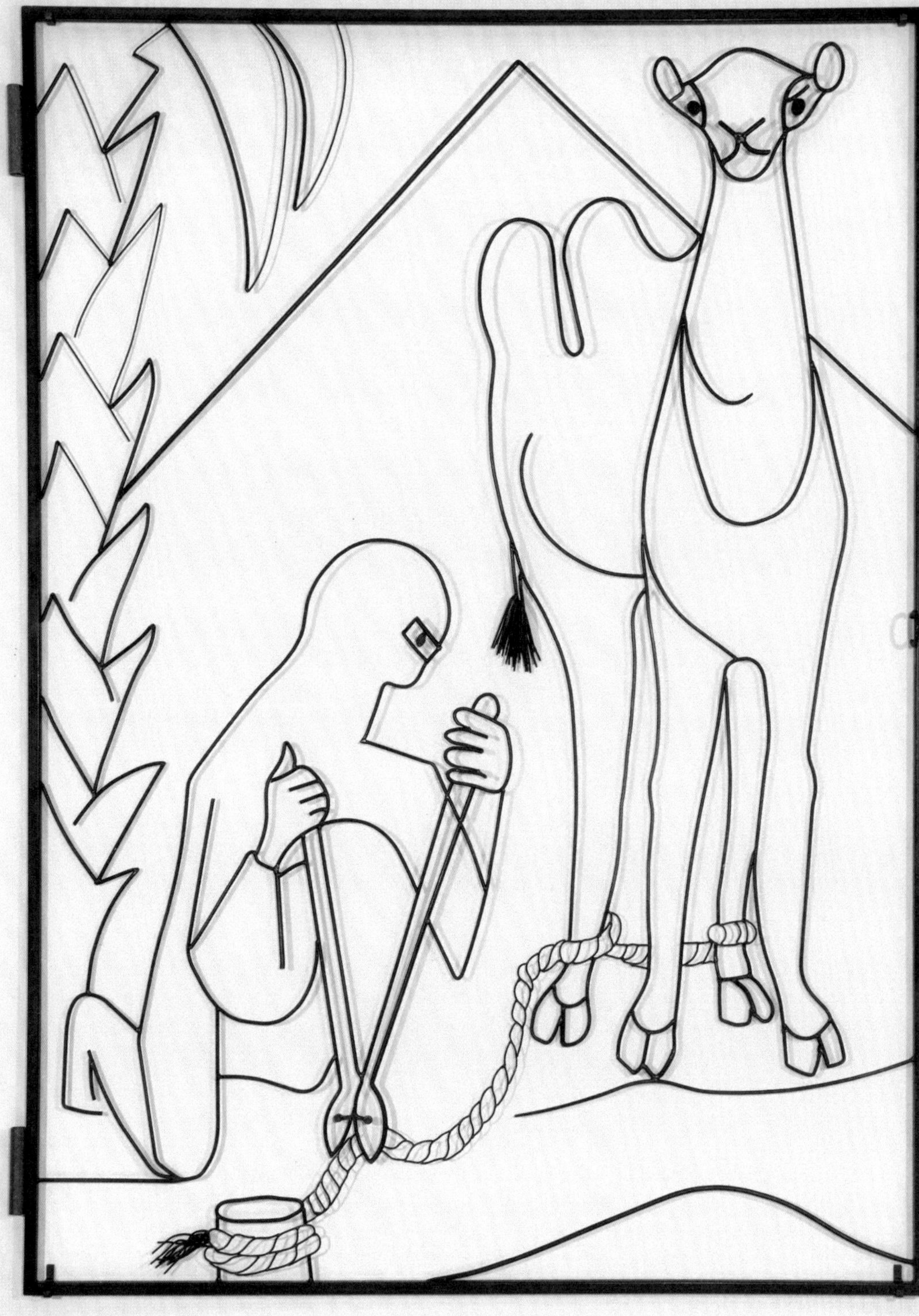

Plate 16. *Cleaner*, 2006, second version 2020
Polystyrene foam, steel, acrylic paint, polyethylene fabric, plastic watering can, dimensions variable

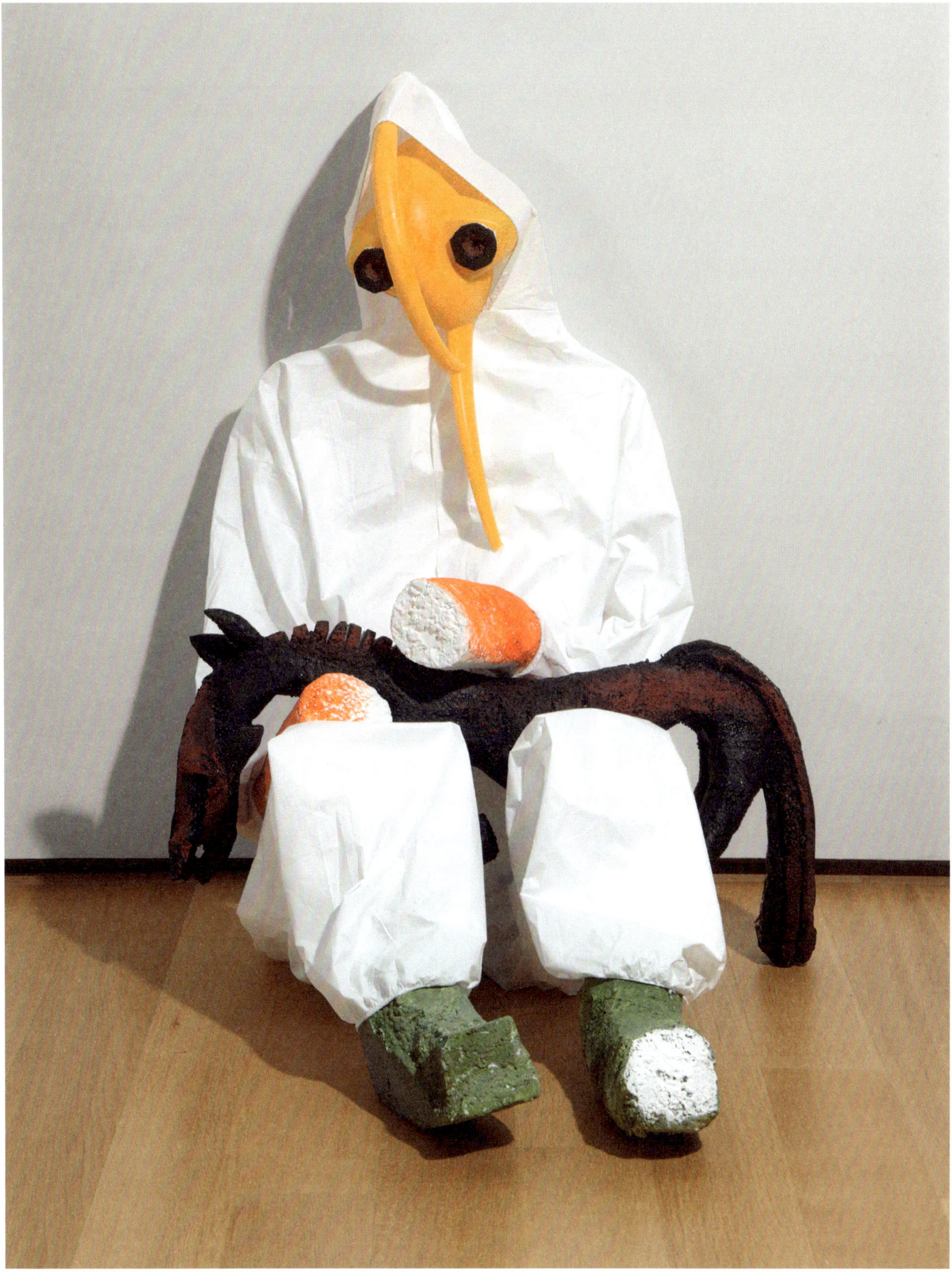

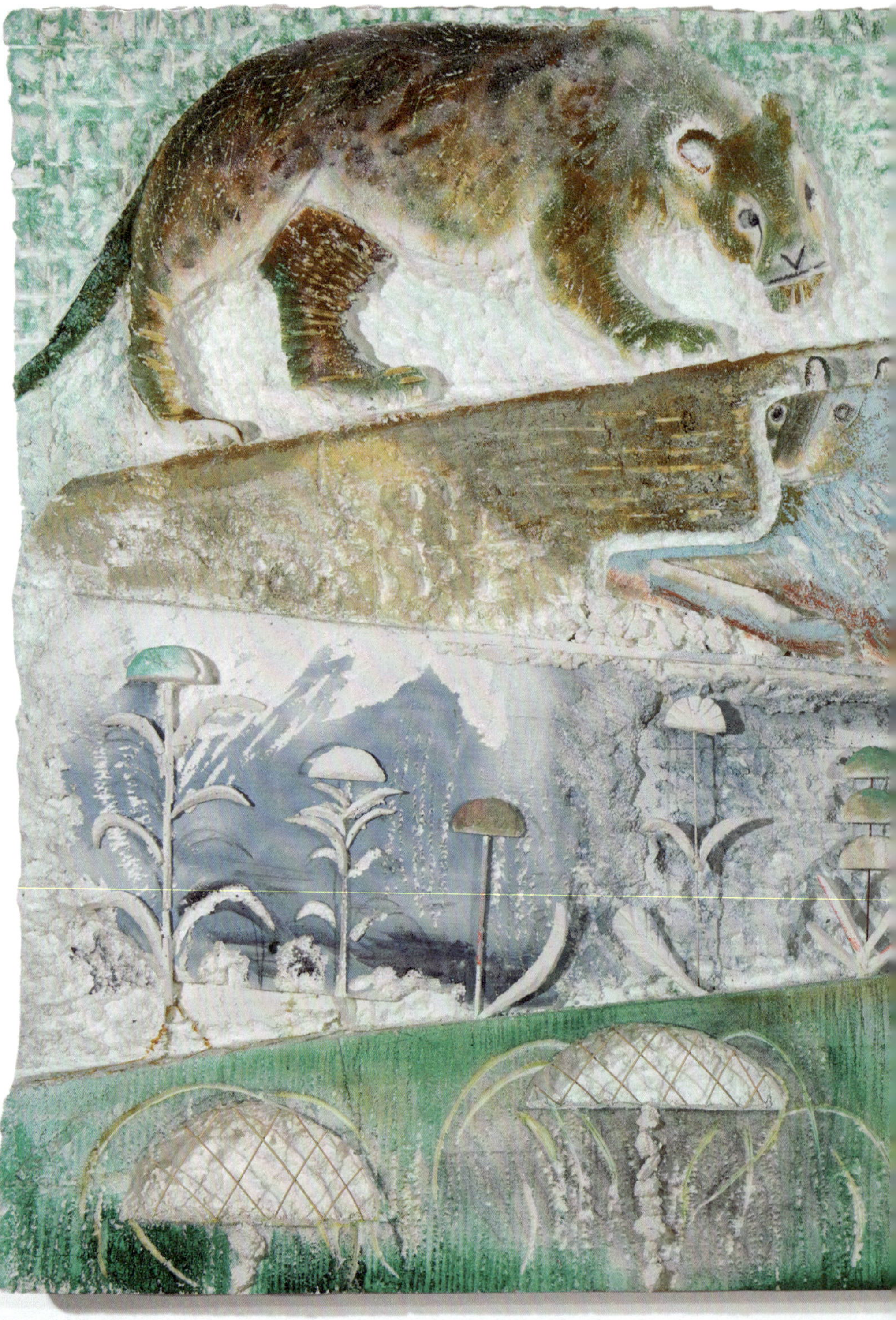

Plate 17. *Mureen/Lion School*, 2016



Polystyrene foam, acrylic paint, steel, wood, plaster, 66 ⅞ × 96 ½ × 7 ½ in. (170 × 245 × 19 cm)

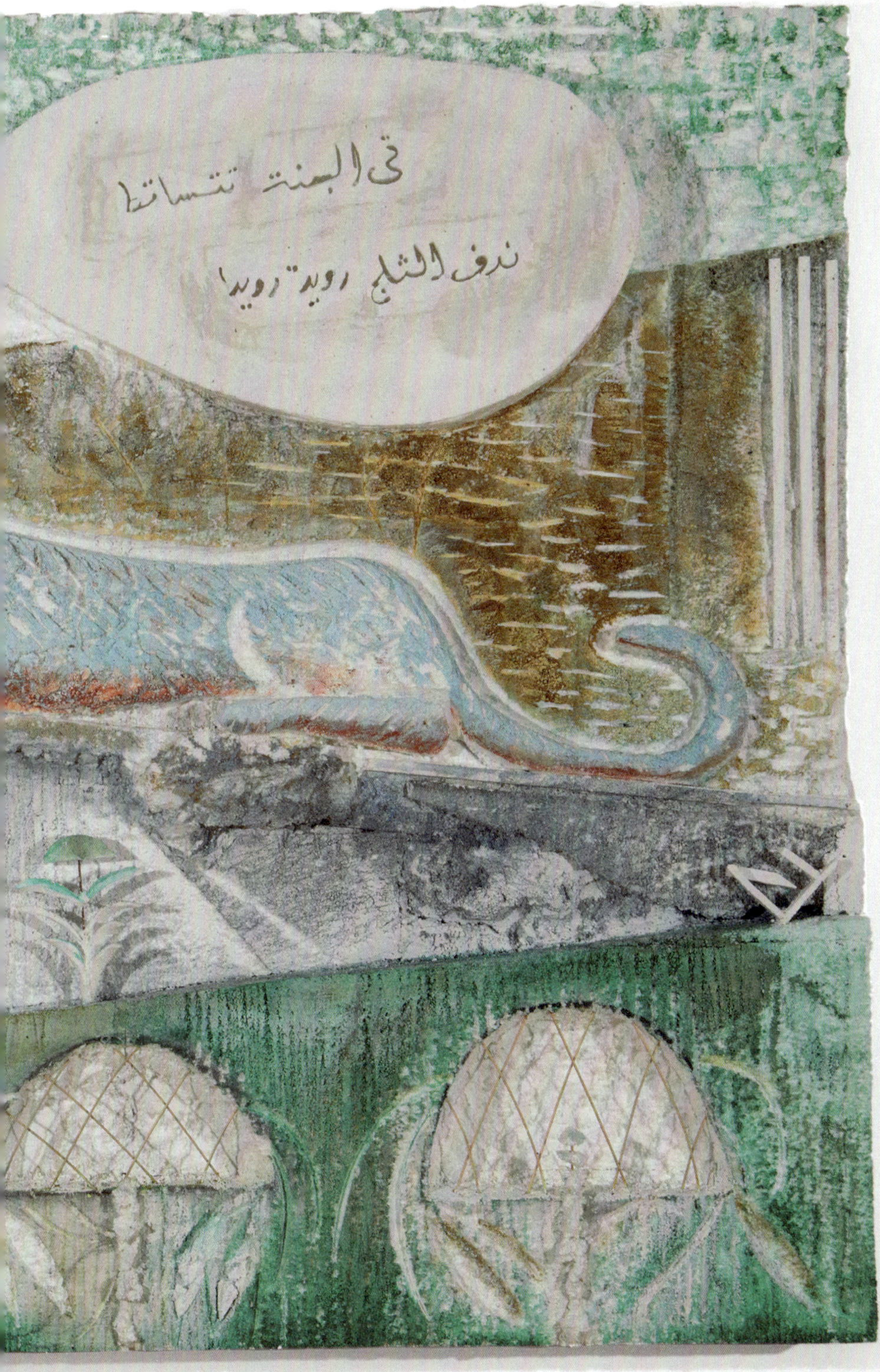

تتساقط
ندف الثلج رويدا رويدا

 *Mureen/Lion School* (detail), 2016

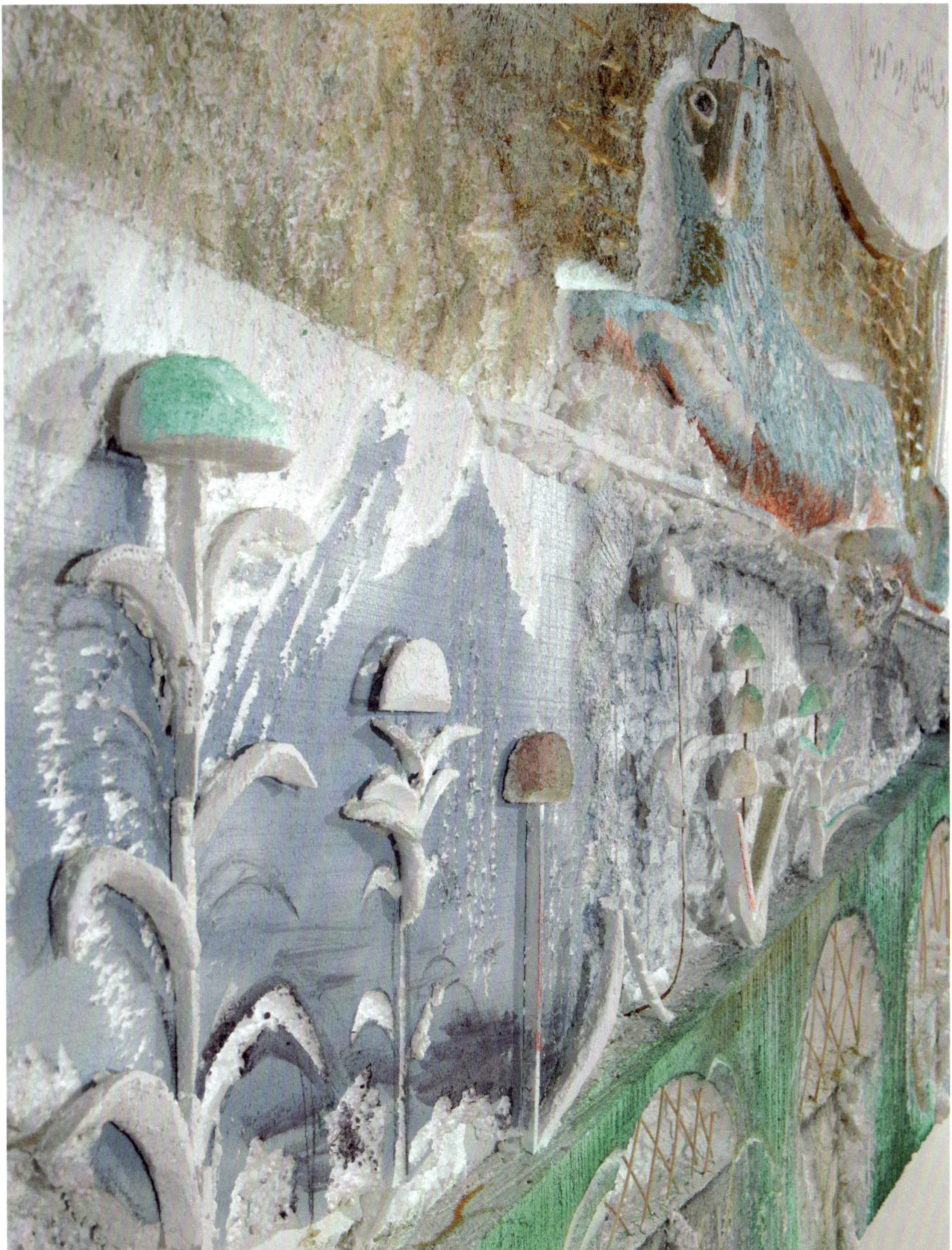

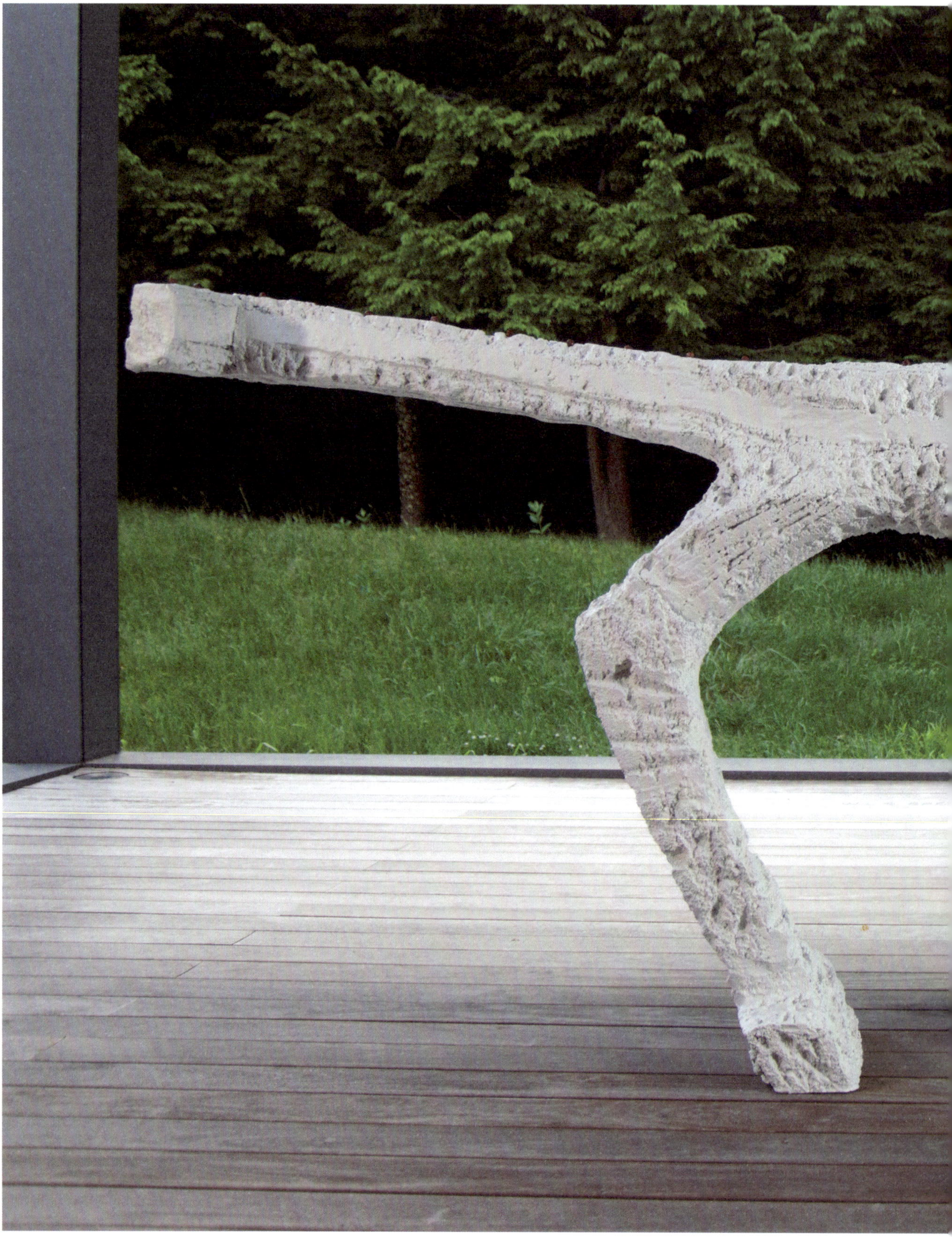

Plate 18. *Thaealab*, 2017
Cast bronze, lacquer, hazelnuts, 56 ¼ × 114 ⅛ × 14 ⅛ in. (143 × 290 × 36 cm)

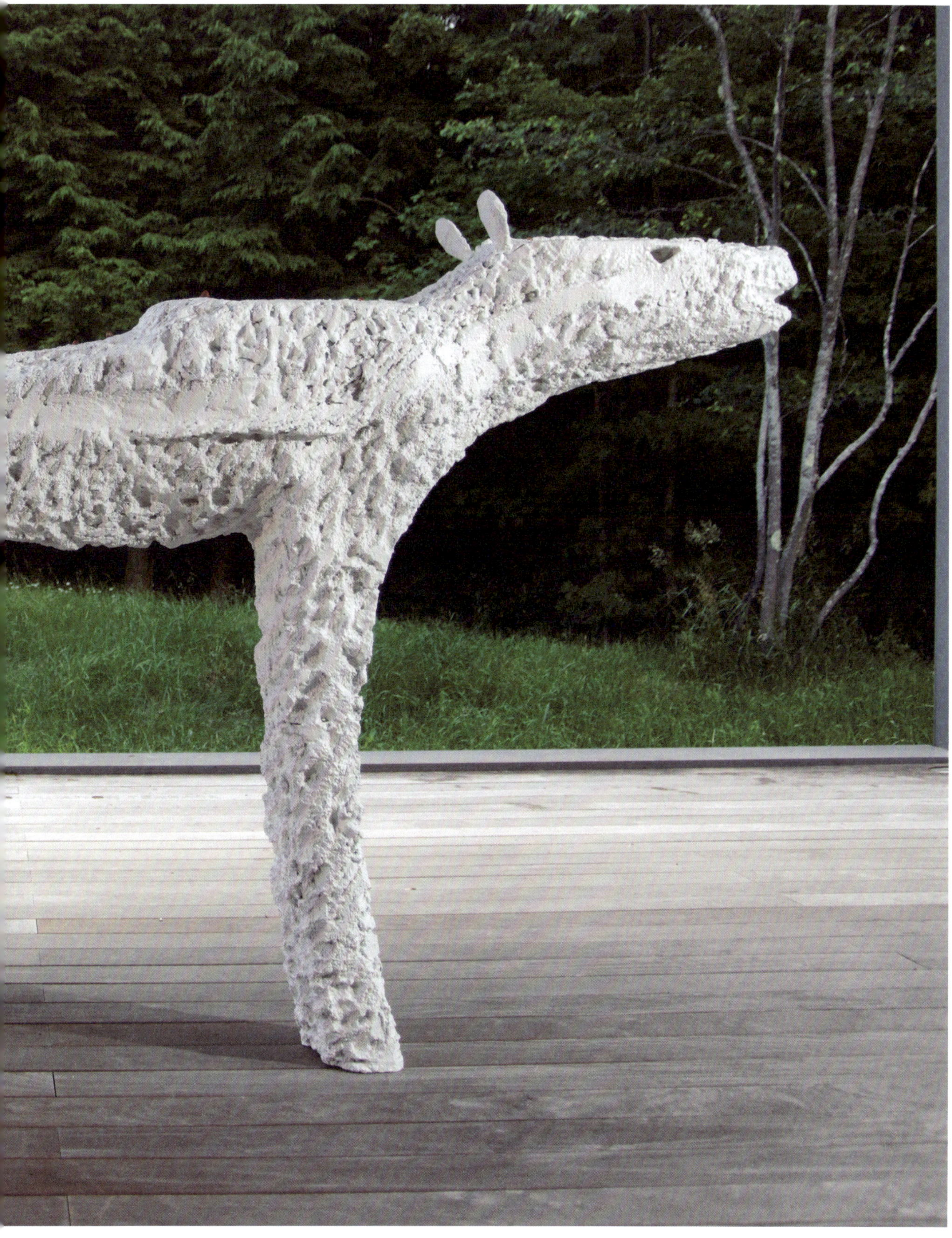

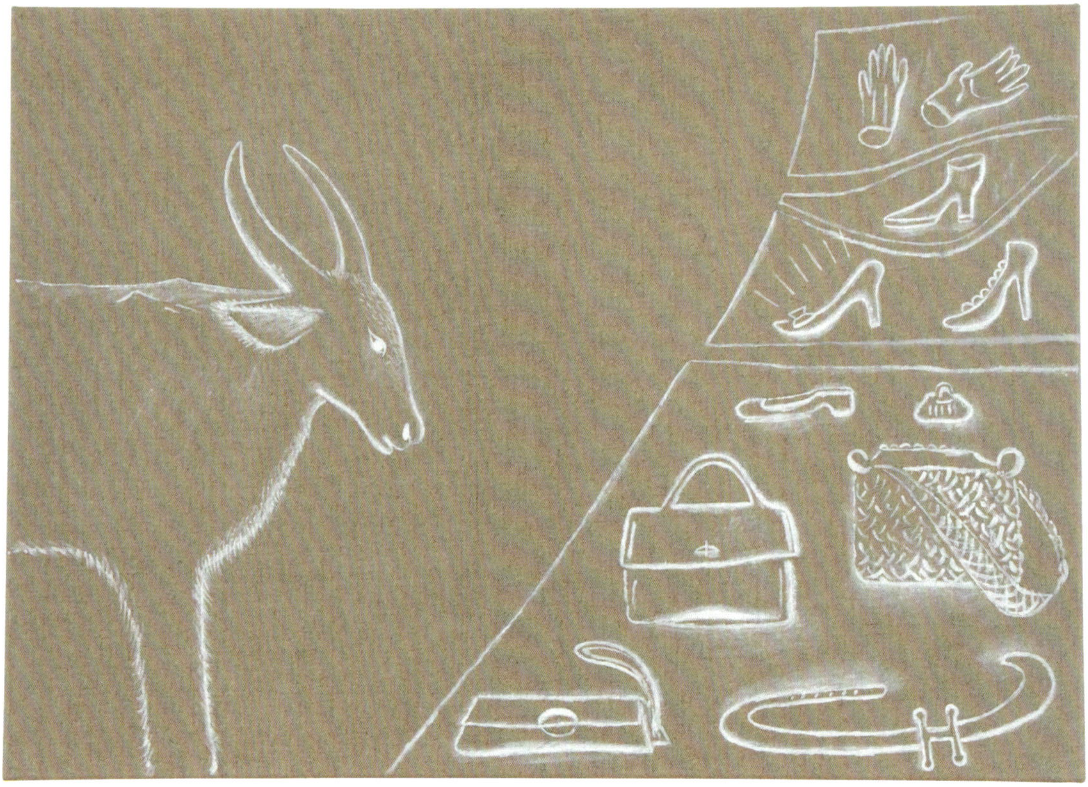

Plate 19. *Aynoor*, 2020
Acrylic paint on canvas, 27 ½ × 39 ⅜ in. (70 × 100 cm)

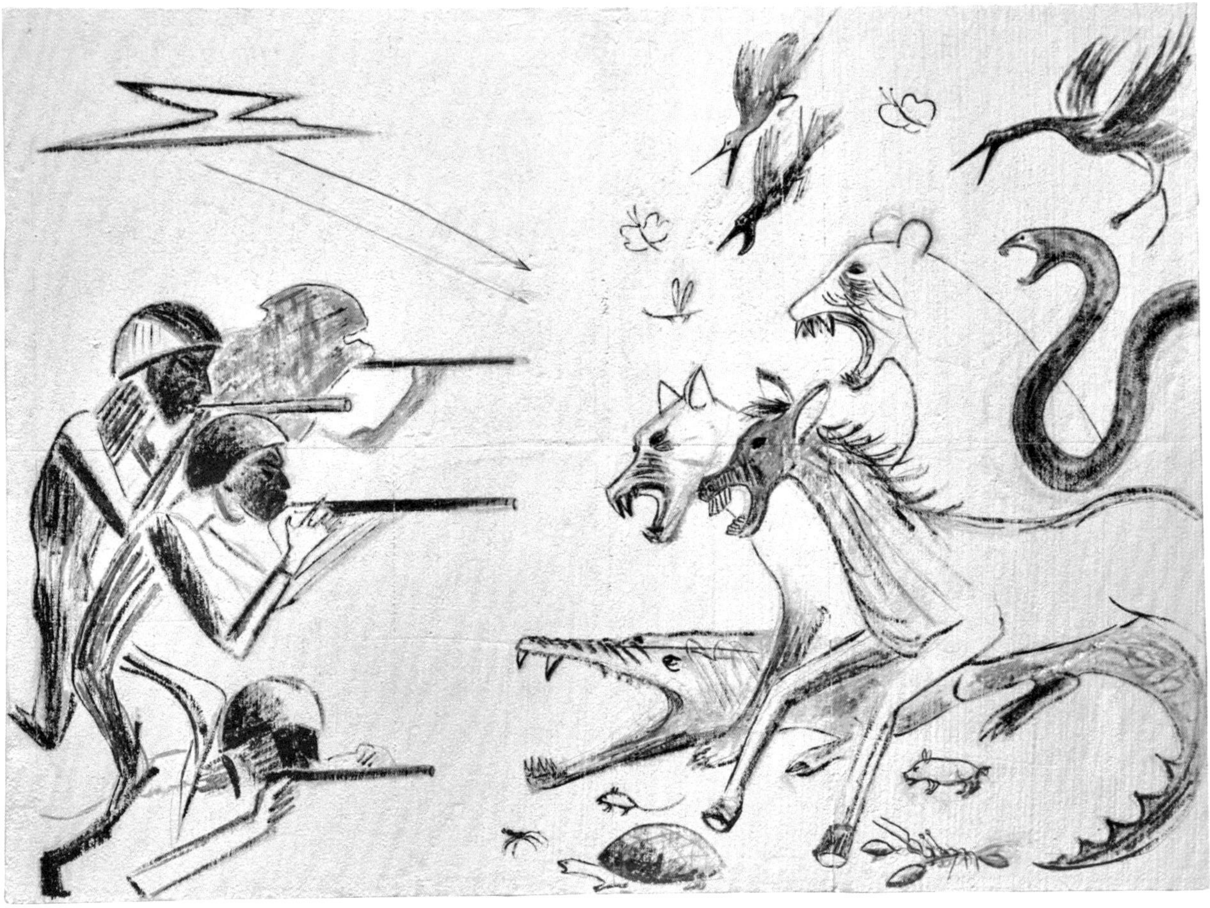

Plate 20. *War*, 2006
Acrylic paint on polystyrene foam, 39 3/8 × 54 3/8 × 1 1/8 in. (100 × 138 × 3 cm)

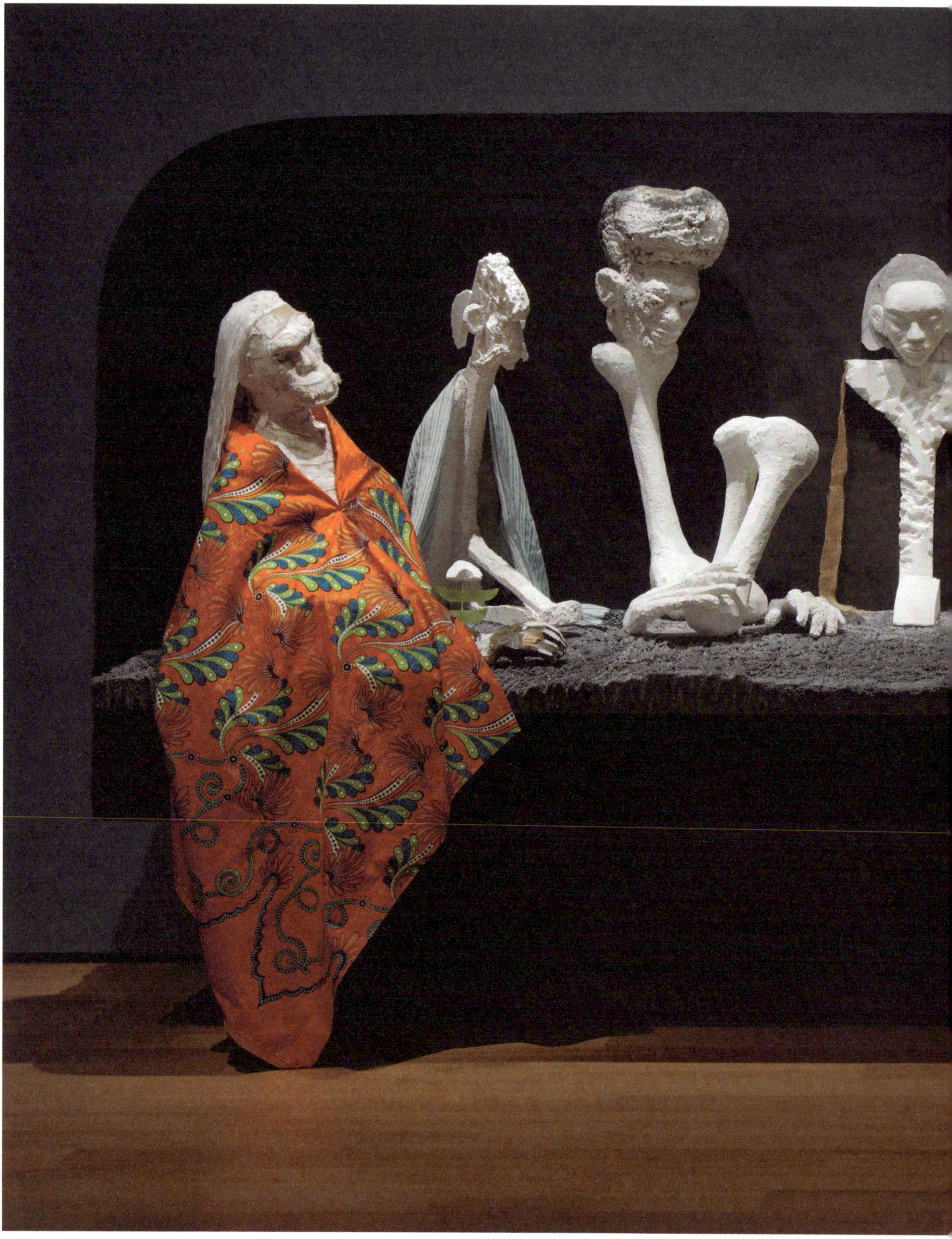

Plate 21. *Seven Sleepers*, 2020
Polystyrene foam, acrylic paint, steel, jute, fabric, paper, plants, glass, water, cotton cord, wood, cardboard, 84 ⅝ × 177 ⅛ × 39 ⅜ in. (215 × 450 × 100 cm)

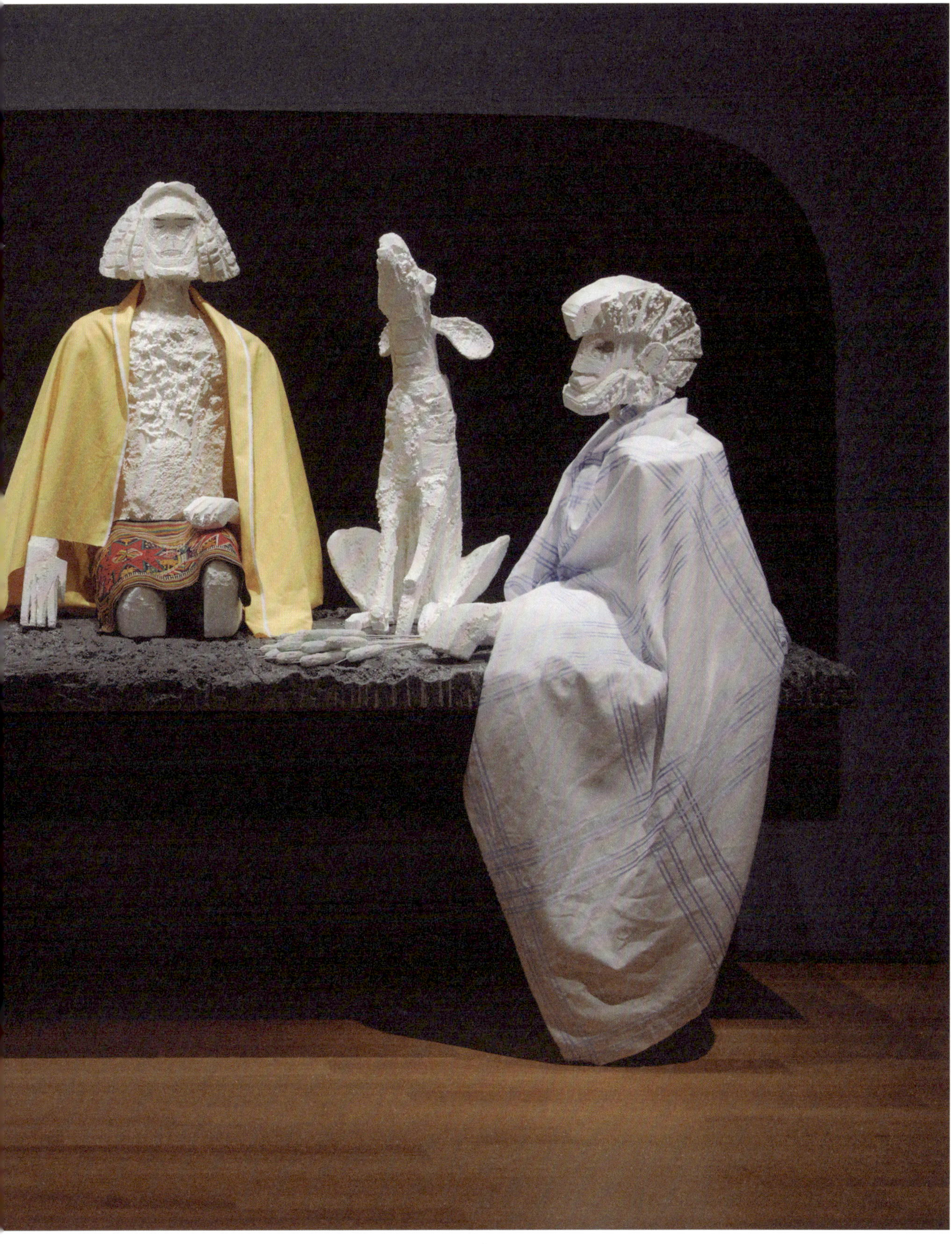

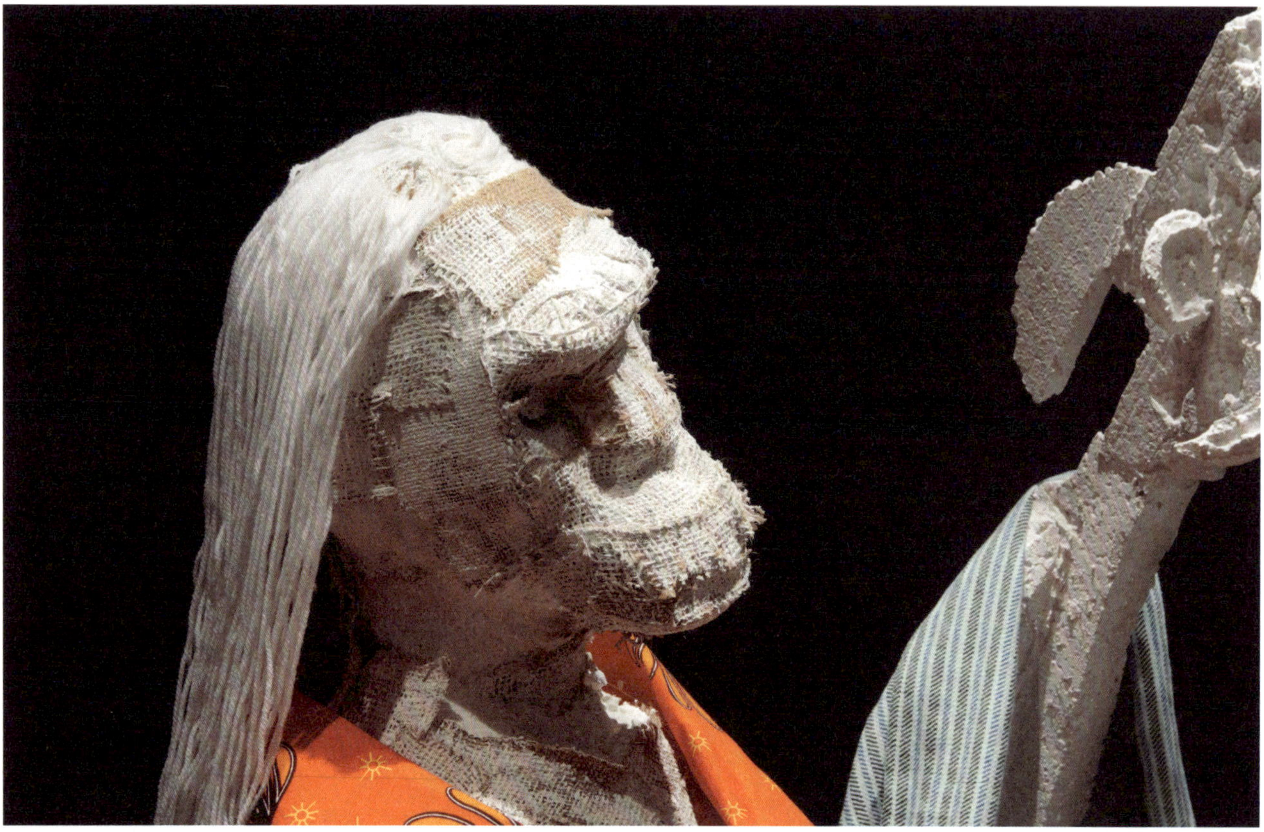

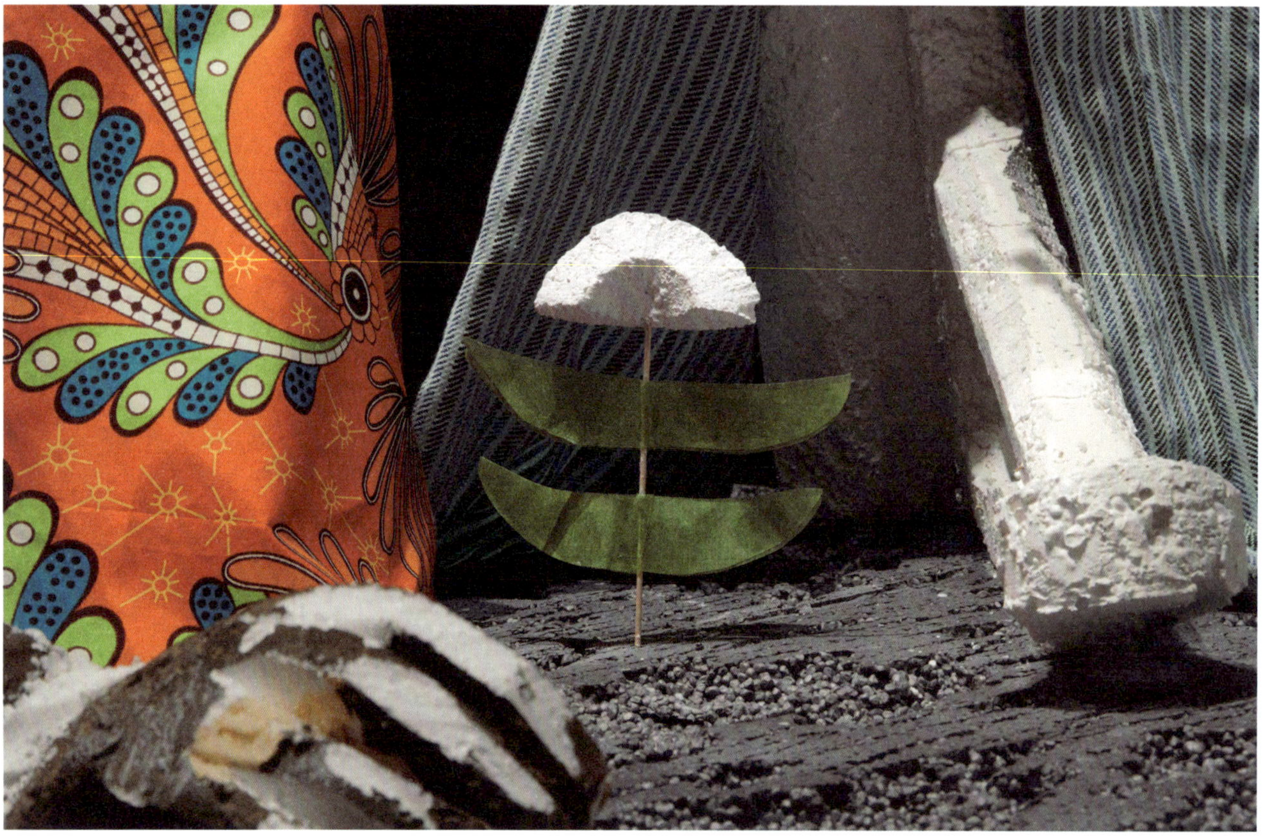

 *Seven Sleepers* (details), 2020

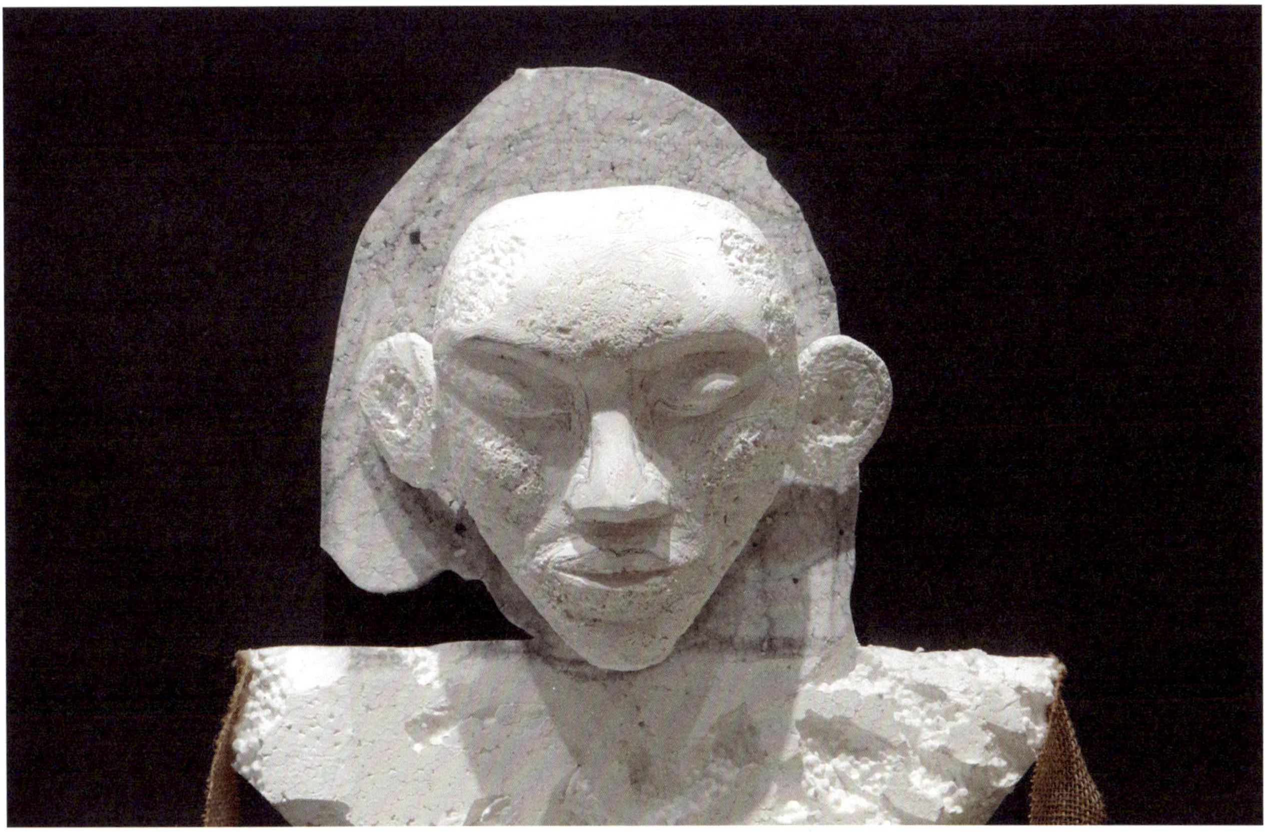

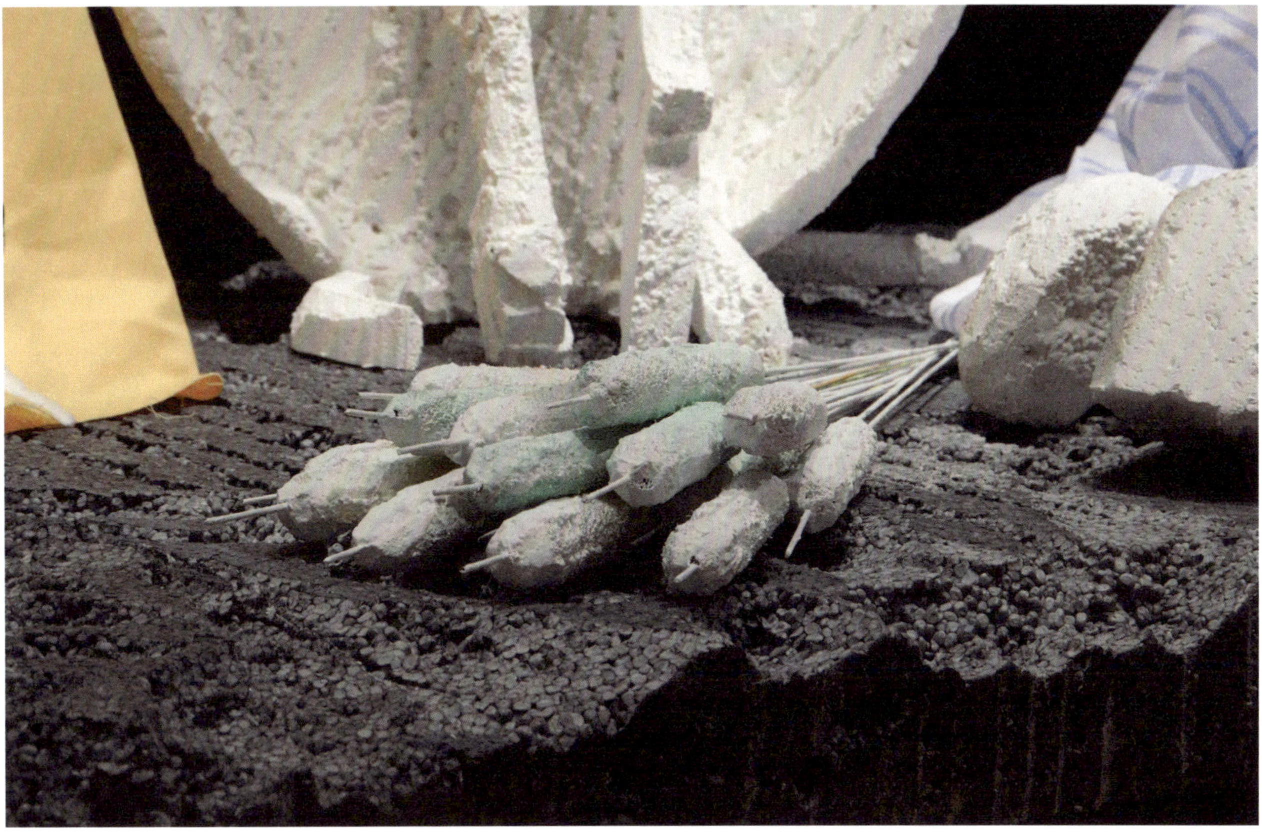

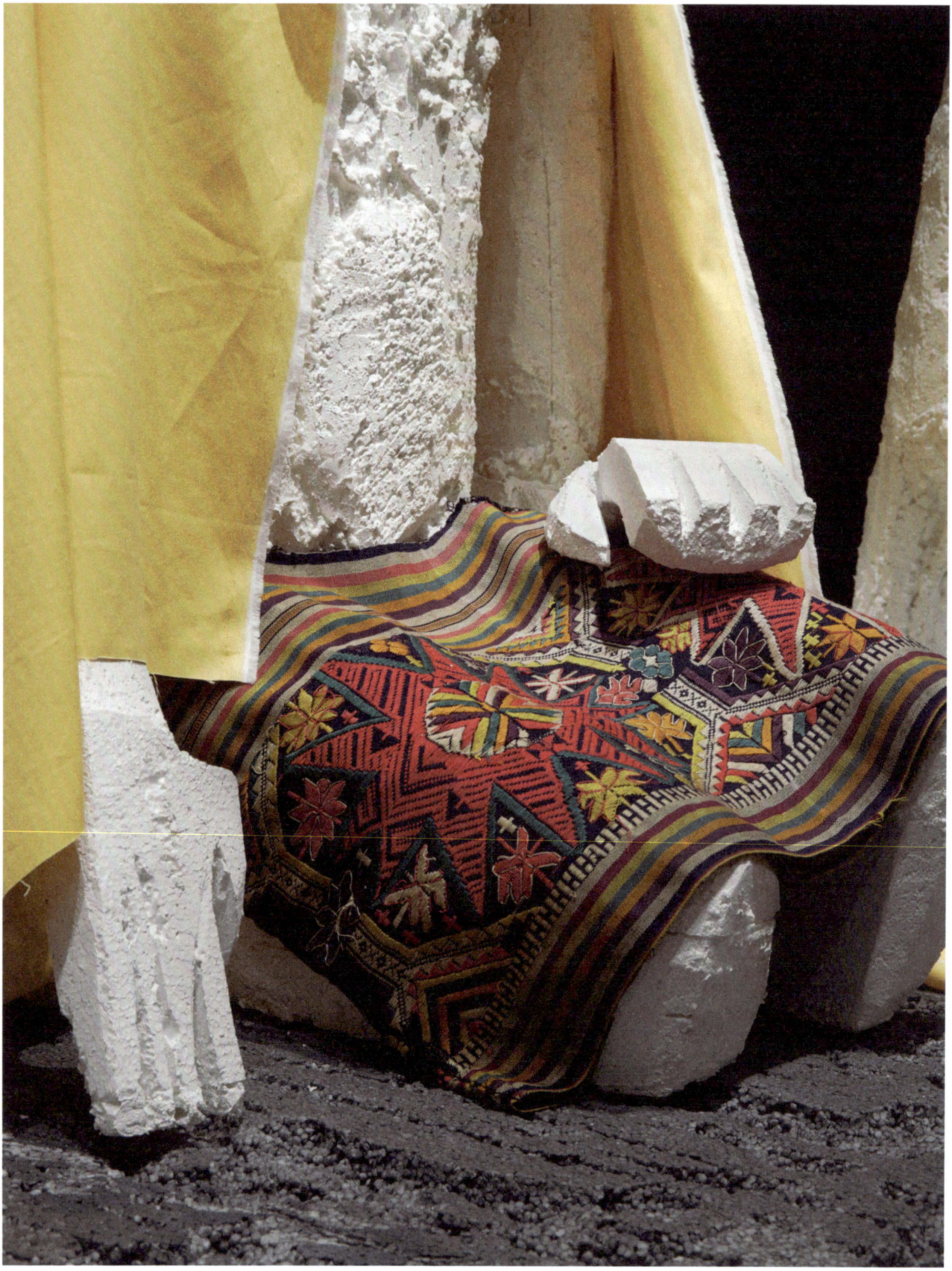

 *Seven Sleepers* (details), 2020

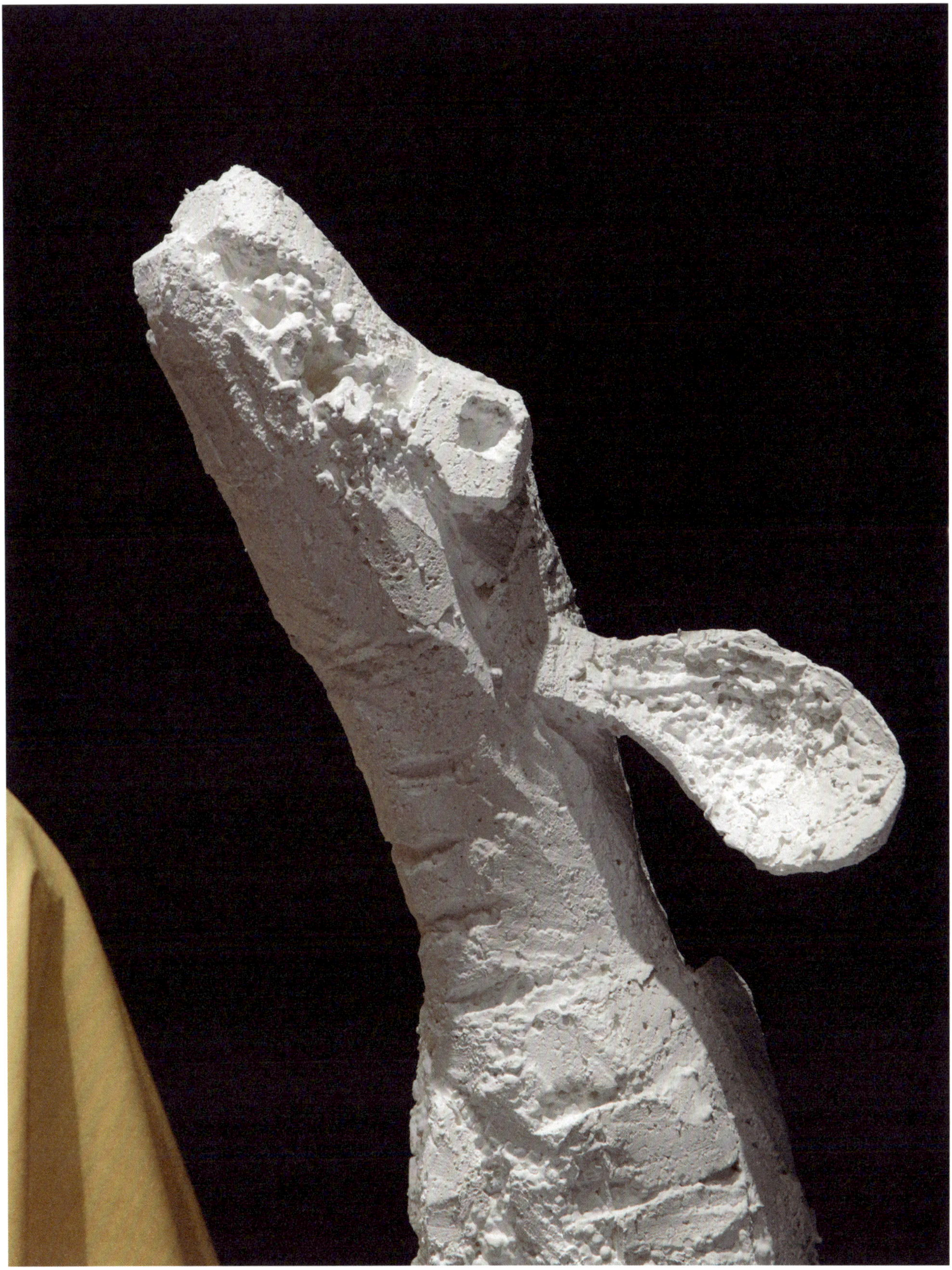

# FABLES

Lin May Saeed

*Hallo zusammen, wie lebt Ihr ?*

*Kaninchen:*
*Wir leben in kleinen Gruppen, keine festen Partnerschaften. Bauen weit verzweigte Gangsysteme, in denen unsere Jungen nackt und blind zur Welt kommen. Wir vermehren uns auch in Gefangenschaft.*

*Hase:*
*Ich lebe solitär. Schlafe in einer flachen Erdmulde. Mein Nachwuchs kommt darin mit Fell und geöffneten Augen zur Welt. Ich bin niemals domestiziert worden.*

*Menschen:*
*Wissen wir noch nicht so genau.*
*Bis wir es herausgefunden haben führen wir Krieg.*

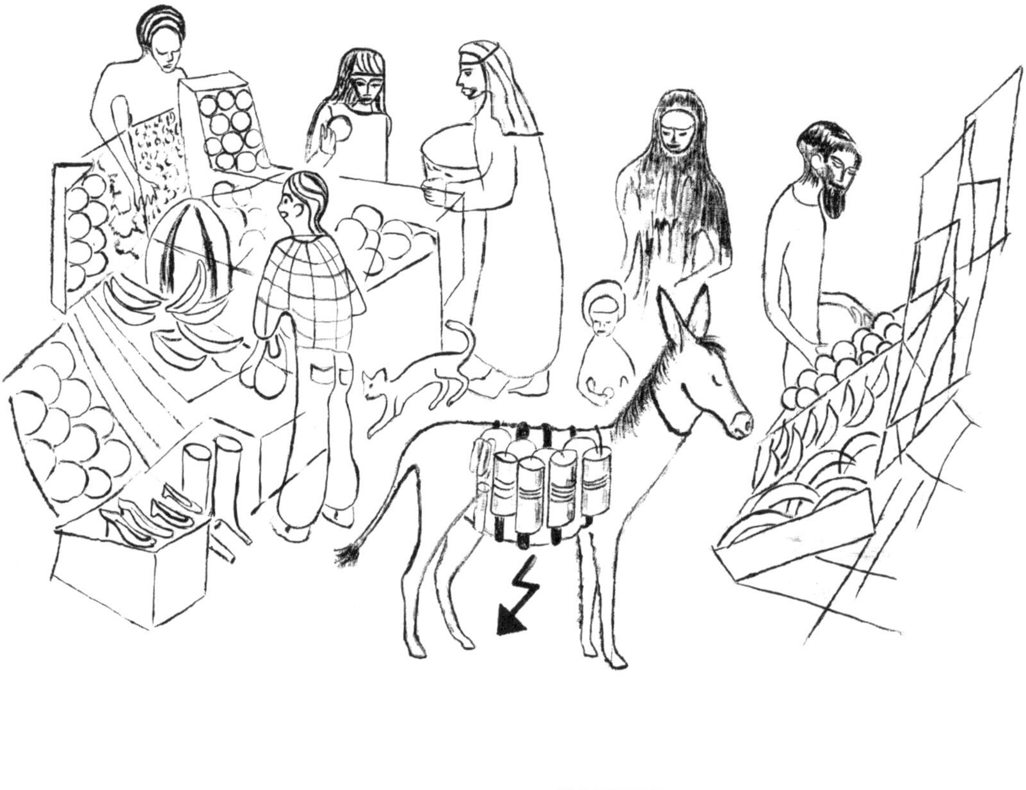

Hi there, how do you live?

Rabbits:
We live in small groups,
have no fixed partnerships.
Build widely branching tunnel systems,
in which our young are born, naked and blind.
We also reproduce when imprisoned.

Hare:
I live solitary. Sleep in a shallow hollow.
My offspring are born with fur and open eyes.
I have never been domesticated.

Humans:
We don't quite know.
Until we find out, we wage wars.

*Das Schweigen der Tiere*

*Es sind verschiedene Gründe denkbar, warum ein Tier nicht antwortet, wenn ihm eine Frage gestellt wird. Zum einen gibt es die etwas esoterisch anmutende Theorie, der Zufolge das Tier schweigt, weil es meditiert. Diese Meditation wäre demnach so tief, dass sie auch dann unaufhebbar ist, wenn das Tier eines gewaltsamen Todes stirbt. Sein Bewusstsein schweigt, während sein Unterbewusstsein Laute von sich gibt, die als „nicht artikuliert“ missverstanden werden und den Raum füllen, der das Tier und seine Widersacher umgibt.*

*Die andere Möglichkeit wäre, dass das Tier tatsächlich sprechen kann, allerdings nur sehr langsam. Bis ein Tier den Satz ausgesprochen hat „Bitte, töte mich nicht!“, vergehen Zeitalter, in einer fast unendlichen Ausdehnung von Silben. Als ob jemand seinen Namen auf die Oberfläche des Mondes schriebe. Entsprechend der jeweiligen Art kann dies hunderttausende Jahre andauern.*

The Silence of the Animals

Different reasons could be imagined why an animal does not answer when it is asked a question. One is the rather esoteric-sounding theory, which claims the animal remains silent because it is meditating. The meditation would be so deep that it cannot even be lifted when the animal dies a violent death. Its super-conscious is silent while its unconscious makes sounds, which are misunderstood as “unarticulated” and fill the space surrounding the animal and its adversary.

The other possibility would be that the animal can actually speak, though only very slowly. Ages can pass before an animal enunciated the sentence, “Please, don’t kill me!,” in an almost infinite expansion of syllables. Like someone writing his name on the surface of the moon. Depending on the particular species, this can take hundreds of thousands of years.

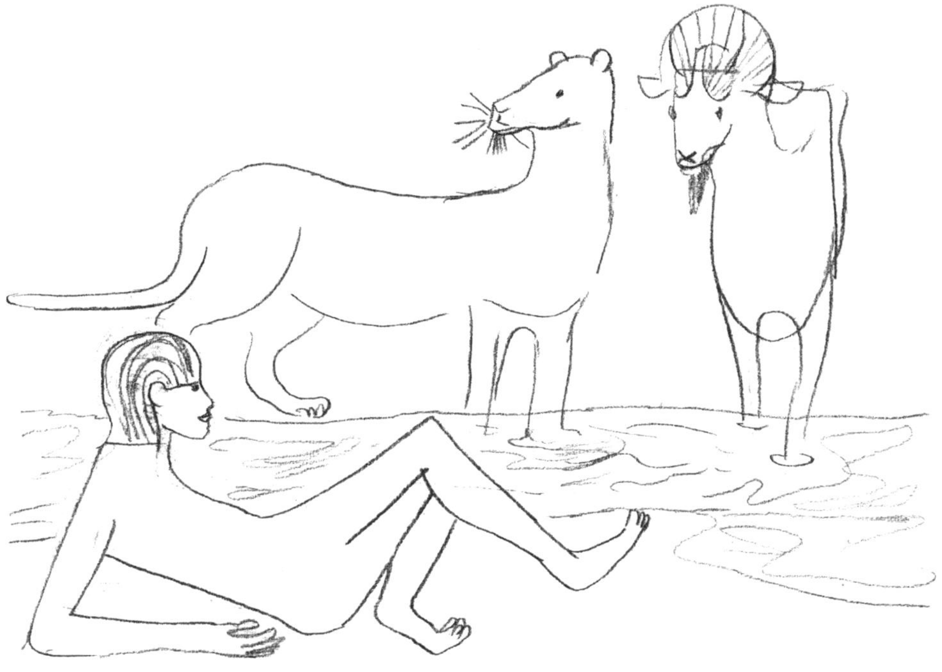

*Eine Zeit lang waren Mensch und Affe gleichauf, bis der Mensch auf die Idee kam, ein Pferd zu besteigen und es zum Laufen zu bringen. Der Affe wollte ihn übertreffen. Er schwang sich auf den Rücken einer Giraffe und kletterte an ihrem Hals hoch wie an einem Baum. Als er oben ange-kommen war und es nicht weiterging, stieg er wieder herunter und schlug sich die Sache aus dem Kopf.*

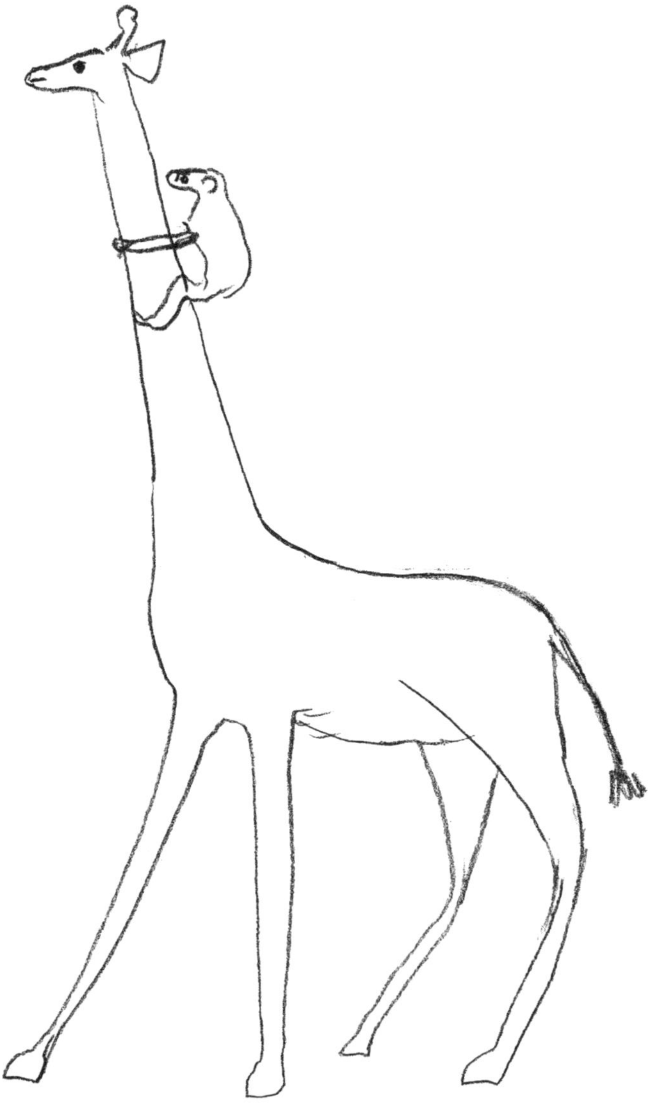

For a time man and ape were equal, until it occurred to the man to mount a horse and get it to run. The ape wanted to surpass him. He swung himself onto a giraffe's back and clambered high up its neck as if it were a tree. When he got to the top and couldn't get any further, he climbed back down and got the matter out of his head.

*Reitversuche mit tödlichem Ausgang*

*Mensch auf*

*>> Löwe – Dauer ca. 2 Sekunden.*

*>> Vogel Strauß – wirft Mensch bei hoher Laufgeschwindigkeit ab. Mensch zieht sich einige kleine Schürfwunden zu; dadurch begünstigt Infektion mit Vogelgrippevirus > Immunsystem kollabiert.*

*>> Hirsch – rennt wie angepiekst durch den Wald > Mensch gelingt es, sich am Geweih festzuhalten und einigermaßen aufrecht zu sitzen > Hirsch rennt unter einem Ast hindurch, der Mensch genau am Kopf trifft.*

*Variante: Hirsch senkt Kopf bei hoher Laufgeschwindigkeit und bremst plötzlich ab > Gegenseitige Durchdringung von Mensch und Geweih.*

Riding attempts with fatal outcome

Man on

>> Lion – Duration c. 2 seconds

>> Ostrich – throws man off at high speed. Man suffers a few small abrasions; resulting in infection with bird-flu virus > immune system collapses.

>> Stag – runs through the forest like electrified. Man succeeds in holding on to the antlers and sitting more or less upright > stag runs under a branch, which hits human exactly in the head.

Variation: Stag lowers head at high speed and then comes to a sudden halt. Reciprocal penetration of man and antlers.

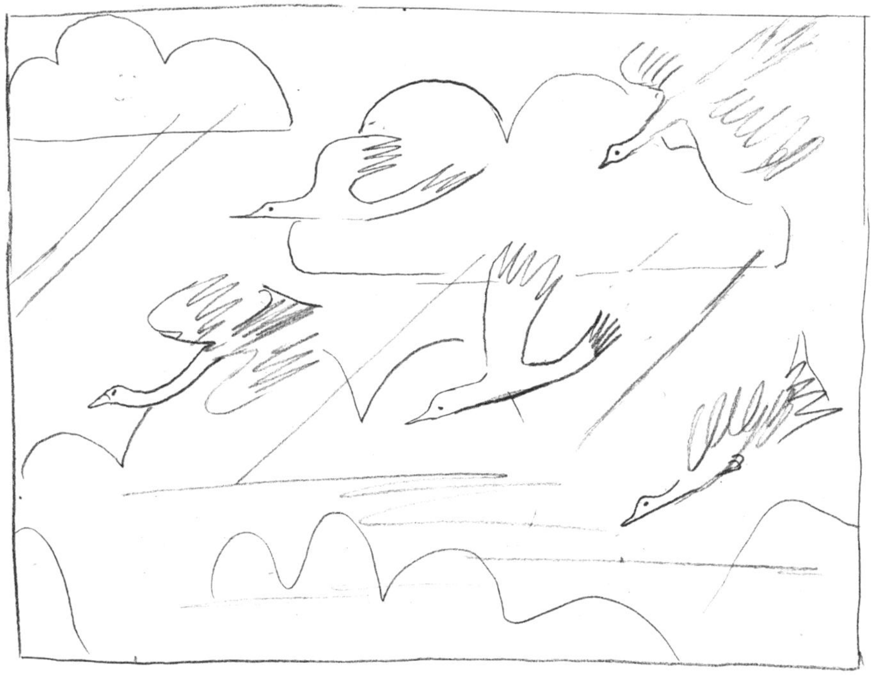

*Ein Hund verließ nachts seinen Körper, seine Käfig und das Labor und ging im Wald spazieren. Dort traf er einen Wolf, der sprach: Es gibt schon alles, also kann man nur mit dem umgehen, was schon vorhanden ist. Aber wie denkst du dann über das, was du tust? fragte der Hund. Ironisch, sagte der Wolf. Ich verstehe, antwortete der Hund, nun muss ich mich verabschieden. Morgen wird ein langer Tag und ich muss sterben. Nur das Eine noch: Ich habe auch schon Alles gesehen, aber es war so dunkel, dass ich nichts erkennen konnte.*

At night, a dog left its body, its cage, and the laboratory and went for a walk in the woods. There he met a wolf, who said: There is nothing new, thus one can only deal with what already exists. But then how do you think about what you do now? asked the dog. Ironically, said the wolf.
I understand, answered the dog, now I must take my leave. Tomorrow will be a long day and I must die. Just one thing more: I too have already seen everything, but it was so dark that I couldn't recognize anything.

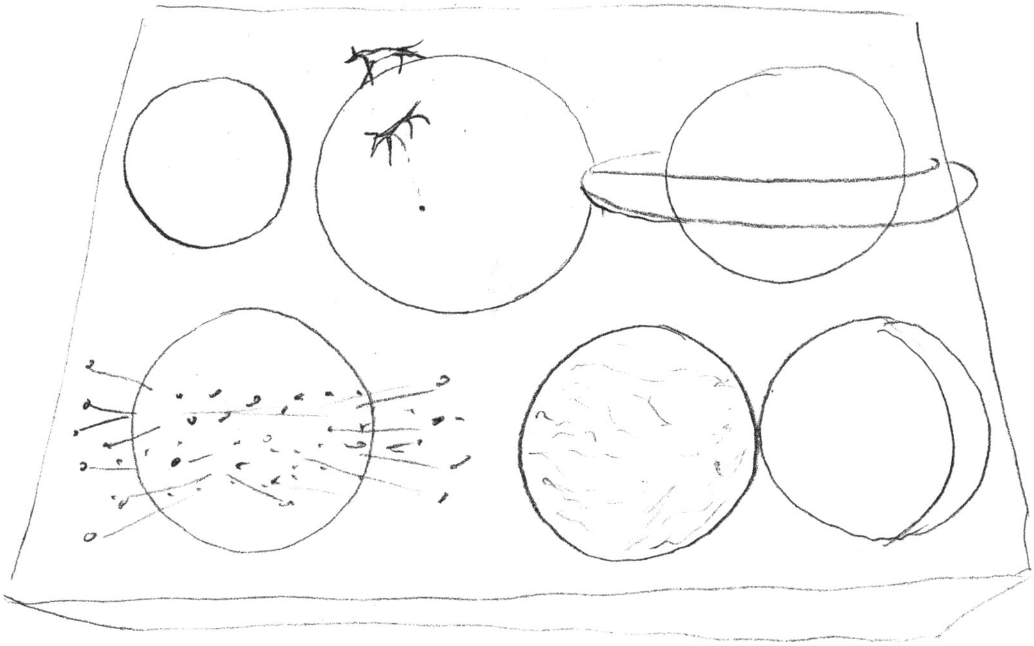

*Zenon rief alle Menschen und Tiere zu sich und sprach: Es ist keine Bewegung möglich, wie ich im Folgenden beweisen werde.*

A C B

*Um von A nach B zu kommen, muss ich zuerst die Hälfte der dazwischen liegenden Strecke zurücklegen. Den Punkt, der die Hälfte der Strecke markiert, nenne ich C. Um zunächst bis zu C zu kommen, muss ich die Hälfte von C zurücklegen, auch davon die Hälfte und so weiter . . . Die Schritte wie Ihr seht, werden also immer kleiner und darum ist es nicht möglich, bei B anzukommen. Wegen der Nichtexistenz von Bewegung werdet Ihr Alle zu Skulpturen.*

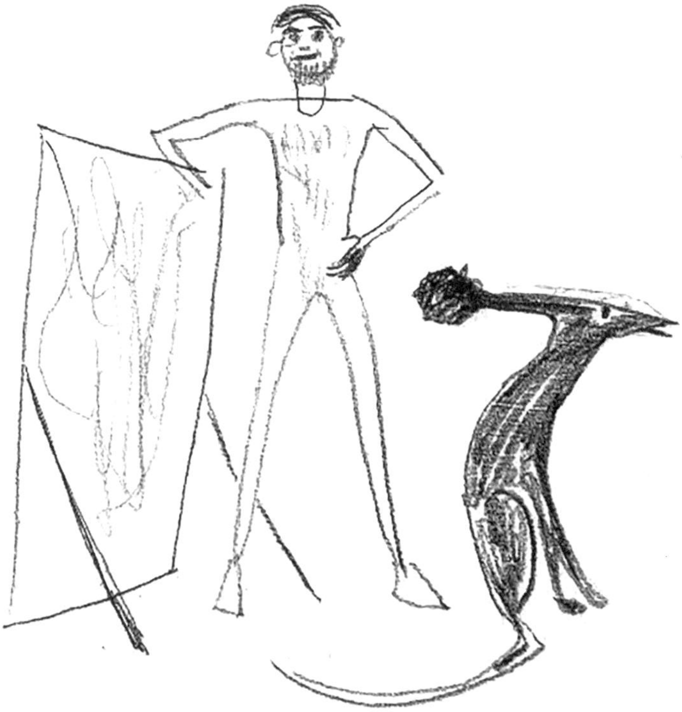

Zeno called all people and animals to him and spoke:
No movement is possible, as I will prove in the following.

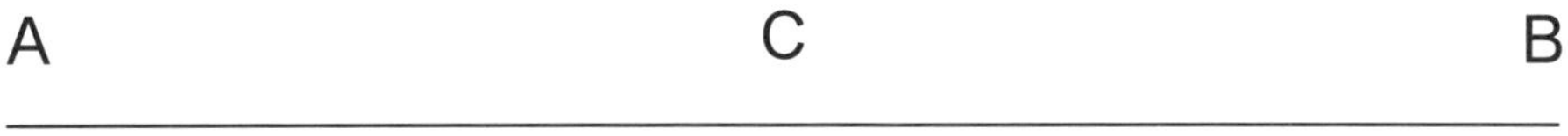


In order to get from A to B, I must first travel half of the distance lying between them. The point that marks one half of the distance I call C. In order to get to C, I must first travel one half of C, and also one half of that distance, and so on . . .  The steps thus become smaller and smaller, as you see, and therefore it is not possible to get to B. Due to the nonexistence of movement you all become sculptures.

Extracts from

# THE SOCIAL CONSTRUCTION OF THE OTHER

*On the Sociological Question of the Animal*

Birgit Mütherich

The problem of the animal, or rather of what is perceived as the animal, begins with its concept; for strictly speaking, "the animal" is a fictive category. Rather, what actually exists is a great diversity of thousands of different species, from the roundworm to the gorilla, which can be said to possess certain features that distinguish them from forms of plant life, among them sense organs, fixed patterns of action, memory, and the ability to learn. Although these features equally apply to human beings, which biological taxonomy would unquestionably categorize as mammals, our culture has been dominated not by an awareness of common features and kinship, but rather by an ontological divide. While many cultures, such as that of ancient Egypt, never developed this kind of terminology because they found no need to draw an absolute distinction between different life forms,[1] the blanket term "animal," undifferentiated, ambiguous and contradictory as it was, progressively mutated into the antonym for "human" under the powerful influence of Western civilization's religious interpretations and philosophical movements.[2] During the early modern period "the animal" went from being a structural element in a triadic world pyramid composed of "god, human, and animal" to being the wholly Other, the very antithesis of humanity's self-image. In so doing, it acquired a crucial social and political function: as an implicitly permanent point of reference within the Western symbolic system, it provided the primary foundation for hierarchical constructions of reality, regimes of inferiority and superiority, and models of legitimation that perpetuate all forms of exclusion, oppression, and violence among human beings themselves.

(...) As Schopenhauer remarked early on, the German language is especially rich in constructions that characterize the animal as something intrinsically Other, as the representative of a separate realm of its own that is styled "nature."[3] Animal individuals[4] are deprived of their individuality as subjects, they are objectified and devalued, and their forms of acting and behaving deliberately estranged—even when these are formally and functionally identical with human forms of behavior. Thus for example, German linguistic conventions would have it that animals *fressen* (devour or eat like animals) rather than *essen* (eat like humans), that they *werfen* ("drop," "litter," "whelp," or "throw") rather than *gebären* (give birth), that they are *trächtig* ("in foal" or "in kitten") rather than *schwanger* (pregnant), and that they *verenden* (die like animals) rather than *sterben* (die like human beings; an analogy might be the term "put down" or "put to sleep" against "euthanize"). They are referred to as *Exemplare* (specimens) rather than as individuals, and their dead bodies, when not being dismembered and served up on platters, are termed *Kadaver* (carcasses) or *Aas* (carrion) rather than *Leichen* (corpses). (...) Historically this hierarchical and patriarchal paradigm, first theocentric, then anthropocentric, proved to be an extremely versatile method of establishing control by means of flexible mechanisms of inclusion and exclusion. (...) Having postulated that humans, or more specifically men, had been made in God's image, and that He had granted them dominion over

Birgit Mütherich's essay "Die soziale Konstruktion des Anderen: zur soziologischen Frage nach dem Tier" was originally published in 2005 by Autonome Tierbefreiungsaktion, Hanover, Germany. The English translation, by Nathaniel McBride, was commissioned by Lin May Saeed. The number following the slash in the notes below indicates the note number in the original essay.

1/2
See Erik Hornung, "Die Bedeutung des Tieres im alten Ägypten," in *Studium Generale* 20, no. 2 (1967): 69–84.

2/3
On the problem of the concept of "the animal" from a sociological, anthropological, biological, juridical, linguistic, philosophical, and archaeological point of view, see Tim Ingold, ed., *What is an Animal?* (London: Routledge, 1988).

3/5
Arthur Schopenhauer, *Preisschrift über die Grundlage der Moral*, chap. 19, no. 7, in his *Werke in fünf Bänden*, vol. III, ed. Ludger Lüdgehaus (Zurich: Haffmans, 1988), 596ff.

4/6
[Trans.: Mütherich uses here the term *tierliche Individuen*, with the note that follows.] "Despite its unambiguously negative connotations, the colloquial term *tierisch* (meaning 'animal,' but with connotations of 'brutal' or 'bestial'), is still in use in the literature. However, it is increasingly being replaced by *tierlich* (which lacks these connotations), and this objective linguistic form is used here throughout." For a critique of the word "tierisch," see Gotthard M. Teutsch, *Mensch und Tier: Lexikon der Tierschutzethik* (Göttingen: Vandenhoeck & Ruprecht, 1987), 190ff., and Heini Hediger, *Tiere Verstehen: Erkenntnisse eines Tierpsychologen* (Munich: Kindler, 1980), 323.

other forms of life,[5] this basic order found that it needed a counterpoint to the human being and the idealized features that distinguished him and which were themselves derived from the doctrine of the *Imago Dei*. In the everyday culture of the ancient world, "the animal" had primarily been regarded as a sacrificial offering or source of meat; but once religious law had defined it as a creature that could and should be dominated, it became the ideal repository for all that was evil, ungodly, and anti-human. This not only made "the animal" both the cause of the Fall in the creation myth and the Antichrist in the Apocalypse of the End Times,[6] it also made it the political symbol for a rising Christianity in its struggle against the old animal deities and powerful competing religions of the period.[7]

(...) [The] human being's immortal soul, his capacity for salvation, his ability to exercise divine reason, and his free will to choose between good and evil are all negative correlates of the animal's abhorrent qualities: its absence of a soul, its lack of reason, its lack of free will and its mortality. The disciplining function of this construction is made clear by the fact that the (conception of the) human being contains both principles, reflected with the same asymmetry and intrinsic value. While the Western project of civilization defines this ideal "inhabitant of two worlds" as one who controls his "inner nature" and physicality by means of his intellect and reason, the construct of the animal is—apart from a few internal functional differences such as that between "work animals" and "pests"—on the whole one-dimensional. In essence this implies a conception of the animal as a piece of "living matter," as a being reduced to its own physicality and devoid of any subjecthood—and this despite the fact that the animal's own capacity for feeling was understood relatively early on. The conception is promoted by growing economic interests in exploiting other species, and accompanied by a progressive desensitization to their mistreatment and killing. In antiquity, the Middle Ages, the Renaissance, and the Enlightenment, down to the first half of the twentieth century, the dominant ideas—those serving the interests of the ruling class—were characterized by a search for features that distinguished humans from members of other species or even presented them as the antithesis of each other. What is significant about these highly influential theories—such as those of Aristotle, Thomas Aquinas, or René Descartes—is not only that they establish axiological hierarchies among life forms and dualist constructions separating human beings from other species, they also consistently justify regimes of permanent inequality among human beings themselves. In both fields, these theories come to be contrasted with more liberal positions and critiques of culture and power that emerge in the early modern period with thinkers such as Michel de Montaigne (an early pioneer of ethnology and animal psychology), David Hume, Jean-Jacques Rousseau, and Jeremy Bentham, down to Leonard Nelson. Nevertheless, the antithesis to "the animal" retained a central importance, not least because of the compatibility between hierarchical political concepts, the actual power interests of feudal (and later class) society, and the traditionally dualistic structure of Western culture. Its dual function as a basic component of the culture's model of order and point of reference and source of legitimation for political strategies led to the formation of lasting collective prejudices, which, passed down by patterns of perception, classification, and behavior, were manifest in every area of society, and—from the beginning of industrialization especially—went through various different processes of institutionalization. In social and political terms, the crucial reason for the construction of "the animal" as the "wholly Other" may have originated in its function as an instrument of education and control in the formation of European civilization. The opposition of idea to appearance, of mind to nature, soul to body, and order to chaos, which had been known since antiquity (Platonic Idealism, Aristotle's concept of nature

5 / 9
Genesis 9:1–7.

6 / 10
For the figure of the Antichrist as "the beast with the number 666," see Revelation 12:7–9 and 13:11–18.

7 / 11
See Jeremy Rifkin, *Beyond Beef* (New York: Plume, 1993), 27–34.

and politics, Stoicism), were crucial in determining that reason, morality, and self-control constituted the fundamental guiding values for an orderly and hierarchical state. The "animal," which was supposedly nonrational, subject to its own nature, and without free will, was both proof of and justification for the idea of a goal-oriented order of being, where nonrational beings had been created to be used and dominated by rational ones. However, this idea was applied far more broadly: for example, all groups of humans that could be described as lacking reason, as being governed by their instincts, as being unable to control their emotions, and therefore as being unalterably "close to nature" were largely regarded as being without rights and as subjects or even objects to be dominated. (...)

The accusation of being backward or having no history, part of the standard repertoire of exclusionary figures of argumentation, originates in a form of thinking that specifically reconstructs history in terms of societies' organizational, technical and material forms of intercourse, and links the concept of history to the productive human (male) subject who aims at appropriating his environment. Combined with the old but still widely accepted model of "natural" evolution, conceived both as having come to an end and as being ordered in a hierarchical series of stages, this pattern of thinking contains a biological prejudice not only against animals but also—and especially—against women. Arguments about a so-called female "nature" are used to interconnect their position with biological and social forms of social reproduction, which in turn are used to establish their supposed lack of history, inability to develop, and "naturally" inferior status. In contrast to work in the sphere of production, which is interpreted as being manly and active and a force for historical progress, women's part in social work is seen as passive, unchanging, and an almost timeless and natural "performance of duties"—as well as one that needs to be preserved as such. "Women," declared the doctor Max Runge at the end of the nineteenth century, "are bound by eternal laws. The best examples of them feel no need to become half-men, but desire rather to be wives and mothers." For the physicist Max Planck there was no doubt that "nature itself has ordained for women their vocation as mothers and housewives, and natural laws can never be ignored without causing serious damage, which would become particularly apparent in the succeeding generation."[8]

(...) The construction of that which is "animal," and its denigration and relegation to a different order of being, cannot be regarded as a purely semantic phenomenon in the history of ideas—any more than racist and sexist forms of speech can be treated as the mere object of theoretical game-playing. Rather, they reinforce the real subjugation of animal individuals, a process that has massively intensified as industrial society's forms of production have continued to expand. The fact that nonhuman beings possess no rights to life or its enjoyment, that they in general are entitled to no form of existence beyond that defined for them by human needs, that their (forced) reproduction, their miserable living conditions in mechanized battery farms and laboratories and the billions of deaths they suffer every day should be controlled by humans to serve our personal needs and growing social consumption is largely regarded as "natural" even today, and justified on the grounds that the "animal" "consents" to it, or on the grounds that it is inferior because it is less rational. (Even though this attitude seems on the face of it to

8 / 51
Quoted in Renate Feyl (ed.), *"Sein ist das Weib, Denken der Mann": Ansichten und Äusserungen für und wider den Intellekt der Frau von Luther bis Weininger* (Darmstadt: Luchterhand, 1984), 63, 71. These comments were part of an 1897 report on "the academic woman" in which "eminent university professors" offered their assessment of "women's aptitude for academic study and professions" (p. 90).

9 / 62
In certain fields of life, particularly the military, a capacity to distance oneself from and destroy others when required is considered highly desirable. In many countries, the training programs for hand-to-hand combat experts, elite soldiers, and torturers include demonstrating the ability to kill animals that are generally positively regarded, such as dogs, as a means of developing aggressive capacities. "Training" often involves particularly brutal forms of mistreatment, such as cutting open and tearing apart live animals, as a means of systematically lowering inhibitions.

be outmoded—as opinion polls or people's own close relationships with their pets would indicate, or as educational interaction with children and animals and the large numbers of viewers for animal documentaries would suggest—the fact cannot be ignored that all manner of individual psychic needs or specific forms of instrumentalization are operative here, which do not run counter to the economic interests and general cultural model of order, but are often part of it.) As a symbol of a commodified, inferior life form, produced to serve particular needs, and as a representative of the underdog, stigmatized as a matter of course, "the animal" is defined in our culture as the very prototype of the Other that must be dominated. As such, it also serves as a model for related forms of behavior, which range from training and manipulation to depersonalization, exploitation, anonymization and annihilation (followed by technical transformation into a dead commodity). This both inculcates and propagates a basic attitude towards the Other which extends from the symbolic level through social systems of norms and values to collective and individual attitudes and patterns of behavior, and which is based on dissociation, degradation, objectification, and violence, and on suppressing elementary commonalities—some physical (feelings of pain), some psychic (the ability to suffer), and some affective, cognitive and social.[9] (...) Like racism, sexism and other forms of discrimination, the social construction of the Other—including the propagation of the image of the enemy—can only be analyzed and problematized as a form of violence through a holistic approach, one that includes the "animal question" and a qualitatively new broadening of the range of those we recognize as other subjects. By analyzing the violence implicit in the construction of the Other, it may become possible to attenuate and perhaps to some extent even overcome it, thereby opening up a broad, new field of research.

# THE GATE AND THE UNREACHABLE

Mel Y. Chen

> Animals have a right to life, freedom, and integrity. There is no justification for keeping animals imprisoned. Not for animal experimentation, and not for food in either intensive or so-called species-appropriate farming. Only freedom can be species-appropriate. The *Soma* exhibition by Carsten Höller shows a pointless animal experiment in the museum Hamburger Bahnhof, Berlin. . . . There is no justification for structural violence against animals through *l'art pour l'art*, especially not through art which borders on science. The animal is the unreachable. Animals must be liberated.[1]
>
> —Lin May Saeed

## I. GATES

In so many contemporary metropolitan imaginations around the world, a gate solidifies as an idiom: keep out. The classed intensification of property in space is vaunted as a collective refusal of publics. Such a gate would seem to keep company with some notions of the "unreachable"—at first glance, in ways that seem quite different from Saeed's allusive use above, which prefaces her demand for animals' liberation. In nominally class-mobile societies, the gate at the opening to a neighborhood is the physical mark of mobility's failure in the face of an increasingly secure—locked—wealth divide. Indeed, gates, even at their most capacious, suggest uneven passage—through irreversible time, or up to levels of spiritual or material betterment, maturation, or privilege. We might also find gates—again primarily closed ones—in Palestinian imaging of Israeli checkpoints; in nation-state borders on the shores of Greece, Spain, or Macedonia, and on the land crossings of Hungary, Germany, or Denmark; in South African reanimations of apartheid as securitized land wealth; in the borders of the United States from directions south. Where ingress seems so physically unlikely, today's gates, across their diverse forms and workings, seem to feel and operate more permanently—closer to walls. A gate, in myth or religious story, suggests more than this (as do, in truth, national borders whose gates work preferentially, not absolutely). This essay is framed around the theme of the gate, beginning with a close look at one of Saeed's gate works in the exhibition and meditating on similarly vexed and preferential human-animal divides.

One of Saeed's most recent works in the *Arrival of the Animals* exhibition, *Toreador Gate* (fig. 13/pl. 2) depicts a bullfighting scene. Its metal strands suggest the schematic qualities of a sketch. This rectangular work is outlined by a thicker frame, with a ringed handle on the right edge and two hinges along the left; thus, is suggested the titular gate. To an embodied human observer, *Toreador Gate* is imposing. As well, however, the work's interior has a structuring element and backdrop in the partial form of an arched gate, inside of which are set a number of perpendicularly crossed bars. Presumably, the bull has been narratively brought forward by opening this gate. Under the bull's forehooves and along the bottom lies a human figure (not obviously gendered, but arguably a masculine toreador) whose hair, directed away from the head, speaks of a violent disheveling—at which point the line of the chest disappears, suggesting dissolution, cutting, or misshaping. Arms are absent or fall below the frame. The toreador's few straight lines of hair and obscured face contrast starkly with the curved lines representing the hair of the bull, whose face is depicted in profile (the bull's finer hair seems an extraordinary and dense detail compared with the vectoral suggestions of the rest of the work). The work thus deploys what Saeed has elsewhere called the "iconography of the victor,"[2] but at face value reverses the victory.

1
Lin May Saeed, "Anlässlich der Ausstellung *Soma* von Carsten Höller in Hamburger Bahnhof, Berlin (November 5, 2010–February 6, 2011), 2011. www.linmay.de/index_e.html.

2
Lin May Saeed and Jochen Lempert, unpublished conversation. Berlin, June 17, 2017. Saeed's reference to an iconography of the victor understands the role of predators as informing schemas of dominance in histories of art: "You're very quickly confronted with the theme of domination, either the domination of the predator over its prey, or the domination of the hunter who has killed the predator, which, by this logic, makes the animal worthy of presentation."

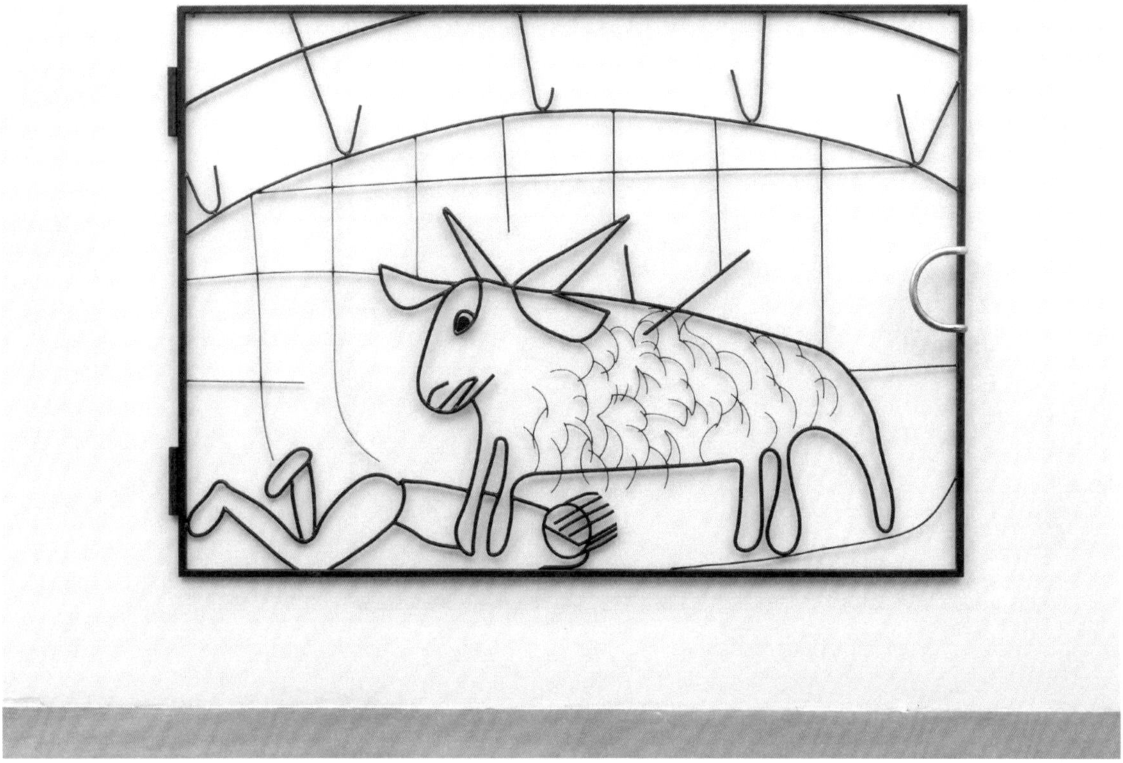

Fig. 13. *Toreador Gate*, 2019. Steel, lacquer, 59 × 83 ⅞ × 3 ½ in. (150 × 213 × 10 cm)

Visual art has long involved changing discourses and edicts of spatial relations: for instance, perspective, proximity as intimacy or taxonomic kin, different surfaces as different worlds. Saeed's *Toreador Gate* is no exception. Encountering the interior, or "second-level," gate is somehow an experience both classic and accessible. The gate's narrativity works by way of spatial and perceptual language; for instance, if the gate bars do not overlap with the figure of the bull, it is because they are understood as situated behind it. The gate represents the unleashing of an extended event, an actual face-off, between human and bull. Note that the toreador is not released by the gate; instead, it is the bull who enters the space in which the person waits. We see that the narrative also marks moments of incursion: the toreador has left two lances in the shoulder flesh of the bull, weapons that here have not resulted in the bull's immediate death. After these incursions, the bull must have, narratively speaking, toppled the toreador and propped its hooves on the person. (Indeed, a "toreador" is not defined as one who must have killed the bull, though the final event would be a sword that reaches through the shoulder blades to stab the heart.) But the bull is injured, and we do not know what will eventually happen: ambiguity is key to Saeed's work, and it may be particularly felt here.

Opening the "first-level" gate—that of the entire metal ensemble—might yield an appreciation of its inside, as well as the blankness or conditionality of the wall space it formerly occupied, which we once were able to see. It might join other works that remark on their facial conditionalities, their sidedness. Here, if we ourselves open the first-level gate, have we thus, in a directly bodily way, positioned ourselves inside the second gate, where the bull was once in wait—and yet still may be found, along with the fallen toreador, in the same space that we inhabit? We face the bull's extensible command of its own liberation. The interior gate thus serves as a symbolic backdrop to an

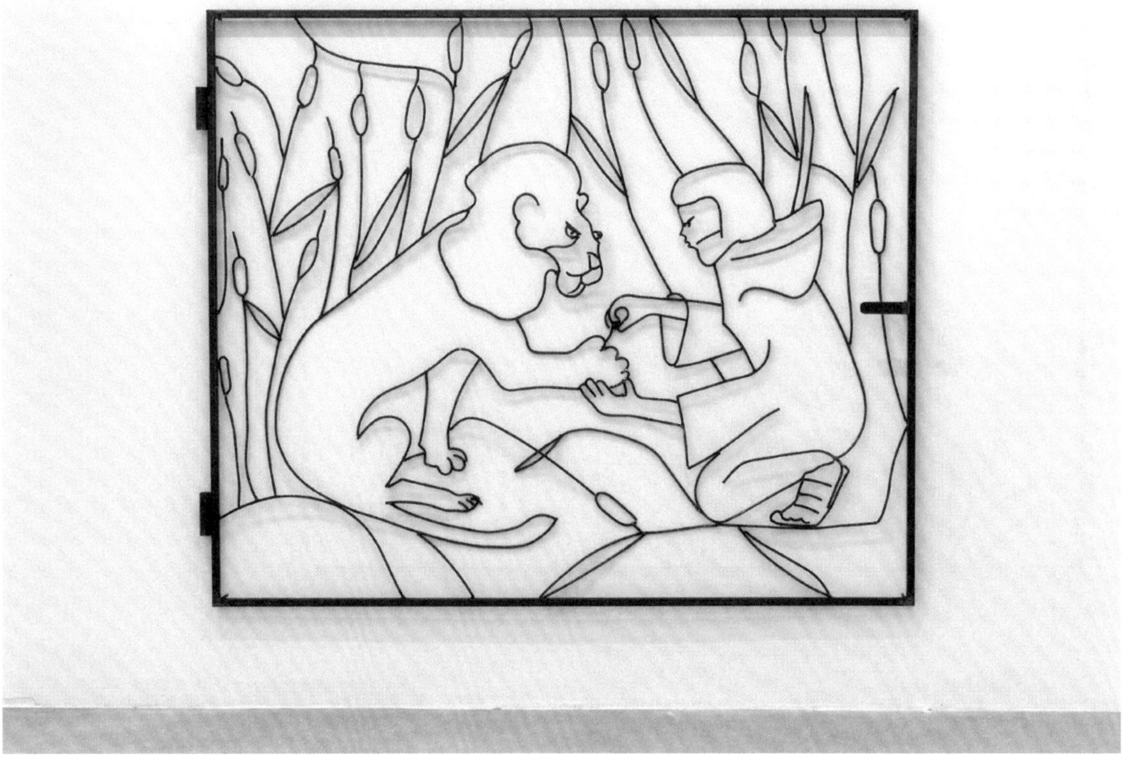

Fig. 14. *St. Jerome and the Lion*, 2016. Steel, lacquer, 59 × 73 ¼ × 3 ⅞ in. (150 × 186 × 10 cm)

opening: that of an imagination of freedom for the bull, as well as a reversal of the gate's preferentiality. That freedom has been conditioned by histories of violence—in both domestication as well as self-liberation—in this case, with subjects and objects that importantly change place.

The same "first-level" gate device is seen in an earlier work of Saeed's in this exhibition, *St. Jerome and the Lion* (fig. 14/pl. 1), with a single linear handle, hinges, and an interior background of (perhaps tongue-in-cheek) cattails that surround the kneeling St. Jerome and the sitting lion. The saint, holding the lion's extended paw in an indication of an intimacy of sorts, faces the lion and grips the thorn; the lion's tail rests on the ground, unthreatened as it curls toward St. Jerome. Saeed has said in an unpublished interview that this scene was not meant to be realistic, since literal representation interrupts the apprehension of the tale as a fictive proposition, a myth. Indeed, the human–animal relationship depicted here, compared to that in *Toreador Gate*, appears as less exploitative, less theatrical, kinder, and gentler: the fantasy of prelapsarian benevolence (if not equity) that underwrites many artistic depictions, including Saeed's. Yet here Saeed chose otherwise, aiming for something like the sly Pink Panther: in her rendering the lion feels no gratitude, and might well eat St. Jerome "after you've finished bandaging my paw." Here, there are no interior gates pitched for reversal, but given the opportunity for reflection at the first level, one wonders at the possibilities of conversation between these two works. In one conversation, the *Toreador Gate*'s compositional analogue is the surround of cattails behind St. Jerome and the lion. Bullfighting, one ritual of "man's" seemingly crafty—yet obtusely over-staged and highly constrained—symbolic victory over nature, might be answered by nature's inevitable surround, and the figurative dominance of one type of animal, in such numbers that they refuse individuation. We might say that Saeed's figurations here are *translations*, ones that necessarily engage shifted perspective; they re-present iconic stories in a way that opens up a productive gap between the philosophical possibility of figural release and the seeming pragmatics of animal liberation.

## II. SPECIES PARABLES

In contemplating *Toreador Gate*, *St. Jerome and the Lion*, and the reflexive, first-level gates that appear in both, we might consider Saeed's work, in its allusive use of stationing-in-relation, mythic reference, non-iconic or iconic animality, and more, as kinds of propositions. Or, better, to escape the attachment to rational thought that propositions might have, to view them as parables, or fables, another writing form Saeed has employed (see Fables, p. 73 in this volume), here in visual or figural form. Here is an untitled parable from 2004:

> At night, a dog left its body, its cage, and the laboratory and went for a walk in the woods. There he met a wolf, who said: There is nothing new, thus one can only deal with what already exists. But then how do you think about what you do now? asked the dog. Ironically, said the wolf. I understand, answered the dog, now I must take my leave. Tomorrow will be a long day and I must die. Just one thing more: I too have already seen everything, but it was so dark that I couldn't recognize anything.[3]

A parable, defined in the Oxford English Dictionary as an allegory, a fable, or a comparison (and secondarily defined as a story linked to moral or spiritual insight), may proceed with narrative determinacy while often arriving without a timestamp, cultural location, or interpretive framework. It is spare, open, and ultimately ambiguous. Saeed's above parable yields little about the dog or the wolf, and their reach for the abstractions or distances of irony; the meditations on novelty versus habit; the anticipation of death; the trans-species reach of a kind of cognizance of darkness and its relationship to knowing. But in beholding their relationship—the encounter between wild and domesticated—one is invited to move or be moved, to think in extension. Laboratories that perform experiments on animals like the dog in the context of their cold domestications might engage perception rather than genuine recognition, and ultimately deliver death, even as their living subjects continue to ask questions; yet the luxury of irony—that of the wolf—happens on their outside, amid the wildness and freedom of interpretation. Such insight becomes the grounds of further action, breaching, for instance, the seemingly constitutional divide between reflection about animals and animal activism.

Saeed's parable, with narrative or conceptual gaps that force contemplation, confusion, meditation, or mere aspirational filling, calls to mind another type of parable, but one perhaps with the possibility of even sparer narrative: Zen koans, some of which themselves carry a history of translation from Chinese to Japanese. And with parables, we return to the gate. *The Gateless Gate*, also translated as *The Gateless Barrier* (Mandarin: 無門關 *Wúménguān*; Japanese: 無門関 *Mumonkan*), is a renowned Zen work comprising forty-eight koans by Wúmén Huìkāi, a Chinese Zen Buddhist master in the 12th–13th centuries.[4] *Gateless Gate* refers, in part, to a gate that in some way fails to operate as such: the feat of traversal in a Zen practitioner's efforts toward enlightenment proves, upon its breaching, to be not what it has seemed, in part because the self is no longer the integrity that would have moved through. In the practice of Zen, these koans are less to be explained periphrastically or theoretically than apprehended directly; at most, they might be commented upon. A dog in fact begins the forty-eight-koan sequence; this koan was historically signal to Wúmén's own spiritual growth, and one of only four that superficially involve nonhuman animals (the next involved a fox that was once a human being, subject to five hundred rebirths; the fourteenth, a cat that is cut in half; and the thirty-seventh, a buffalo whose tail presents a problem for its passage to butchery).

3
Lin May Saeed, untitled, 2004

4
An English translation can be found in Reginald Horace Blyth, *Mumonkan: The Zen Masterpiece* (Tokyo: Hokuseido Press, 2002).

> A monk asked Zhàozhōu, "Does a dog have Buddha nature or not?"
>
> Zhàozhōu said, "Wú." (Wú means "no," "not have," "not being.")

As Wúmén commented on this koan: "To realize Zen, one has to pass through the barrier of the patriarchs. Enlightenment always comes after the road of thinking is blocked. . . . You may ask, What is a barrier of a patriarch? This one word, Mu [Wú], is it. . . . Do not believe it is the common symbol meaning nothing. It is not nothingness, the opposite of existence."[5] The koan is therefore not a puzzle to be resolved. Rather, it is a seat for contemplation of what seems the fundamental "gate," or barrier, which looks like—but is not—pure negation. And at its heart, the subject of the question that might or might not be a Buddhist "subject," is the dog. The "usefulness" of koans is not that they have intellectual power and resolvability; rather, they provide a means for spiritual development.

The significance of asking whether dogs have access to Buddha nature speaks to a widespread (but not universal) transcultural valuation of dogs as symbolically "low." Dogs have frequently served as examples of the abject, a ripe opportunity for "pure (social) negation," cultured humanity's Other (despite, in some cultural spaces, also being "man's best friend.") Thinking back to Saeed's parable, it was not the wolf (*Canis lupus*), but the dog (*Canis lupus familiaris*) that, even as the species might have been an agent of its own domestication, still fell victim to laboratory research, a research practice in which meaning lies in the replication and hence the individuated disposability of the lives of animals. If the dog of the koan did not speak, the koan, in refusing to deny the possibility of its Buddha nature, tugs against the dog's silence. Bénédicte Boisseron, in *Afro-Dog: Blackness and the Animal Question*,studies the actual historical contingencies between Black people and dogs in the transatlantic West, including colonial impositions of human animality and dog-proximity in chattel slavery and its consequential echoes.[6] Following critical animal studies investments in trans-species justice, Boisseron notes that merely decrying these forms of embedded coercion and violence risks an implicit acceptance of the abjectness of dogs. She pushes beyond such accountings and the simplicity of a label of "animalization" to encourage not the replication of their conceptual commingling (which an academic analysis can inadvertently further), but the search for cultures and signs of *defiance*—whether among the dogs, the people subject to such proximity, or both. Defiance coalesces with self-liberation. In the 2014 Hungarian film *White God*, directed by Kornél Mundruczó, a sustained face-off is depicted between urban human denizens and the city's stray dogs that become a massive group of actors. The dogs have the explicit sheen of a racialized, classed Other as the focal dog, Hagen, has been determined by the state to be an unacceptably mixed breed for domestic ownership and is taken from his human companion and "master," Lili. The final scene shows the dogs—including Hagen—in confident defiance, having not defeated, but rather made tentative peace with Lili and her human comrades. (The production's dog actors were all strays, and by design, each was eventually adopted into a home after the completion of the film; a re-domestication.) Though the conflation of humans and animals is decidedly not her project, Boisseron's search for defiance doubles as a trans-species claim that defiance is possible, and a right, and an expression. It is also a claim that a dog's defiance is, precisely, *reachable*, not least to her and other readers. Returning to Saeed's parable, I wonder if perhaps a dog's lament, reflection, should also be reachable. Its "speech," after all, does not come in quotes.

It should be noted, however, that the very idea of reachability—or unreachability, for that matter—requires the imagination of a gap over which relating, or relatedness, is a possibility,

5 *The Gateless Gate*, by Ekai, trans. Nyogen Senzaki and Paul Reps [1934], at sacred-texts.com.

6 New York: Columbia University Press, 2018

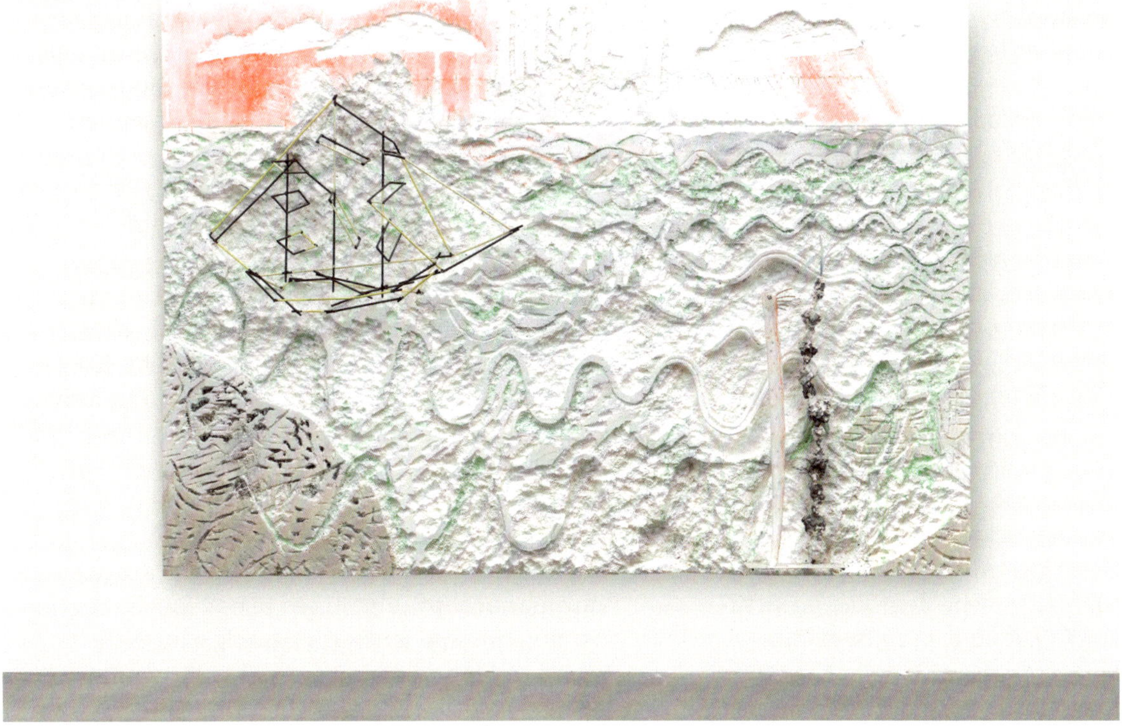

Fig. 15. *Ghost Ship Relief*, 2013. Polystyrene foam, acrylic paint, steel, plaster, paper, 69 ¼ × 98 ⅞ × 13 ½ in. (176 × 251 × 34 cm)

not a given. Such a view goes against many philosophies of being that run through histories of domination and colonization. For instance, indigenous thinkers have decried the self-presented novelty of the recent “ontological turn” and its challenge of the divide between nature and culture. As Zoe Todd states: “I think that if we’re going to talk about the nature–culture divide, we need to be explicit about scholarly work as a colonial tool, and indigenous legal structures as credible, robust, and dynamic ways of thinking. And also ways of asserting and thinking through relationships between people, whether they’re human or not.”[7] As Todd offhandedly presumes here, for many indigenous people and cultures of relational knowledge, personhood is a feature of being that is not reducible to species, or even biological notions of life; one can recognize the personhood of stones, rivers, mountains, and understand them as being agentive. For instance, Vine Deloria writes of the relationality of the world and of knowledge among the Western Teton Sioux, such that conditions of categorial isolation and vast constitutional gaps between species are insupportable abstractions.[8]

## III. THE LOW AND THE LOWLY

In a colonial world, however, the symbolic interdependencies among nonhuman animals and human animalities are many, and once understood, they are overwhelming. Saeed’s *Ghost Ship Relief* (fig. 15/pl. 3), a carved styrofoam

7
Aaron Vasintjan, “Decolonizing nature, the academy, and Europe: An interview with Metis writer Zoe Todd” in Uneven Earth: Where the ecological meets the political (Sept. 21, 2015). http://unevenearth.org/2015/09/decolonizing-nature-the-academy-and-europe.

8
Vine Deloria, “If You Think About It, You Will See That It Is True,” in *Spirit and Reason: The Vine Deloria, Jr. Reader* (Golden, CO: Fulcrum Publishing, 1999), 40-62.

relief of an oceanic scene, at first looks like a distant view of autonomous peace. At top are storm clouds and rain; below them at left, a ship is afloat, with no human sailors in evidence; below the ship, depths of water, down to a deep-sea hydrothermal vent, an analogous storm around which rich ecosystems thrive, beside which sits an oarfish—perhaps a visual pun and another form of mirroring. There is the sense of a vast gap between two systems of movement and perception even as the carrier of humans has been abandoned or as the humans themselves have, in effect, disappeared. Reading from the present moment's climate-change framing of the Anthropocene as a geological era induced by human influence, this may serve as a proposition that nature, possessed of relatively human-independent forms of ecosystem nourishment, might well be indifferent to humankind's self-erasure.

This work also haunts me because it reaches forward in time to remix, in both form and message, a catastrophic fire in the neighborhood adjacent to mine, the Fruitvale District of Oakland, California, on December 2, 2016, which killed thirty-six people at a music event. It became national news in the way it brought gentrification's shifting underside to the urgent fore. Many of the fire's victims were residents; among the attendees were many people living at intersections of marked race, gender, sexuality, and class. Several who died were trans, nonbinary, and/or queer people of color, communities in which I take part and which are regularly subject to judgments of inhumanity. Accounts by former residents and members of their communities spoke to the stresses and municipal abandonments of vulnerable populations through processes of gentrification. Their voices added to the structural understanding of precarity and the compromises that can occur when one barely manages to avoid homelessness. They lived what amounted to various survival strategies, including collective living and forms of worldmaking, in structurally unsound conditions that doubled the effects of a patriarchal modernity that already imagined their queer and queered beings as disposable symbolic excess or structural threat. "Ghost Ship" was the nickname for the sprawling, ticky-tacky construction that served as residences, art studios, and event space: it was a place whose irregular shapes and forms of crafted living among people striving for creative self-determination was greater than the sum of its parts.

Saeed's intentionally "low" and "ugly" found base material of Styrofoam, which forms the choppy surface of *Ghost Ship Relief*, is a painful metonym for the found materials that formed their own relief structures in Oakland's "Ghost Ship," comprising scavenged resources for ad-hoc building: barriers, makeshift stairs, and decoration, beautiful assemblage. Those materials formed, for the fire, a perfect storm of kindling. Saeed's oarfish, planted at the bottom of the sea near a deep-sea vent, faces this history as a lone witness, yet it, too, has turned away. Or it might never have noticed in the first place, again the proposition: unreachable, but also, unreaching. Which being actually desires the encounter?

The human animalities of precarious homing and homelessness, and of abandonment by civic structures, raise questions about nomination itself. The phrase "human animal" embeds several aspects of contradiction in one. If not all animals are human, all humans are animal, so why the redundancy, the conflation of sets? Because, outside of moments of voluntaristic self-regard, not all humans are animal. "Animal," as a concept, has been cultivated not only as a placeholder for creatures in the wild or agricultural laboring bodies or diverse food supply, but also as a place of deferral, death, and Otherness: in the preferential conception, there are human humans, and human animals, and the human animals are those thought immanent to an abject nature or failing to achieve the forms of rarefied "human nature" proper to a few. In this way, human animals are those deferred from proprietary humanity, those who may well be imagined to serve to define, as its negation, the very existence of the human. Thus, certain denigrated human animals share with certain other debased animals an utterly exhaustive imagination of being that is in some perverse way trans-species: it exists in a cynical state calculus of expulsion, displacement, captivity, violence, control, extraction, and exploitation. The hierarchical violence against the low that underlies the exploitation and abuse of animals—what Saeed refers to as speciesism, "an ideology in which you think that you can do things to animals because they're lower beings than we are," works hand in hand with intrahuman violences, participating in the same shared intersectional systems.[9] Here, the two forms of unreachability at the top of this essay come together. "They are treating them like animals" is a protest heard all too often as if it were defiant surprise, yet the simile simply registers the unspeakable intraspecies truth of domination, enslavement, coloniality, and Othering (while denying the diversity of actual treatment of nonhuman animals—including the cultures and economies of pets, the neglect of noncharismatic megafauna, and so on). The asymmetric gates that have become revivified at national borders around the world, as well as in virtual forms of access, speak directly to the actualities today (not imaginary futurities) of human animality, much as those identifications might be defiantly disowned by those forced to live by them.

The proposition that many people living in alienated relationship to nature have to face here and there, when the gates open in uncanny fashion, is the (nonrelational) idea that animals are fatally unreachable, condemned to metaphorical silence. The outreached hand by an orangutan in a reserve to a naturalist in a pond where he was trapping snakes, in what the orangutan apparently felt was a state of danger, is one such open gate. Studies in animal communication that increasingly demonstrate the abundance of communicative sophistication among nonhuman animal species challenge (religious and nonreligious, Western scientific and non-Western scientific) hierarchical traditions, constative schematics, by which a massive group defined as a negation of what is human could not possibly match the communicative capacities of humans as a species. A claim this sweeping is deeply suspect, and clearly ignores both the diversity of language use and the possibility of diverse language-related capacities (including what are understood as disabilities) among both humans and animals.

Indeed, if animals themselves are unreachable, one has also to ask: must this mean that humans themselves are unreachable to the animals? And if animals are unreachable, doesn't this mean that humans, as animals, are also unreachable to one another? Critically, how, thinking of the expression above, in either circumstance, do we define unreachability—as communication, understanding, inclusion in a community? We learn, in an unpublished interview, that Saeed's rabbits (an animal she has had all her life) don't seem all that interested in her: "They only ever interact among themselves, I am almost always left out." What is to be reached; what can be won; what can be felt, if touched?

## IV. UNNAMING

In an apprehension of animals, one can find strategies of accumulation, such as taxonomic description, and subtraction, such as indeterminacy, suffusion, and there is retreat. Science fiction writer Ursula K. Le Guin's feminist fable, "She Unnames Them," uses the upsetting of language, not its proliferation, to effect a companion proximity. The fable tells of a woman named Eve (whose husband is tellingly named Adam) who has the capacity and will to expunge the gross names of animals, a casual form of reference for nonhumans by humans who commonly live in alienated relationship to their natural surrounds. While many of the animals object to Eve's unnaming of them, others find it useful to return to "anonymity." Le Guin begins the story without an antecedent for "them," forcing us not only to imagine the referent of "them" as fullest subjects capable of indifference and acceptance, but also later to ask: was it the animals?

> Most of them accepted namelessness with the perfect indifference with which they had so long accepted and ignored

9
Una Meistere, "Why haven't animals revolted against humans yet? A conversation with German-Iraqi artist and animal activist Lin May Saeed," Arterritory.com, Jan. 8, 2020. http://www.arterritory.com/en/texts/interviews/8612-why_havent_animals_revolted_against_humans_yet/.

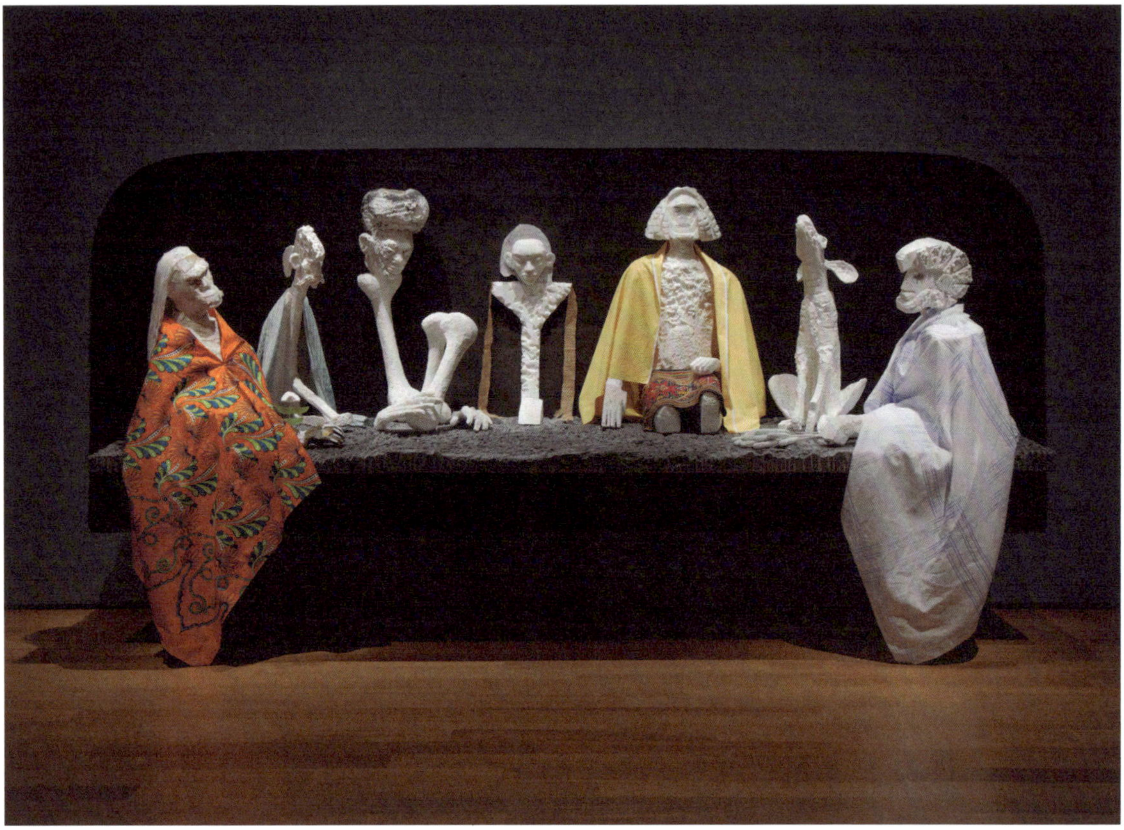

Fig. 16. *Seven Sleepers*, 2020. Polystyrene foam, acrylic paint, steel, jute, fabric, paper, plants, glass, water, cotton cord, wood, cardboard, 84 ⅝ × 177 ⅛ × 39 ⅜ in. (215 × 450 × 100 cm)

> their names. Whales and dolphins, seals and sea otters consented with particular alacrity, sliding into anonymity as into their element. A faction of yaks, however, protested. They said that "yak" sounded right, and that almost everyone who knew they existed called them that. . . . Soon after the beginning of the thaw, their agreement was reached and the designation "yak" was returned to the donor.[10]

The tale ends with the narrator leaving her husband, announcing she is "going now. With the. . . With them, you know," using the same uncertain antecedent the story began with. By "names," Le Guin's story refers not only to major species groupings, but also to what linguists call basic-level categories: each name—not likely the most specific possible for a member of that group, for instance, "bird" not "wren"—represents a material swath that might have a conceptual basis for humans but which varies, in specificity and groupings, among language-using human societies. She writes that not one of the animals "had the least objection to parting with the lowercase (or, as regards German creatures, uppercase) generic appellations 'poodle,' 'parrot,' 'dog,' or 'bird,' and all the Linnaean qualifiers that had trailed along behind them for two hundred years like tin cans tied to a tail."[11]

Such basic-level categories had attached to the animals in ways that taxonomically dragged on, rather than augmented, their being, against their own desires for address—except for the yaks, who apparently never had to struggle with what to do in the face of a nominal displacement. For the narrator, her singlehanded

10 Ursula K. Le Guin, "She Unnames Them," *The New Yorker*, January 21, 1985. 27.

11 Le Guin, 1985.

removal of names has brought all the animals (including herself) closer, along with newly entangled affects like fear and uncertainty, such that their holder would become indistinct from the rest. "I could not now, in all conscience, make an exception for myself." I note, too, the possibility that complexly gendered encounters, such as the yaks' unnaming by Eve and the determination by the female yaks that this could be advantageous, could span species divides, reminding us of the intricacies of mapping gender both within and beyond human confines.

Le Guin, the daughter of anthropologist Alfred Kroeber, surely knew that the name "yak" was not Germanic like the rest; it comes from the Tibetan language, speaking to its locally precise appellation. If the fact that "almost everyone who knew they existed called them that" became a foundation for the yaks' easeful return of their name to its donor, there might be a lesson about the colonial violence of certain languages that are carried over to their animals by way of systems of radical domintion, displacing indigenous nominations along with the forms of relation that accompany them.

If the German equivalent of "unreachable," *unerreichbar*, contains more than reach but also the notion of "unbroachable," then we are concerned not just with nonspeech, or silence, but also *unspeakability*. There is intense, almost unmappable traffic in the movement between direct address and topical possibility. Saeed's works, in their wily juxtapositions, enfacings, figural ambiguities, and supplantations, violate both temporal and spatial orders, remixing narratives and bringing them to and beyond their interpretive limit. I am thinking here of Saeed's multispecies *Seven Sleepers* (fig. 16/pl. 21): according to the Christian and Islamic parables about a group of human male youths, these young men would have slept together in their cave for hundreds of years. In Saeed's interspecies version, there is a truth of coexistence and potentially risky, intimate proximity—whether among young men or among species—that all too many deny. The message of Saeed's work is only complexly linked to liberation. For capture symbolizes captivity, the seizure of living things, and representation itself (of that which is, and isn't, reachable). There is also, to me, a kind of intellectual capture, a neat trick of linguistic and conceptual tying up as if all (wild) possibilities have been exhausted. If liberation is the undoing of capture and perhaps capture's effects, Saeed also refuses, much in the manner of parable, ready resolution for the animals, and perhaps also the human animals. Seated not in indigenous philosophies, in which the above questions might be very much retold, but in the readily inquisitive position of—to take one example—a biracial Jewish and Arab citizen of a German state, Saeed chooses the challenge of broad transtemporal sweeps and major/minor terms of animality, bringing questions of religion, history, myth, and figure to the animals. Whether or not in language, one might say that Saeed participates in their figural unnaming, conspiring to set alternative terms for liberation.

# CLARK COLLECTION WORKS

Plate 22
Nicolò Boldrini (Italian, born c. 1500, active c. 1530–1570),
after Raphael (Italian, 1483–1520)
*Hercules Wrestling with the Nemean Lion*, 16th century
Woodcut on paper
11 7/8 × 16 1/2 in. (30.7 × 41.8 cm)
Clark Art Institute, 1988.221

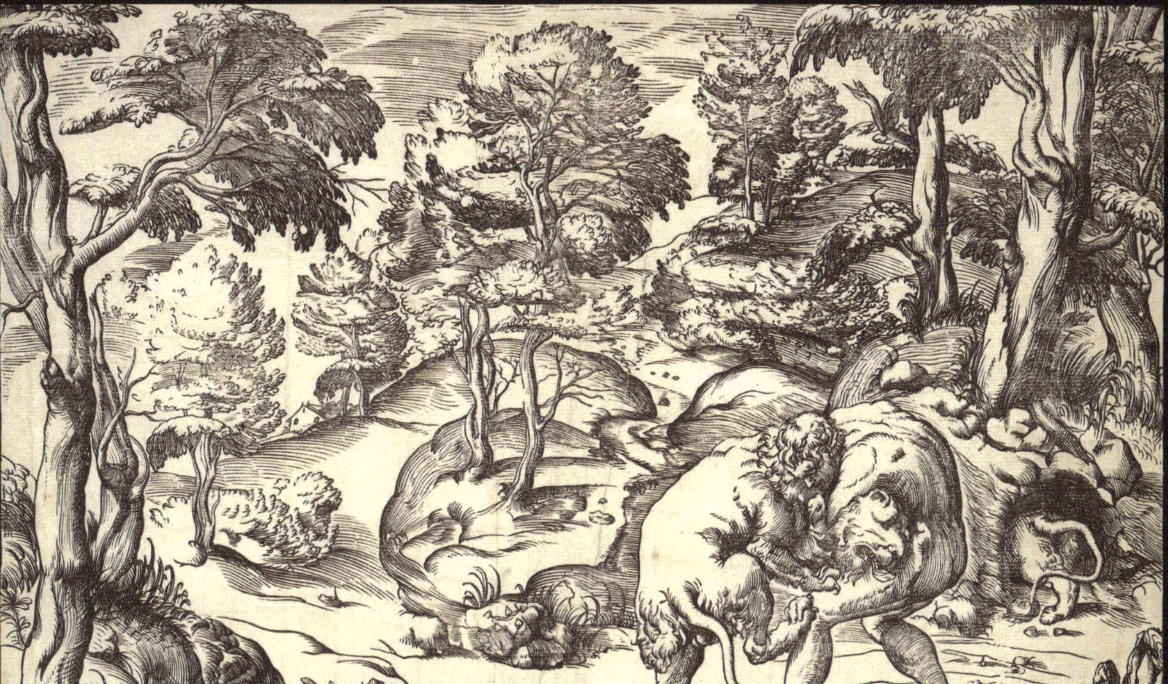
RAPHEL·VR·IN

Plate 23
Michael Snyders (Flemish, 1586–1672)
*Studies of Animals, Insects. Heads, etc.*, 17th century
Etching and engraving on laid paper
6 ⅞ × 9 ½ in. (17.5 × 24 cm)
Clark Art Institute
William J. Collins Collection, 1960.257

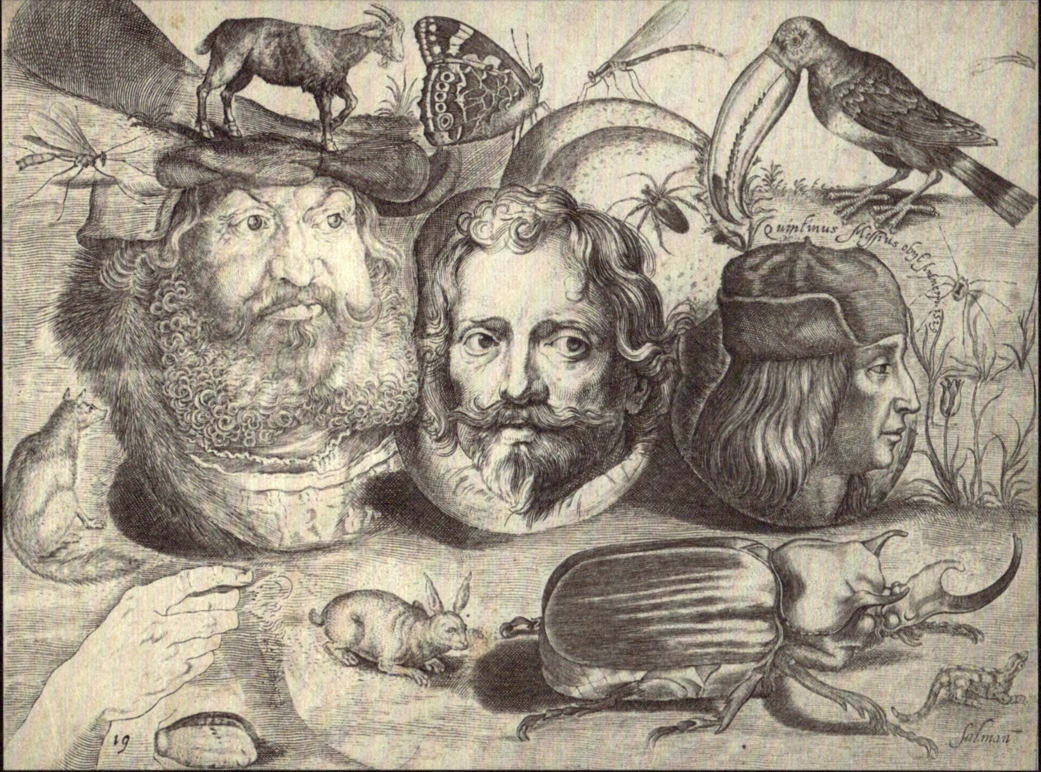

Quintinus Messius
19
Salman

Plate 24
Albrecht Dürer (German, 1471–1528)
*The Little Passion: The Fall of Man*, 1510–11
Woodcut on paper
9 ½ × 6 ⅜ in. (24.1 × 16.2 cm)
Clark Art Institute, 1968.136

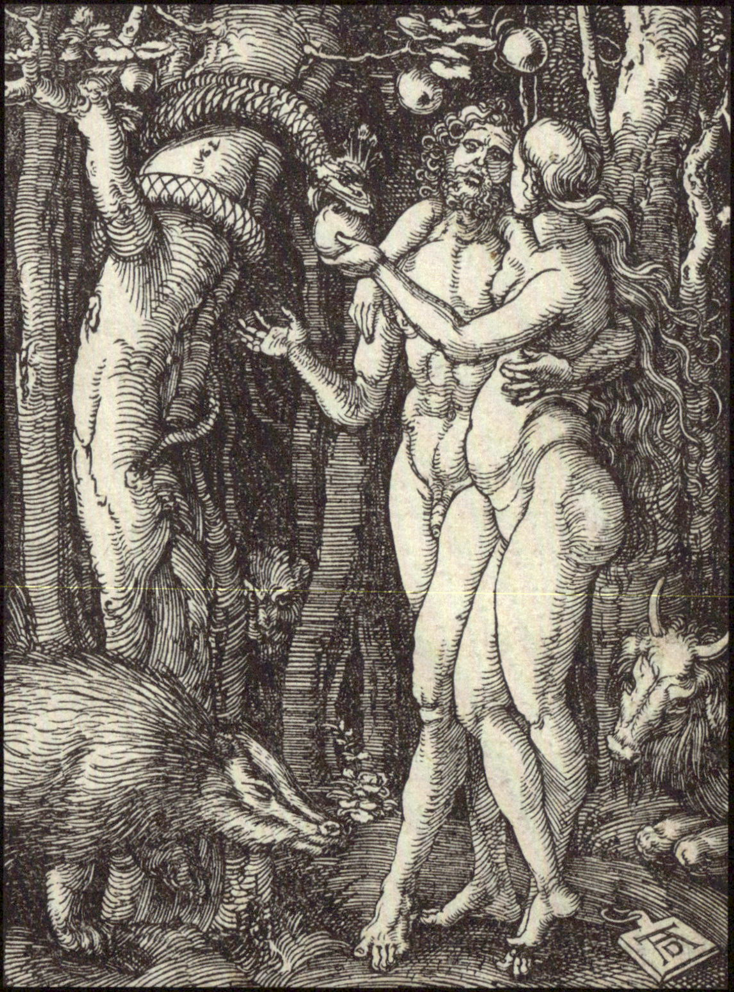

Plate 25
Albrecht Dürer (German, 1471–1528)
*Saint Jerome in His Cell*, 1511
Woodcut on paper
9 ⅜ × 6 ½ in. (23.8 × 16.5 cm)
Clark Art Institute, 1968.250

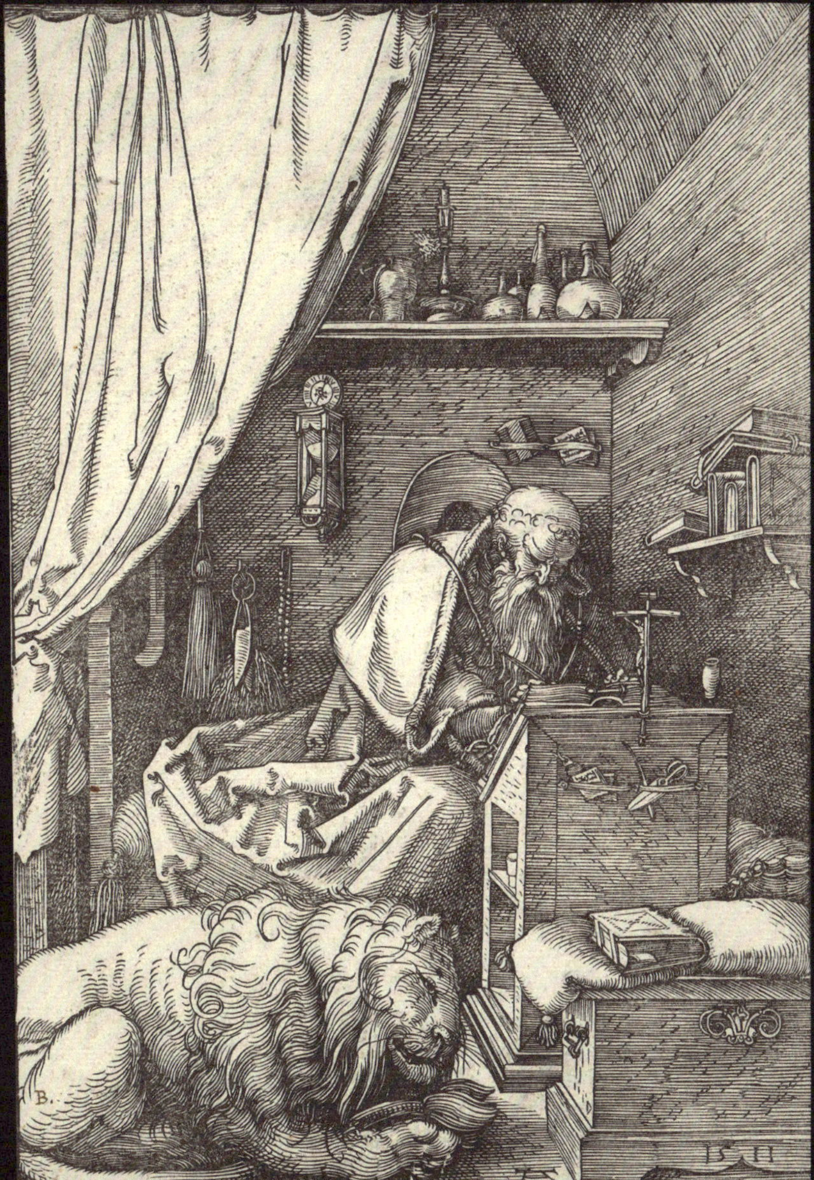

Plate 26
Rosa Bonheur (French, 1822–1899)
*Studies of a Lioness*, 19th century
Pencil on white wove paper
$6\frac{5}{8} \times 9\frac{3}{4}$ in. (16.7 × 24.8 cm)
Clark Art Institute
Gift of Denison B. Hull, 1976.23

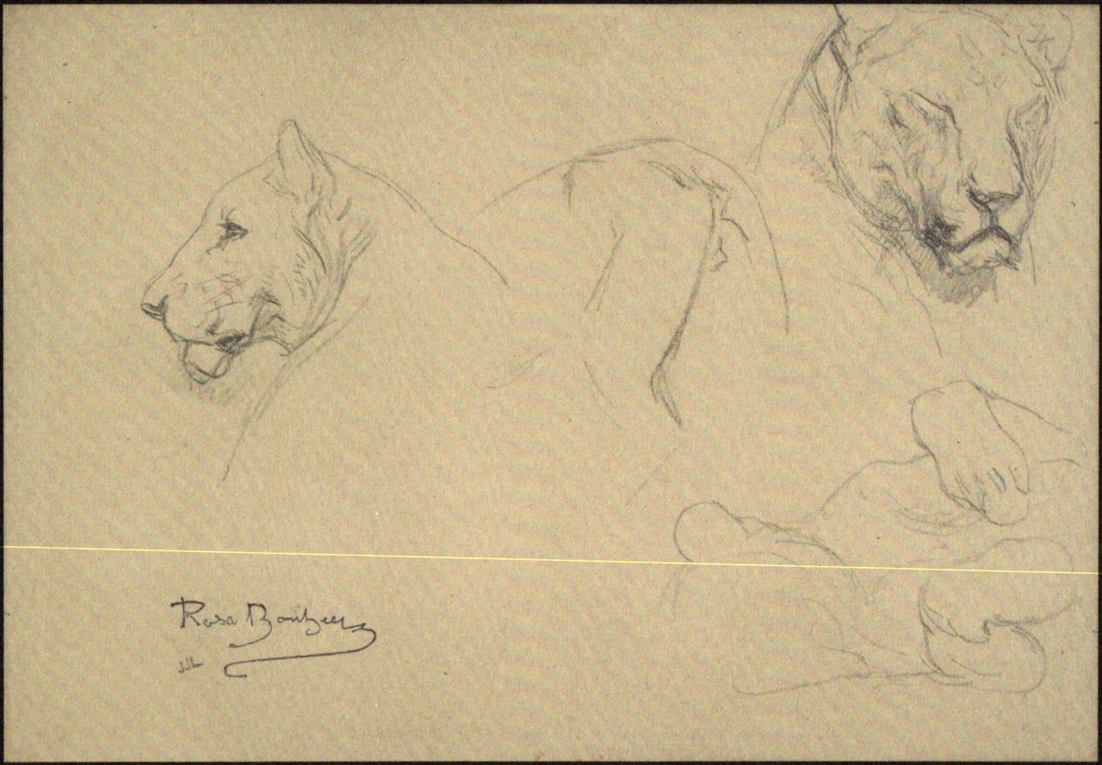

Plate 27
Eugène Delacroix (French, 1798–1863)
*Studies of a Crouching Tiger*, 19th century
Pencil on paper
5 ½ × 8 ⅞ in. (14 × 22.5 cm)
Clark Art Institute, 1955.1424

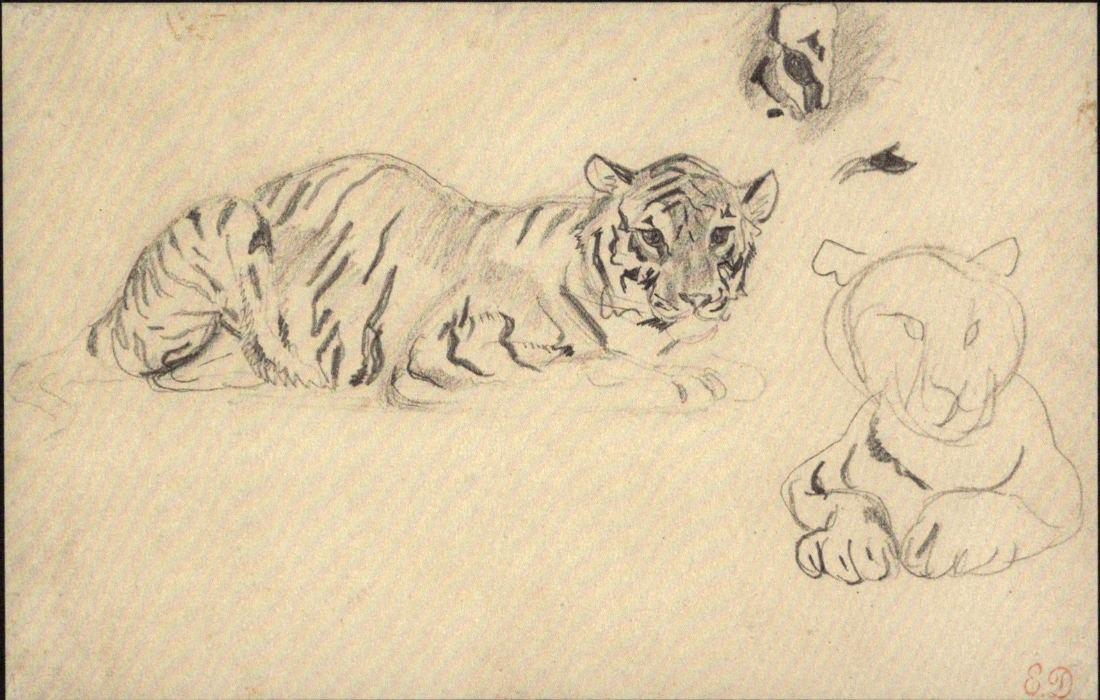

*Flemish Horses (Chevaux flamands)*, 1822
Lithograph on paper
9 ½ × 14 ⅛ in. (24 × 36 cm)
Clark Art Institute
Gift of James A. Bergquist, 1998.35

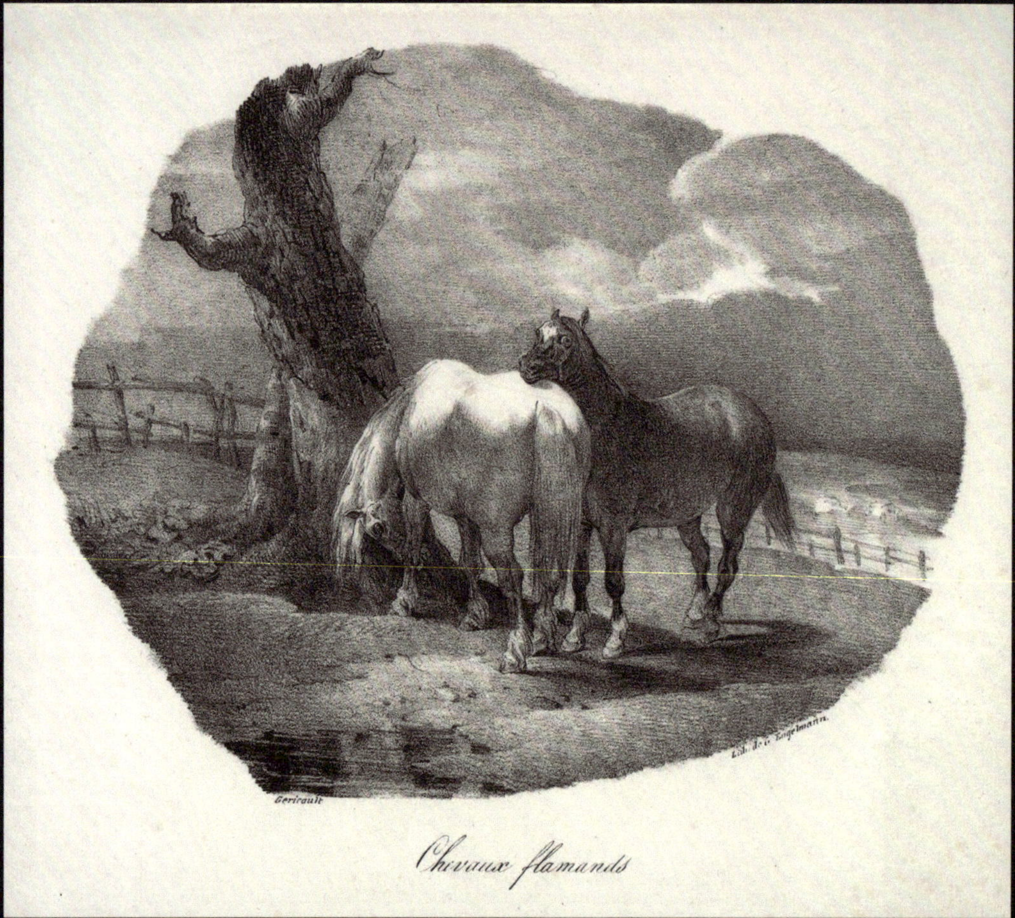

Félix Bracquemond (French, 1833–1914)
*The Moles (Les Taupes)*, 1854
Etching on laid paper
16 ⅝ × 12 ⅝ in. (42.1 × 32.2 cm)
Clark Art Institute, 1980.11

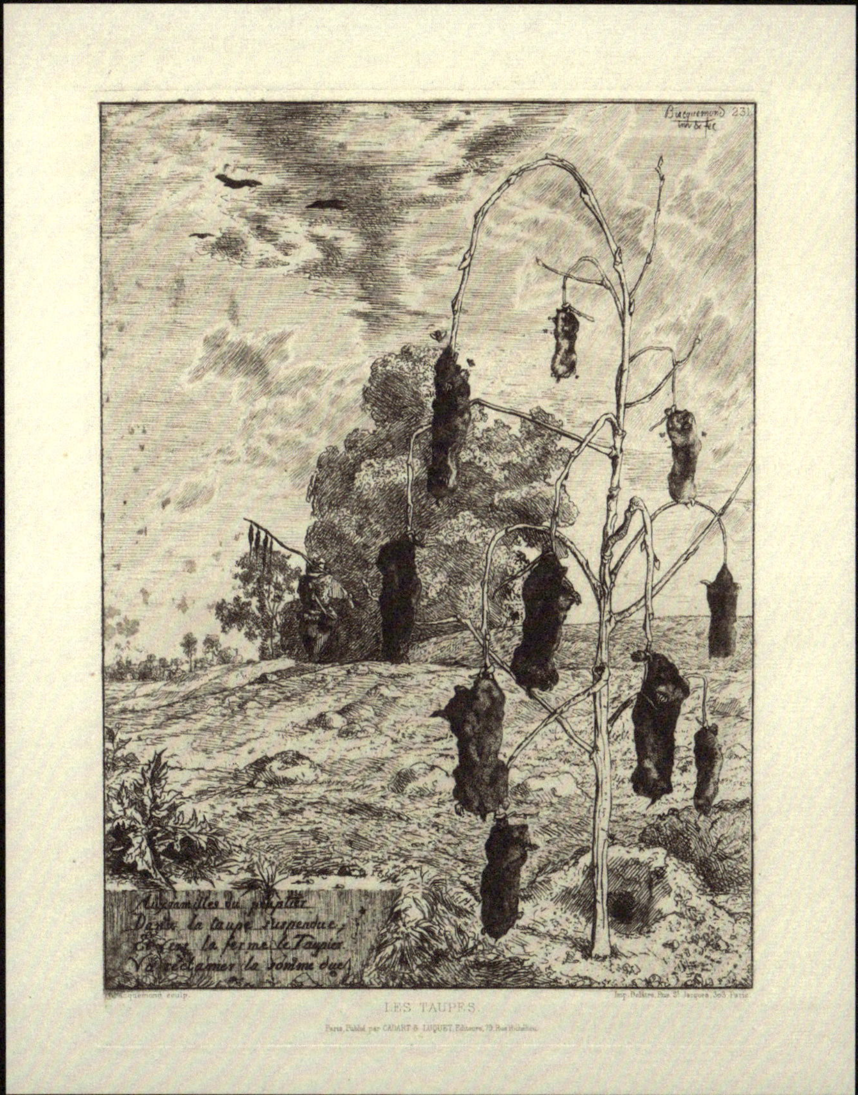

Plate 30
Théodore Chassériau (French, born
present-day Dominican Republic, 1819–1856)
*Moorish Women of Constantine*, 1851
Etching and soft ground etching on chine collée on paper
8 ¾ × 12 in. (22.2 × 30.5 cm)
Clark Art Institute
Gift of Jay McKean Fisher in memory of his parents,
Suzanne and Frederick Fisher, 2003.6

Salon de 1850-51

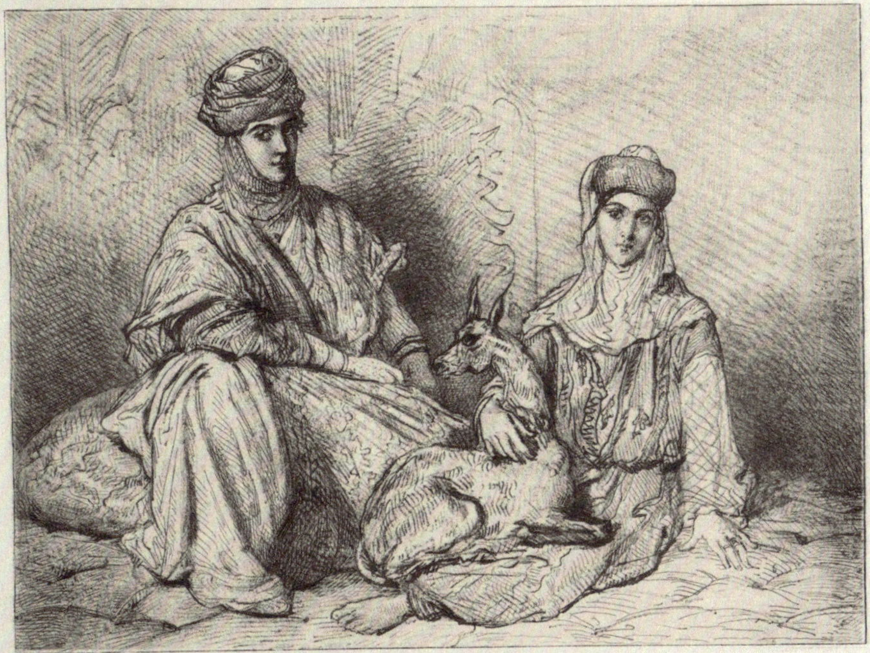

Th. Chassériau 1851

FEMMES MAURESQUES

(de Constantine)

# INSTALLATION VIEWS

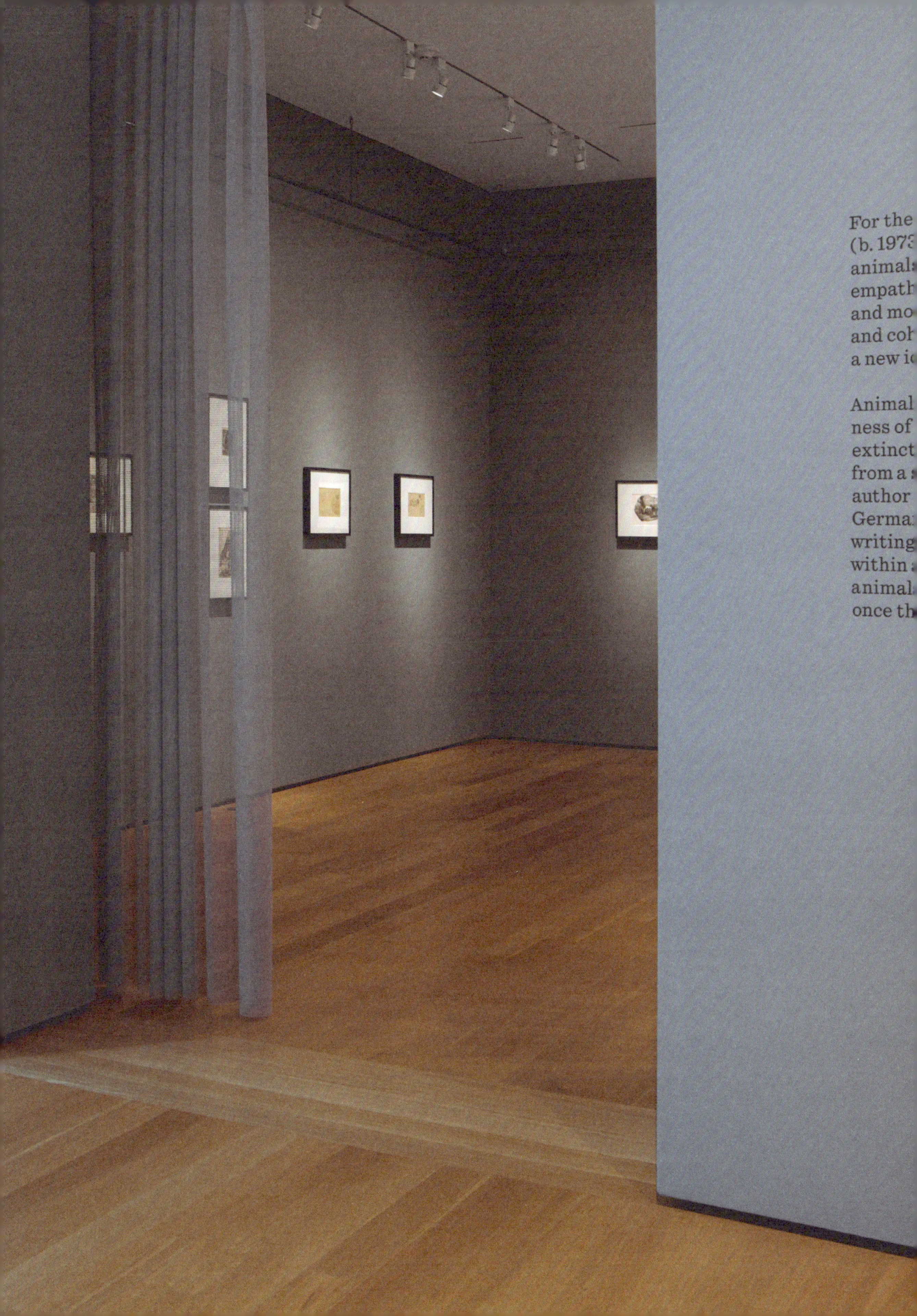
For the
(b. 197
animal
empath
and mo
and coh
a new i
Animal
ness of
extinct
from a
author
Germa
writing
within
animal
once th

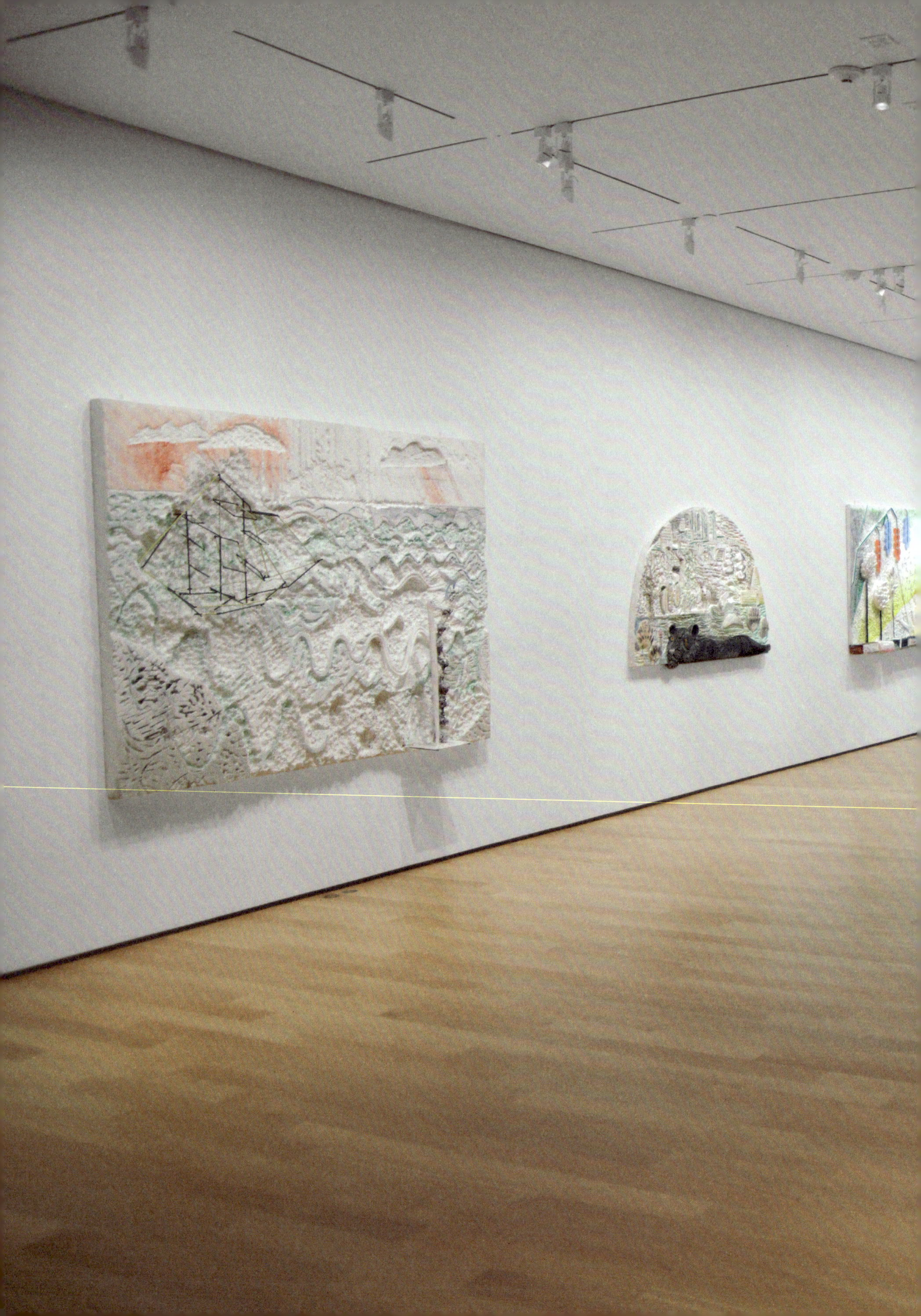

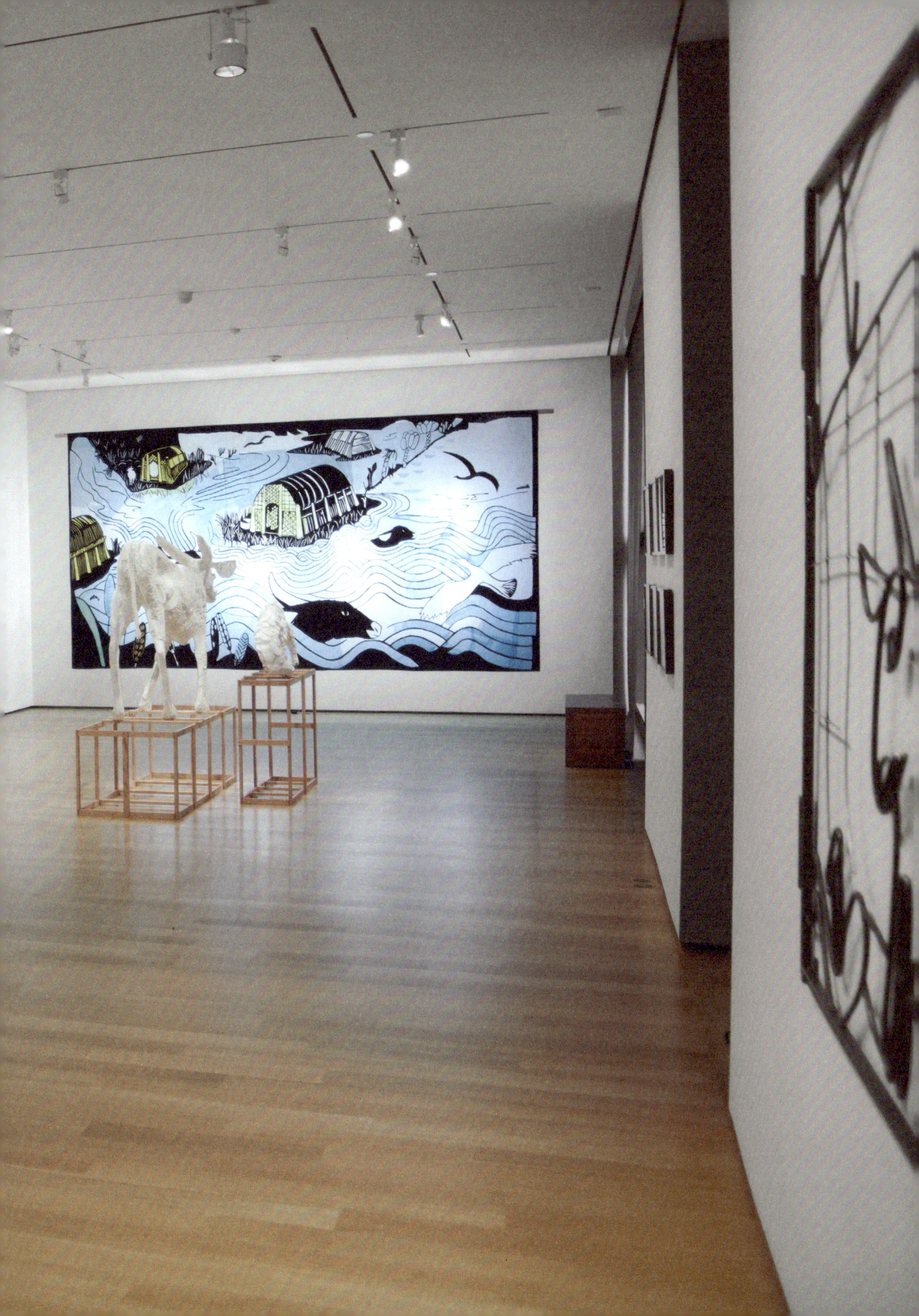

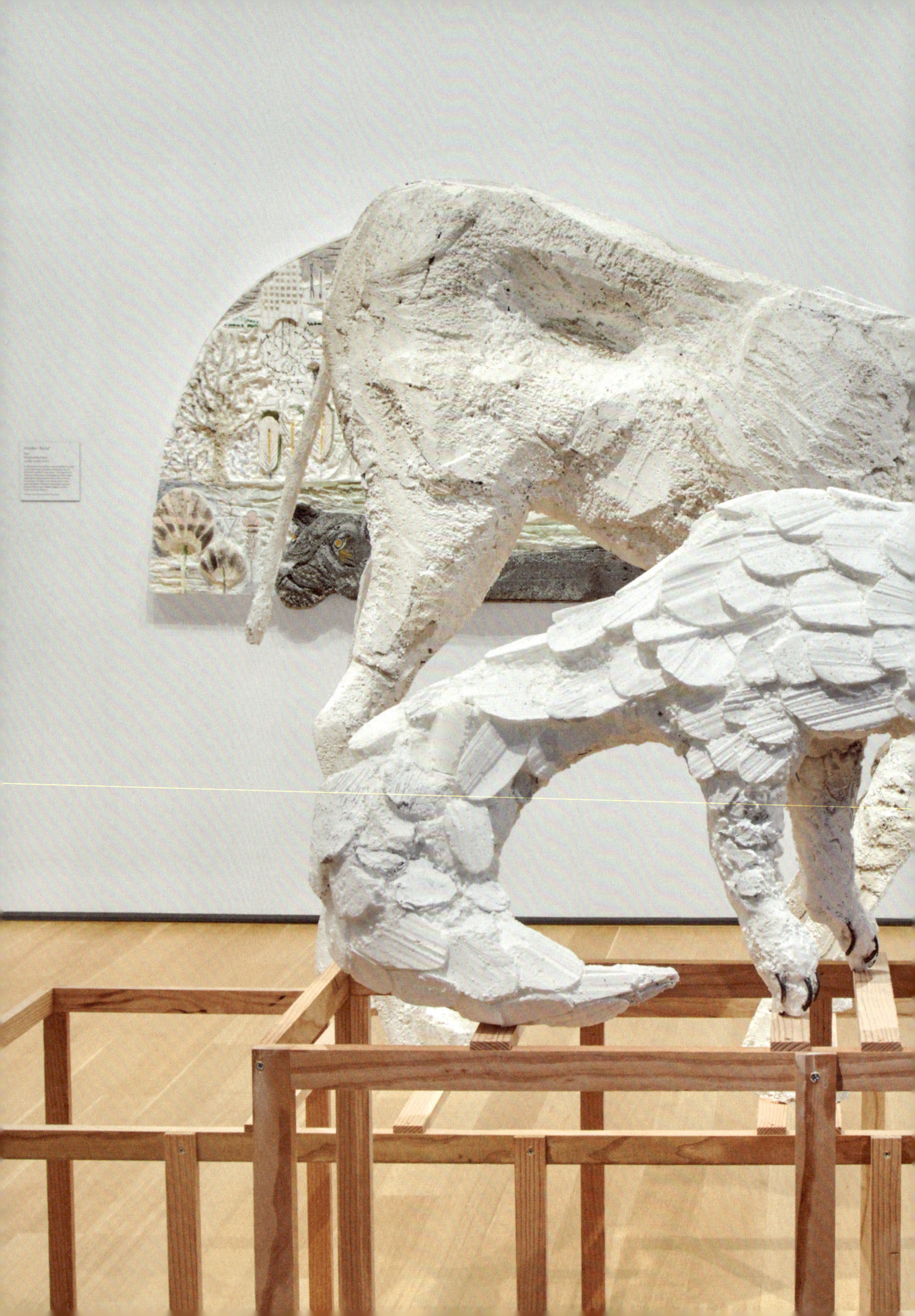

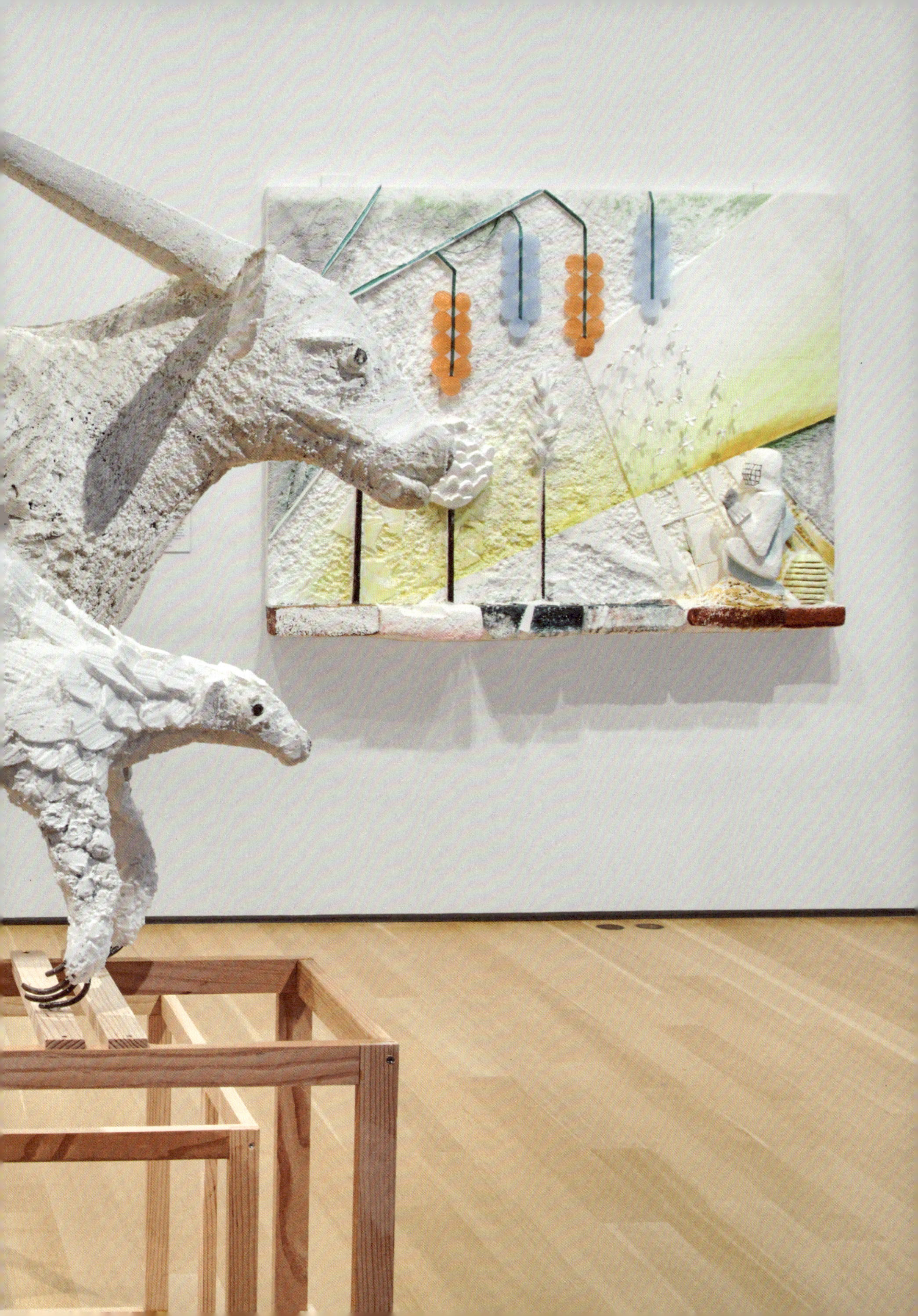

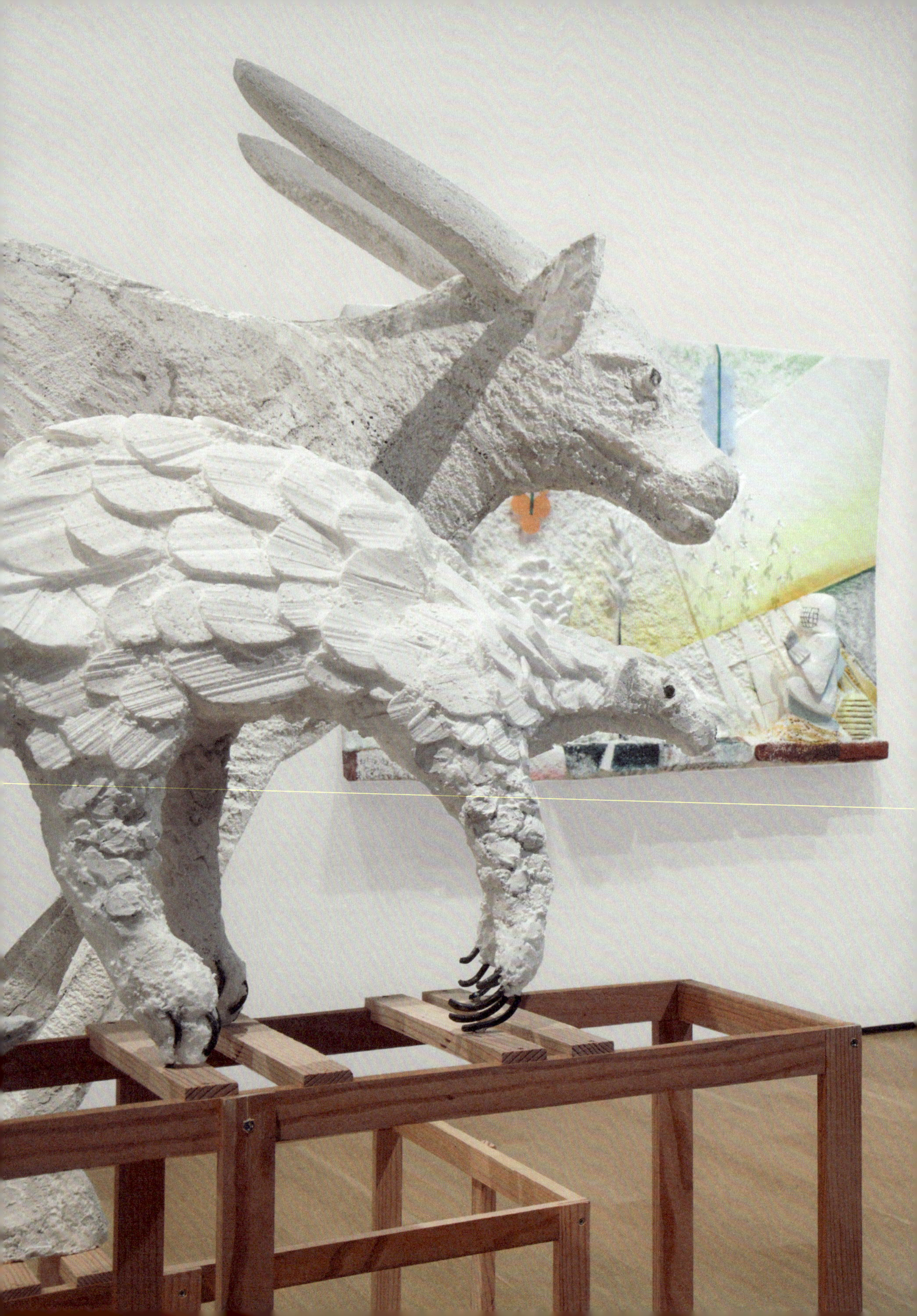

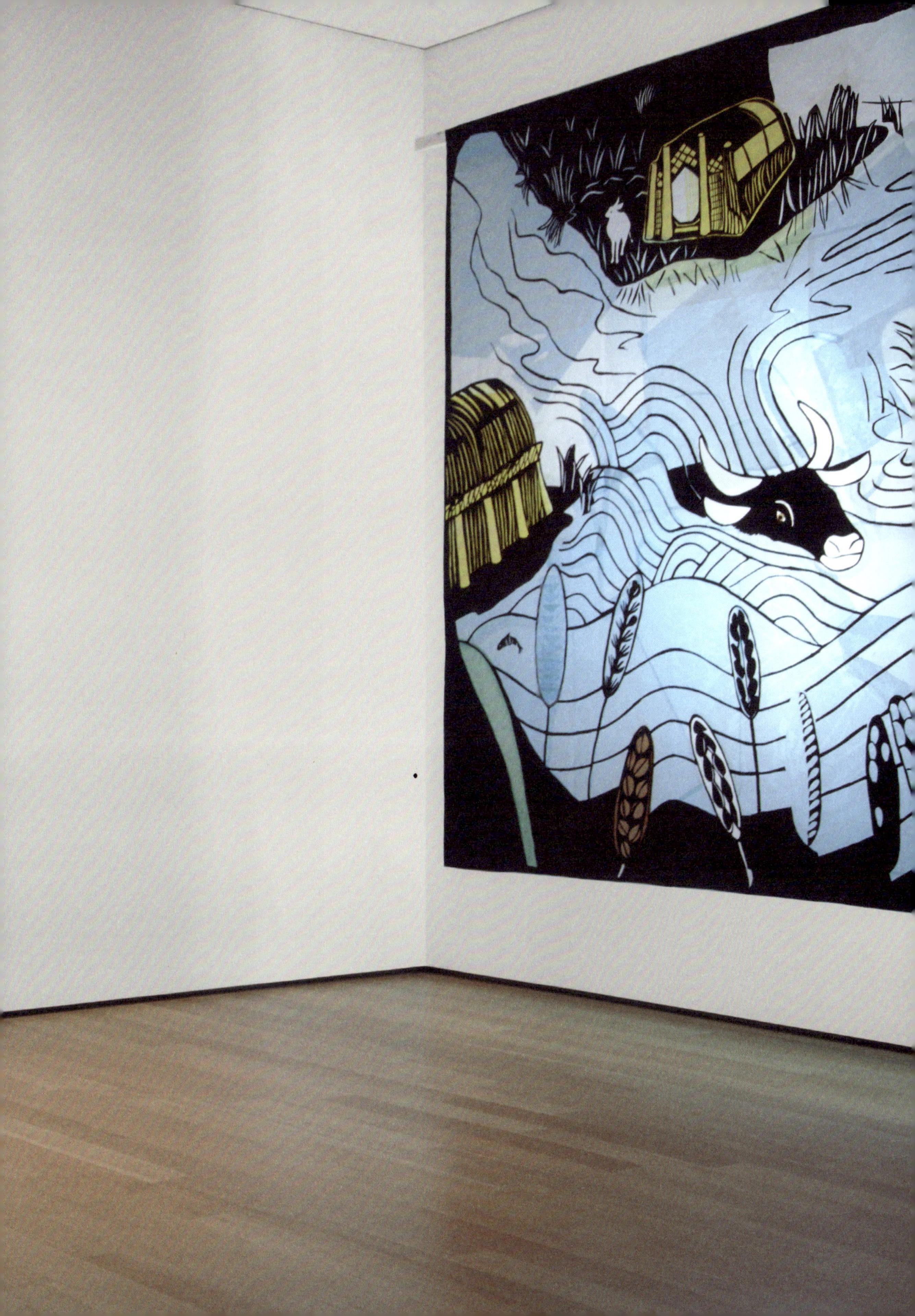

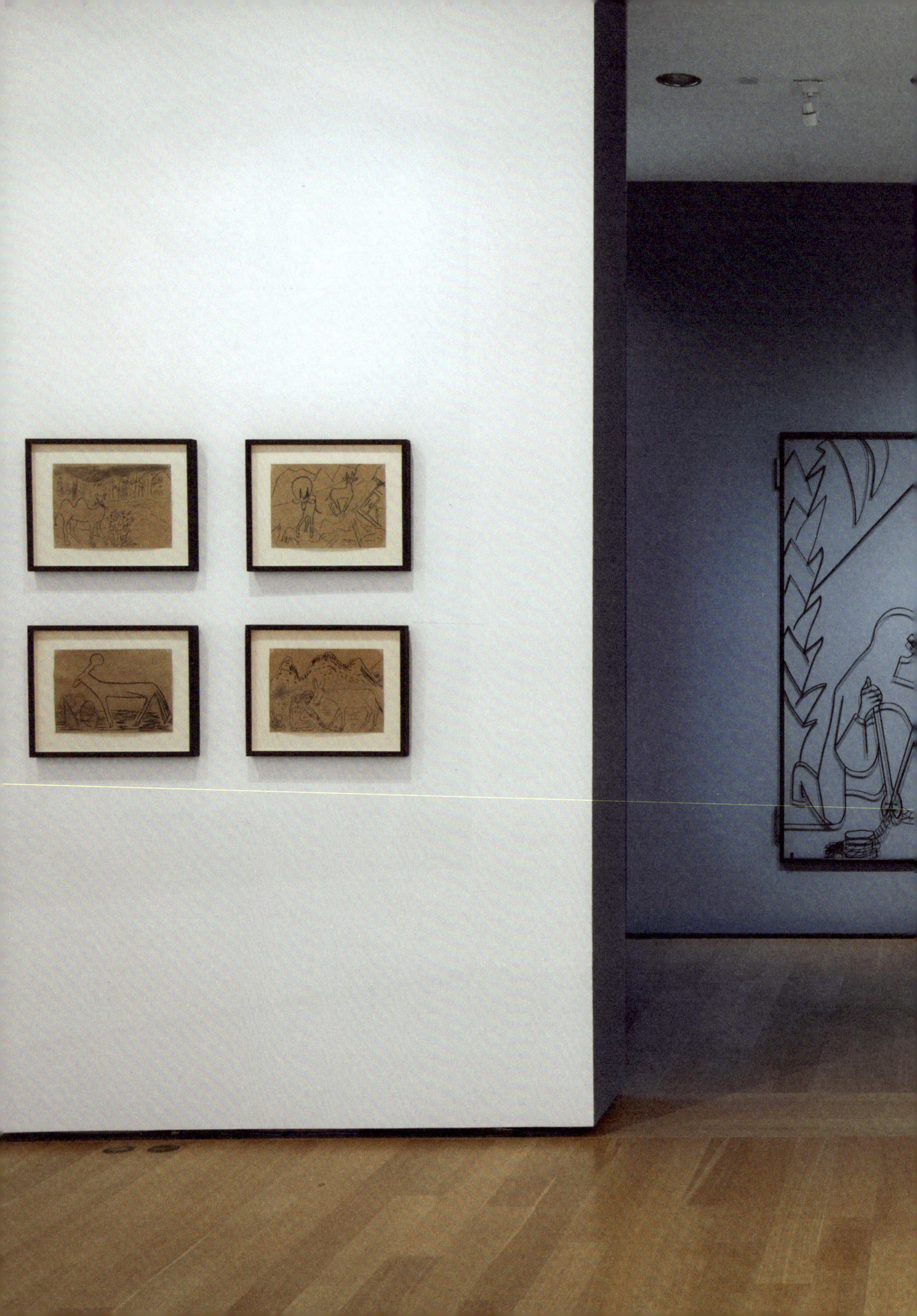

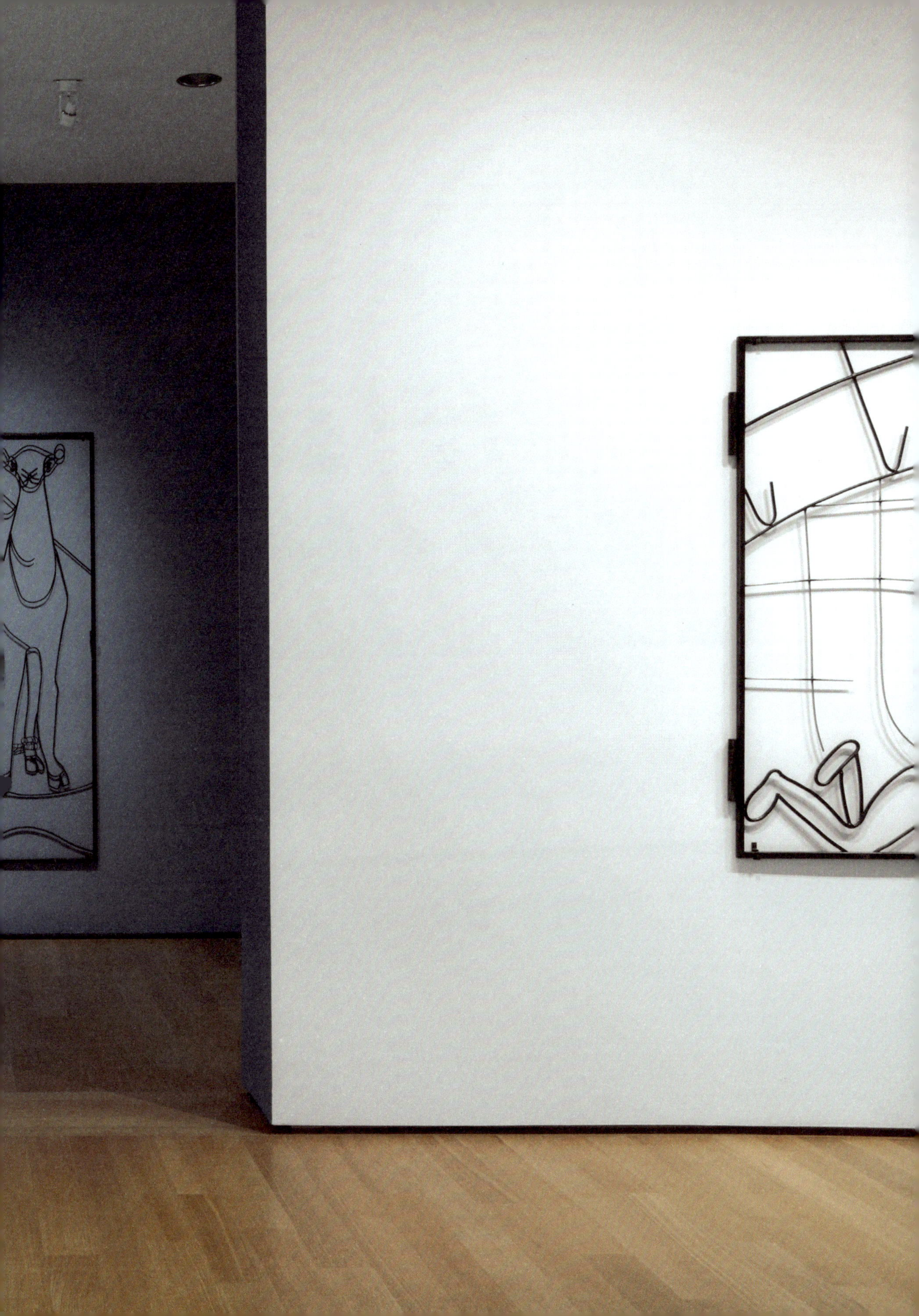

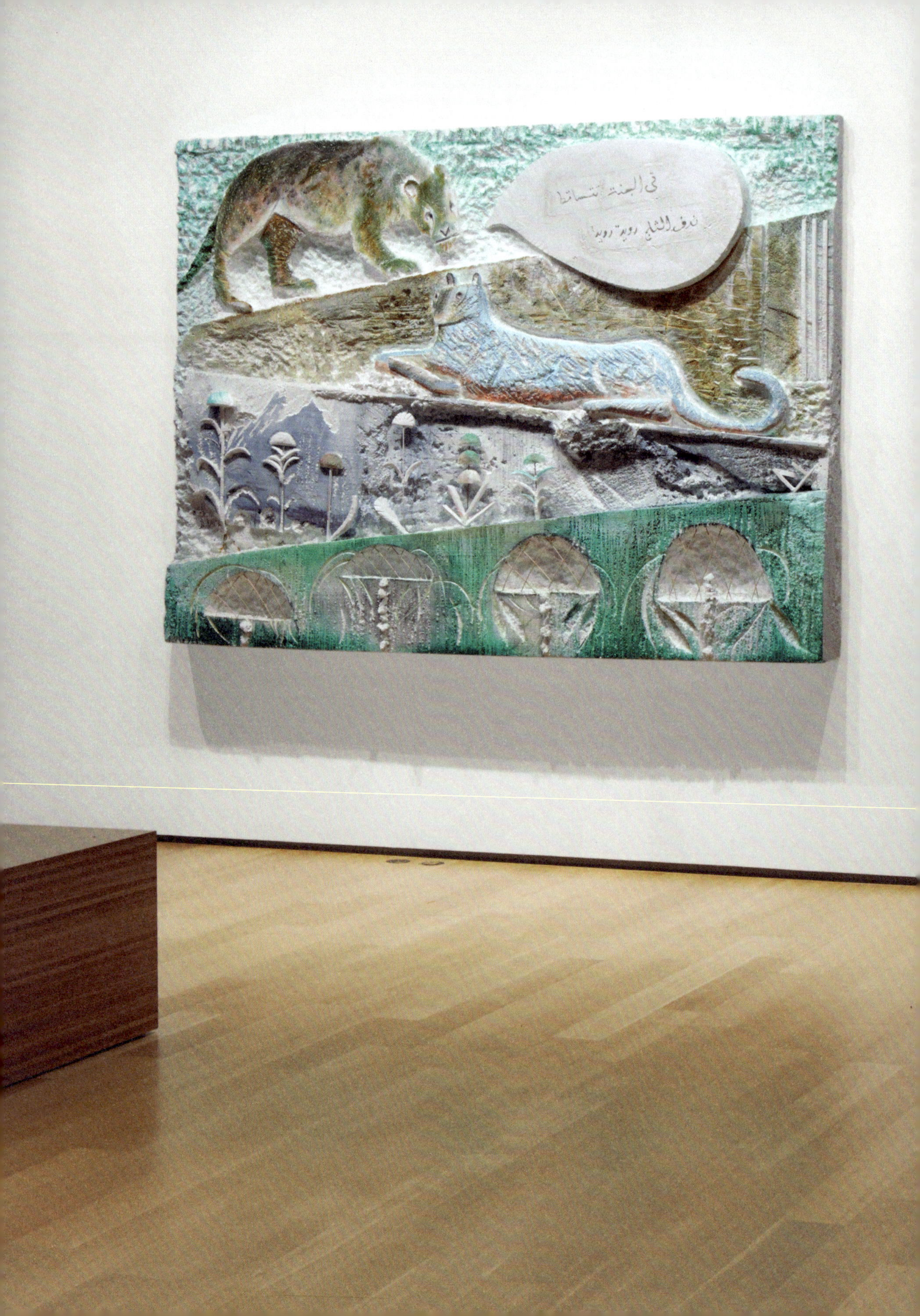
في الجنة تتساقط
ندف الثلج رويدا رويدا

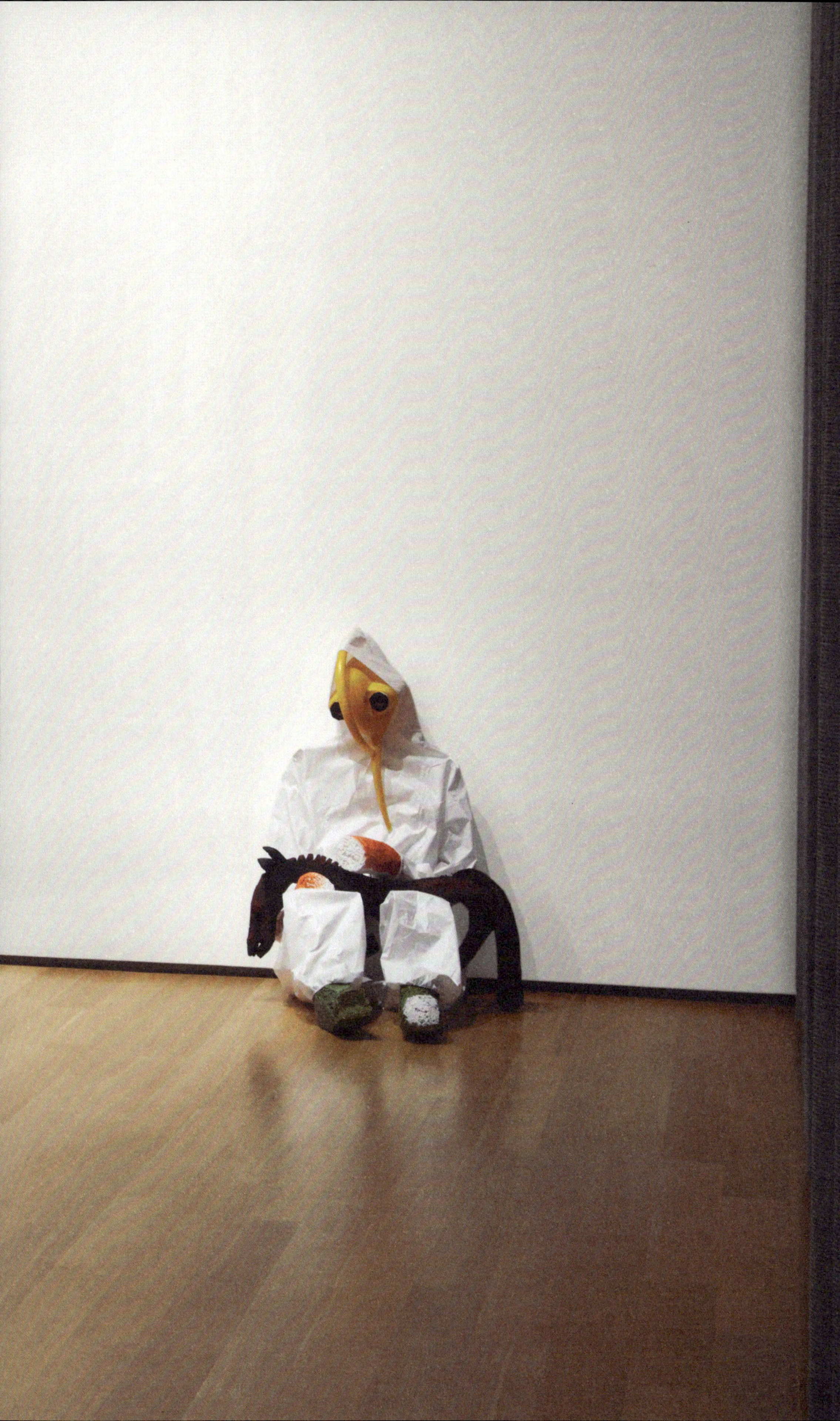

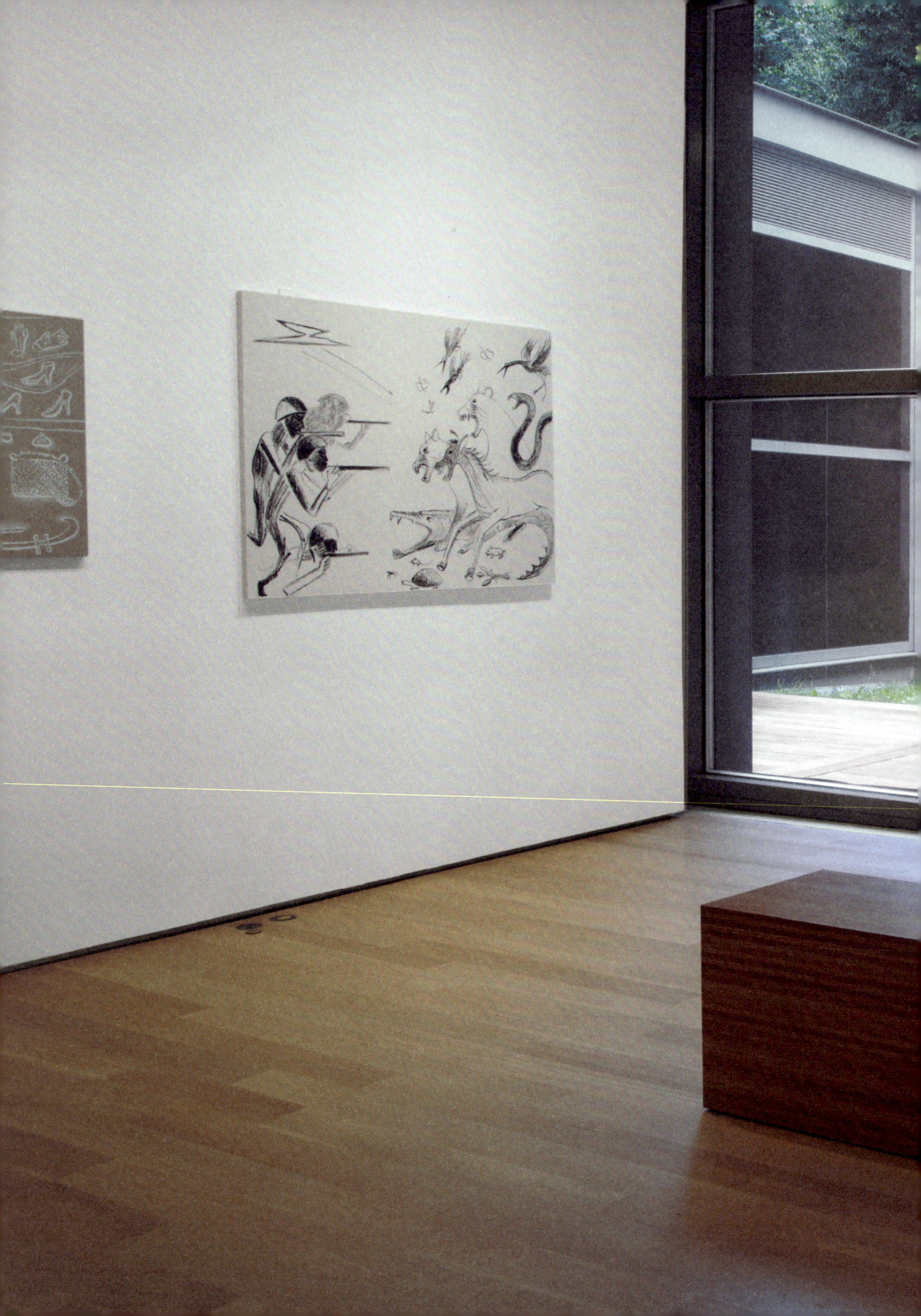

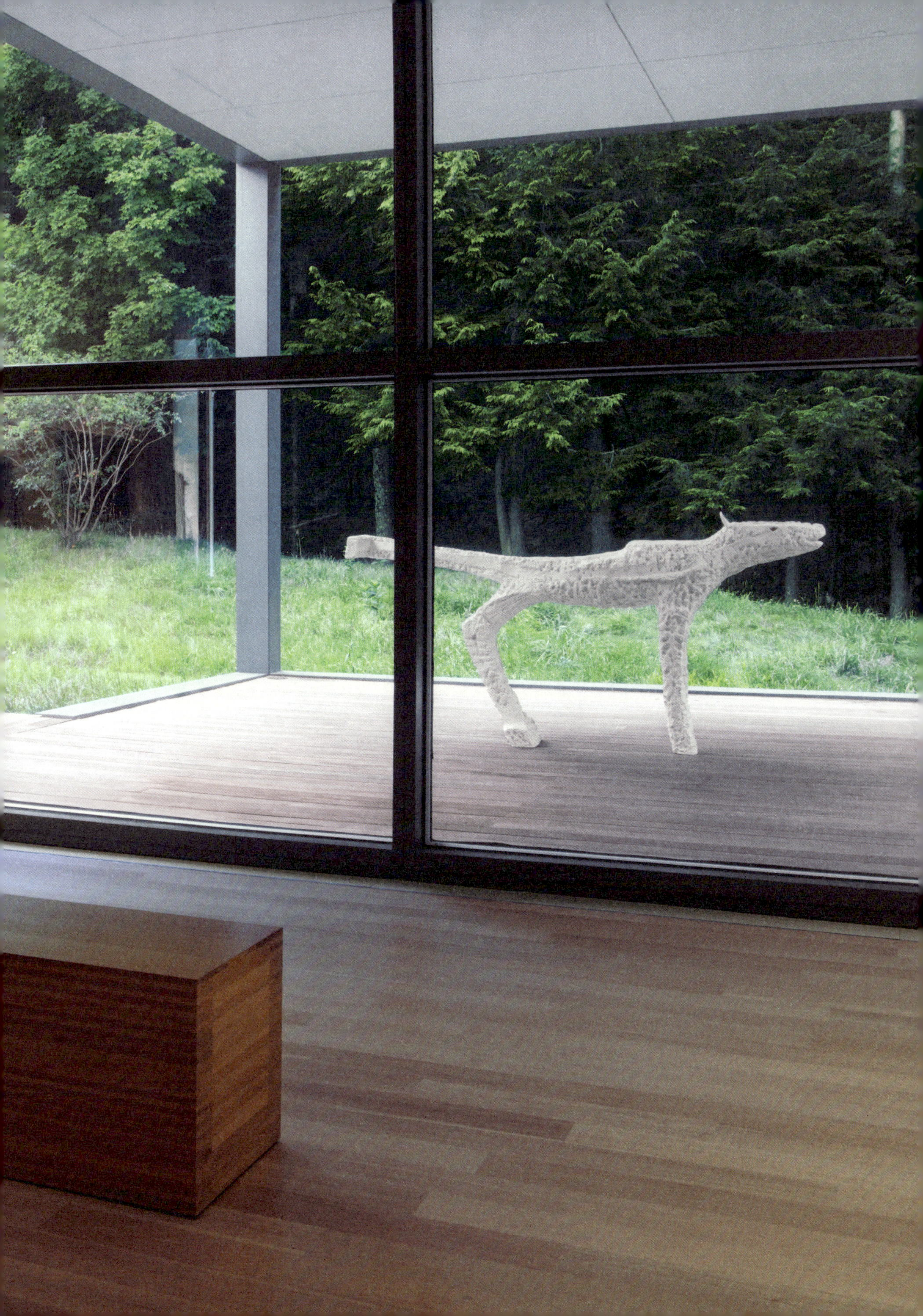

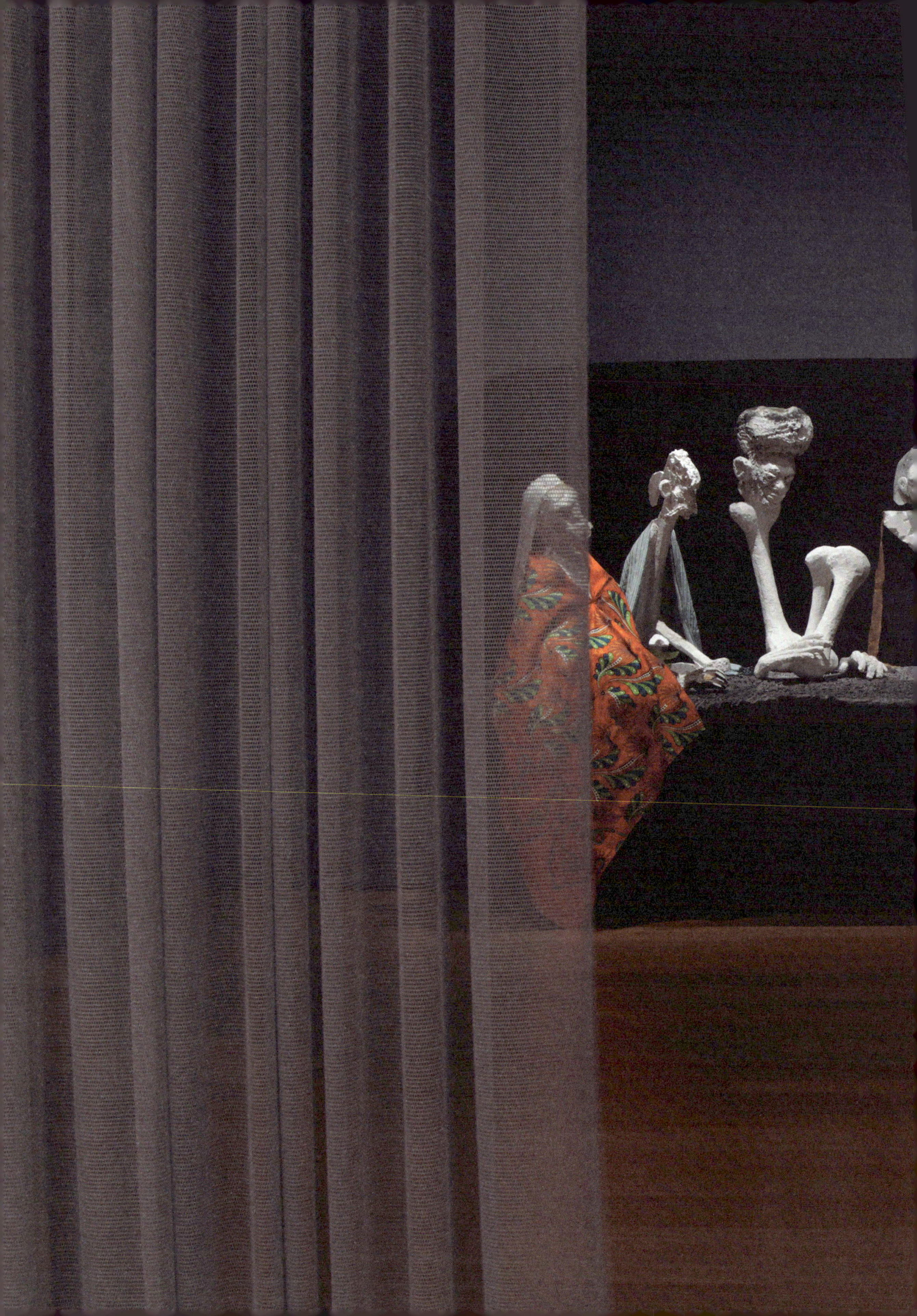

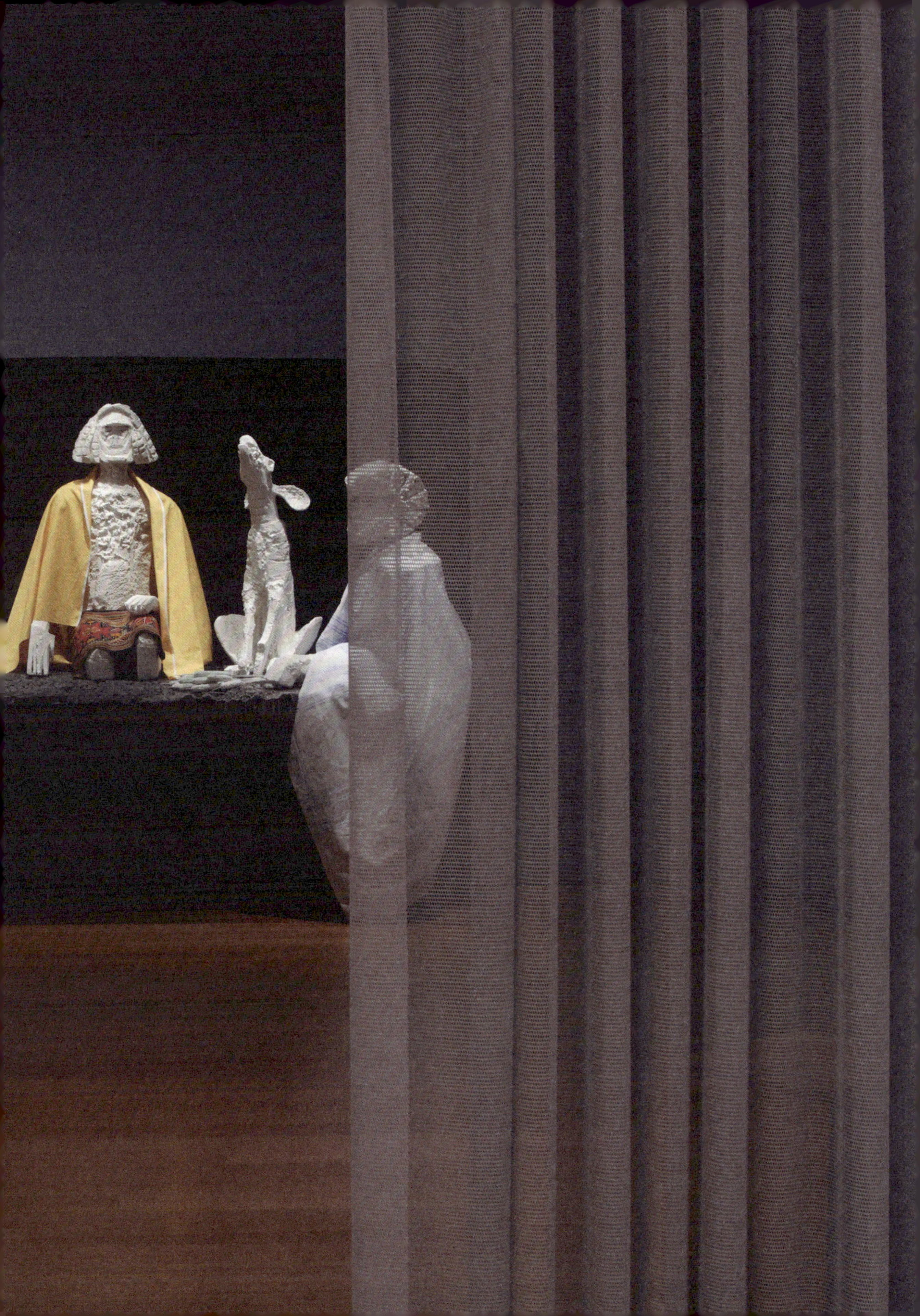

# CHECKLIST

WORKS BY LIN MAY SAEED
(b. 1973, Germany)

26–27 *St. Jerome and the Lion*, 2016
Steel, lacquer
$59 \times 73\frac{1}{4} \times 3\frac{7}{8}$ in.
(150 × 186 × 10 cm)
Courtesy of the artist; Jacky Strenz, Frankfurt; and Nicolas Krupp, Basel

28–29 *Toreador Gate*, 2019
Steel, lacquer
$59 \times 83\frac{7}{8} \times 3\frac{1}{2}$ in.
(150 × 213 × 9 cm)
Courtesy of the artist and Jacky Strenz, Frankfurt

30–31, 33 *Ghost Ship Relief*, 2013
Polystyrene foam, acrylic paint, steel, plaster, paper
$69\frac{1}{4} \times 98\frac{7}{8} \times 13\frac{1}{2}$ in.
(176 × 251 × 34 cm)
Courtesy of the artist and Jacky Strenz, Frankfurt

34–35 *Panther Relief*, 2017
Polystyrene foam, acrylic paint, wood
$44\frac{1}{8} \times 72\frac{1}{2} \times 4\frac{1}{8}$ in.
(112 × 184 × 10.5 cm)
Courtesy of the artist and Nicolas Krupp, Basel

36–37 *Bee Relief*, 2018
Polystyrene foam, acrylic paint, steel, wood, paper
$53\frac{1}{8} \times 70\frac{7}{8} \times 8\frac{5}{8}$ in.
(135 × 180 × 22 cm)
Courtesy of the artist and Jacky Strenz, Frankfurt

38–39 *Hawr al-Hammar/ Hammar Marshes*, 2020
Cardboard, paper, wood, fluorescent lights
$102\frac{3}{8} \times 200\frac{3}{4} \times 25\frac{5}{8}$ in.
(260 × 510 × 65 cm)
Courtesy of the artist and Jacky Strenz, Frankfurt

40 *Noel*, 2019
Charcoal on brown paper
$9\frac{1}{2} \times 13\frac{3}{8}$ in. (24 × 34 cm)
Courtesy of the artist and Jacky Strenz, Frankfurt

41 *Davos*, 2019
Charcoal on brown paper
$9\frac{1}{2} \times 13\frac{3}{8}$ in. (24 × 34 cm)
Courtesy of the artist and Jacky Strenz, Frankfurt

42 *Doha*, 2019
Charcoal on brown paper
$9\frac{1}{2} \times 13\frac{3}{8}$ in. (24 × 34 cm)
Courtesy of the artist and Jacky Strenz, Frankfurt

43 *Anmar*, 2019
Charcoal on brown paper
$9\frac{1}{2} \times 13\frac{3}{8}$ in. (24 × 34 cm)
Courtesy of the artist and Jacky Strenz, Frankfurt

44 *Hathor*, 2019
Charcoal on brown paper
$9\frac{1}{2} \times 13\frac{3}{8}$ in. (24 × 34 cm)
Courtesy of the artist and Jacky Strenz, Frankfurt

45 *Cro-Magnon*, 2019
Charcoal on brown paper
$9\frac{1}{2} \times 13\frac{3}{8}$ in. (24 × 34 cm)
Courtesy of the artist and Jacky Strenz, Frankfurt

# CHECKLIST

47–49 *Calf*, 2018
Polystyrene foam, steel, acrylic paint, charcoal, clay, wood
Overall: 72 ⅞ × 70 ⅞ × 27 ½ in. (185 × 180 × 70 cm); calf: 50 ¾ × 66 ⅞ × 26 in. (129 × 170 × 66 cm)
Courtesy of the artist and Jacky Strenz, Frankfurt

50–51, 53 *Pangolin*, 2020
Polystyrene foam, steel, plaster, acrylic paint, wood
Overall: 53 ⅞ × 42 ½ × 14 ⅛ in. (137 × 108 × 36 cm); pangolin: 20 ½ × 41 × 11 ⅜ in. (52 × 104 × 29 cm)
Courtesy of the artist and Jacky Strenz, Frankfurt

55 *The Liberation of Animals from Their Cages XXIII / Djamil Gate*, 2020
Steel, lacquer
82 ⅝ × 61 ¾ × 3 ⅞ in.
(210 × 157 × 10 cm)
Courtesy of the artist and Jacky Strenz, Frankfurt

57 *Cleaner*, 2006, second version 2020
Polystyrene foam, steel, acrylic paint, polyethylene fabric, plastic watering can
Dimensions variable
Courtesy of the artist and Jacky Strenz, Frankfurt

58–59, 61 *Mureen/Lion School*, 2016
Polystyrene foam, acrylic paint, steel, wood, plaster
66 ⅞ × 96 ½ × 7 ½ in.
(170 × 245 × 19 cm)
Courtesy of the artist; Jacky Strenz, Frankfurt; and Nicolas Krupp, Basel

62–63 *Thaealab*, 2017
Cast bronze, lacquer, hazelnuts *
56 ¼ × 114 ⅛ × 14 ⅛ in.
(143 × 290 × 36 cm)
Courtesy of the artist and Jacky Strenz, Frankfurt

64 *Aynoor*, 2020
Acrylic paint on canvas
27 ½ × 39 ⅜ in. (70 × 100 cm)
Courtesy of the artist and Jacky Strenz, Frankfurt

65 *War*, 2006
Acrylic paint on polystyrene foam
39 ⅜ × 54 ⅜ × 1 ⅛ in.
(100 × 138 × 3 cm)
Courtesy of the artist and Jacky Strenz, Frankfurt

66–71 *Seven Sleepers*, 2020
Polystyrene foam, acrylic paint, steel, jute, fabric, paper, plants, glass, water, cotton cord, wood, cardboard
84 ⅝ × 177 ⅛ × 39 ⅜ in.
(215 × 450 × 100 cm)
Courtesy of the artist and Jacky Strenz, Frankfurt

* Hazelnuts were not included in the exhibition to avoid attracting bears.

# CHECKLIST

CLARK COLLECTION WORKS

107 Nicolò Boldrini
Italian, born c. 1500,
active c. 1530–1570
after Raphael
Italian, 1483–1520
*Hercules Wrestling with the Nemean Lion*
16th century
Woodcut on paper
11 ⅞ × 16 ½ in. (30.7 × 41.8 cm)
Clark Art Institute
Acquired by the Clark, 1988
1988.221

109 Michael Snyders
Flemish, 1586–1672
*Studies of Animals, Insects, Heads, etc.*
17th century
Etching and engraving on laid paper
6 ⅞ × 9 ½ in. (17.5 × 24 cm)
Clark Art Institute
Williams J. Collins Collection
1960.257

110 Albrecht Dürer
German, 1471–1528
*The Little Passion: The Fall of Man*
1510–11
Woodcut on paper
9 ½ × 6 ⅜ in. (24.1 × 16.2 cm)
Clark Art Institute
Acquired by the Clark, 1968
1968.136

111 Albrecht Dürer
German, 1471–1528
*Saint Jerome in His Cell*
1511
Woodcut on paper
9 ⅜ × 6 ½ in. (23.8 × 16.5 cm)
Clark Art Institute
Acquired by the Clark, 1968
1968.250

112 Rosa Bonheur
French, 1822–1899
*Studies of a Lioness*
19th century
Pencil on white wove paper
6 ⅝ × 9 ¾ in. (16.7 × 24.8 cm)
Clark Art Institute
Gift of Denison B. Hull
1976.23

113 Eugène Delacroix
French, 1798–1863
*Studies of a Crouching Tiger*
19th century
Pencil on paper
5 ½ × 8 ⅞ in. (14 × 22.5 cm)
Clark Art Institute
Acquired by the Clark, 1955
1955.1424

114 Théodore Géricault
French, 1791–1824
*Flemish Horses (Chevaux flamands)*
1822
Lithograph on paper
9 ½ × 14 ⅛ in. (24 × 36 cm)
Clark Art Institute
Gift of James A. Bergquist
1998.35

115 Félix Bracquemond
French, 1833–1914
*The Moles (Les Taupes)*
1854
Etching on laid paper
16 ⅝ × 12 ⅝ in. (42.1 × 32.2 cm)
Clark Art Institute
Acquired by the Clark, 1980
1980.11

117 Théodore Chassériau
French, born present-day Dominican Republic, 1819–1856
*Moorish Women of Constantine*
1851
Etching and soft ground etching on chine collée on paper
8 ¾ × 12 in. (22.2 × 30.5 cm)
Clark Art Institute
Gift of Jay McKean Fisher in memory of his parents, Suzanne and Frederick Fisher, 2003.6

# LIN MAY SAEED EXHIBITION HISTORY

## SOLO SHOWS

2019 What Pipeline, Detroit
*Lin May Saeed & Max Brand*
September 27–November 9

Jacky Strenz, Frankfurt
*Girl with Cat*
May 10–July 15

2018 Studio Voltaire, London
*Biene*
June 29–August 26

2017 Lulu, Mexico City
*Djamil*
September 30–November 18

2016 Nicolas Krupp, Basel, Switzerland
*St. Jerome and the Lion*
September 3–October 29

Jacky Strenz, Frankfurt
*Lin May Saeed*
January 30–April 4

2015 Julius Caesar, Chicago
*The Skyscraper/A Horizontal View*
October 11–November 8

2014 Galerie Thomas Flor, Berlin
*Notes on Animals*
September 9–November 29

2013 Jacky Strenz, Frankfurt
*Der Wolkenkratzer*
November 16, 2013–January 18, 2014

Jacky Strenz, Frankfurt
*Grane*
September 7–October 28

2012 Bonner Kunstverein, Bonn, Germany
*Peter Mertes Stipendium 2011: Lin May, Miriam Schwedt*
March 10–May 13

2010 Galerie Thomas Flor, Düsseldorf
*Liberation*
November 5–December 23

Jacky Strenz, Frankfurt
*Nelly Sachs Park* (with Jens Ullrich)
February 5–March 13

2009 Jacky Strenz, Frankfurt
*Ankunft der Tiere*
May 8–July 4

2008 Glaspavillon an der Volksbühne, Berlin
*Arm und Reich* (with Alex Jasch)
October 3–12

2007 Center, Berlin
*Freie Liebe* (with Maria Loboda)
April 22–May 19

Jacky Strenz, Frankfurt
*vor Christus*
January 26–March 31

2006 Galerie Thomas Flor, Düsseldorf
*culpta´gy + dwoonings*
March 24–May 6

2005 Galerie Thomas Flor, Düsseldorf
*Willkommen zur Eröffnung*
(with Jens Ullrich)
May 7–June 18

Adeline Morlon Art Direction, Düsseldorf
*Frühes 18. Jahrhundert*
(with Jens Ullrich)
February 25–April 25

# EXHIBITION HISTORY

GROUP SHOWS

2021 Castello di Rivoli Museo d'Arte Contemporanea, Torino, Italy
*Espressioni*
October 4, 2021–February 27, 2022

IUCN World Conservation Congress, Marseille, France
January 8–13

Fondation Carmignac, Porquerolles, France
*La mer imaginaire*

2020 Air de Paris, Romainville, France
*El oro de los tigres*
January 12–March 14

2019 The International Centre of Graphic Arts, Ljubljana, Slovenia
33rd Ljubljana Biennial of Graphic Arts: *Crack Up–Crack Down*
July 7– September 29

Villa Merkel, Esslingen am Neckar, Germany
*Good Space-Communities, oder das Versprechen von Glück*
June 2–September 1*

Ujazdowski Castle Centre for Contemporary Art, Warsaw
May 29–October 11, 2020

2018 Schirn Kunsthalle Frankfurt, Frankfurt, Germany
*Wildnis*
November 1, 2018–February 3, 2019*

The Approach, London
*Splendor Solis*
June 28–September 23
mumok, Vienna
*Class Reunion. Works from the Gaby and Wilhelm Schürmann Collection*
June 23–November 11*

T293, Rome
*Predatory Behavior*
June 22–July 28

Zürich
*Neuer Norden Zürich: Art in Public Space*
June 9–September 2

Künstlerhaus Dortmund, Germany
*I Wanna Be Your Dog II: Animal Liberation in Contemporary Art*
May 5–July 1*

Castello di Rivoli, Turin
*Metamorphoses—Let Everything Happen to You*
March 6–September 2*

2017 KölnSkulptur #9, Skulpturenpark Köln, Cologne
*La Fin de Babylone. Mich wundert, dass ich so fröhlich bin!*
October 16, 2017–June 16, 2019*

Galerie Krobath, Vienna
*The Happy Fainting of Painting #2*
September 15–October 12

Brennan & Griffin, New York
*The World Without Us*
July 27–August 25

2016 Neue Gesellschaft für bildende Kunst (nGbK), Berlin
*ANIMAL LOVERS*
October 15–November 27*

# EXHIBITION HISTORY

KW Institute for Contemporary Art, Berlin
In Centre for Style, *Dress Rehearsal at 9th Berlin Biennale for Contemporary Art*
June 4–September 18*

Centro de Arte Fundación Ortiz Gurdian, Managua
*X. Bienal de Nicaragua*
February 11–May 14

2015 Städtische Galerie Waldkraiburg, Germany
*Animal Turn—die Hinwendung zum Tier*
September 25, 2015–January 10, 2016*

Martos Gallery, Los Angeles
*Blocking*
July 23–August 22

2014 Kunsthalle am Hamburger Platz, Berlin
*Brücke im Dschungel*
November 13–28

Bergen Kunsthall, Bergen, Norway
*Corruption Feeds*
October 31–December 14*

2012 Fridericianum, Kassel, Germany
In Tue Greenfort, *The Worldly House* at dOCUMENTA (13)
June 9–September 16*

reception, Berlin
*Feierabend*
April 28–June 9

2011 White Flag Projects, St. Louis, Missouri
*Impossible Vacation*
May 7–June 4

2010 Perla-Mode and Dienstgebäude, Zurich
*ich tier! (du mensch)*
April 10–25*

2008 Kunstverein Schwerte, Germany
*Societate su i ma logica*
May 29–July 13

2004 Center, Berlin
*Travellers Health*
February 28–March 30

2003 Center, Berlin
*Bitte schreiben Sie eine vernichtende Kritik über meine Spezies, wir können nur überleben wenn wir wenige bleiben*
March 28–April 5

* indicates accompanied by a publication

# CONTRIBUTORS

LIN MAY SAEED is a German-Iraqi artist who lives and works in Berlin.

ROBERT WIESENBERGER is associate curator of contemporary projects at the Clark Art Institute and a lecturer in the Graduate Program in the History of Art at Williams College.

MEL Y. CHEN is associate professor of gender & women's studies and director, Center for the Study of Sexual Culture at the University of California, Berkeley. They are the author of *Animacies: Biopolitics, Racial Mattering, and Queer Affect* (2012).

BIRGIT MÜTHERICH (1959–2011) was a German sociologist, animal-rights activist, and researcher at the University of Dortmund. She was the author, among other titles, of *Die Problematik der Mensch-Tier-Beziehung in der Soziologie: Weber, Marx und die Frankfurter Schule* (2000).

Published by the Clark Art Institute on the occasion of the exhibition *Lin May Saeed: Arrival of the Animals*, Clark Art Institute, Williamstown, Massachusetts, July 21–October 25, 2020

*Lin May Saeed: Arrival of the Animals* is organized by the Clark Art Institute, Williamstown, Massachusetts. Major support for the exhibition is provided by Denise Littlefield Sobel. Additional funding is generously provided by Katherine and Frank Martucci.

Produced by the Publications Department
of the Clark Art Institute
225 South Street
Williamstown, Massachusetts 01267
clarkart.edu

Anne Roecklein, managing editor
Kevin Bicknell, editor
Samantha Page, assistant editor
David Murphy, rights and licensing associate
Elisama Llera, publications intern

Copyedited by Sharon Herson
Proofread by Kara Pickman, Pickman Editorial

Catalogue design by Mark Owens
Typeset in Quadrant Text and Quadrant Text Mono by Vincent Chan and Syndicat Grotesk by Adrien Menard
Printed on Munken Polar Rough
Printed and bound in Belgium by die Keure



Distributed by
Yale University Press
302 Temple Street
P.O. Box 209040
New Haven, Connecticut 06520-9040
yalebooks.com/art

10 9 8 7 6 5 4 3 2 1
Library of Congress Cataloging-in-Publication Data

Names: Saeed, Lin May, b. 1973. Works. Selections. | Wiesenberger, Robert. Speciesism. | Chen, Mel Y. Gate and the unreachable. | Mütherich, Birgit. Soziale Konstruktion des Anderen. English. | Sterling and Francine Clark Art Institute, organizer, host institution.
Title: Lin May Saeed : arrival of the animals / Robert Wiesenberger ; with contributions by Mel Y. Chen, Lin May Saeed, and Birgit Mütherich.
Description: Williamstown, Massachusetts : Clark Art Institute, 2020. |
Includes bibliographical references.
Identifiers: LCCN 2020016235 |
ISBN 9781935998440 (Clark Art Institute) |
ISBN 9720300250862 (Yale University Press)
Subjects: LCSH: Saeed, Lin May, b. 1973--
Exhibitions. | Animals in art--Exhibitions. |
Human-animal relationships in art--Exhibitions.
Classification: LCC NB588.S235 .A4 2020 | DDC 730.92--dc23
LC record available at https://lccn.loc.gov/2020016235

Photography credits include: Thomas Clark: pl. 2, 3, 5, 6, 14–21, fig. 16, pp. 120–135; Art Evans: pl. 22–30; Wolfgang Günzel: fig. 3, 5, 13, 15; Serge Hasenböler: pl. 1, fig. 14; Jens Heine: fig. 4, 8, pl. 4, 7–13; Frank Kleinbach: fig. 1; Eric Tschernow: fig. 7; Armen Vanetsayan: fig. 11

Front cover: *Pangolin*, 2020; back cover: *St Jerome and the Lion*, 2016; p. 74: *Suq Al-Mansoor*, 2017; p. 77: *Cato*, 2019; p. 78: *Ape and Giraffe*, 2019; p. 81: *Sketch for Bird Gate*, 2019; p. 83: *Sketch for Planet Relief*, 2019; p. 84: *Zeno in front of the Cave*, 2006